Edgar Poe:

seer and craftsman

Edgar Poe:

seer and craftsman

by Stuart Levine

EVERETT/EDWARDS, inc.

POST OFFICE BOX 1060
DELAND, FLORIDA 32720

Library of Congress Catalog Card Number 75-89576
Everett/Edwards, inc., DeLand, Florida 32720
© 1972 by Stuart Levine, All Rights Reserved
Printed in the United States of America

Second Printing, November, 1973

For Aaron and Allen and Rebecca

About the Author

Stuart Levine holds a Ph.D. from Brown University and is Professor of American Studies at the University of Kansas, where he was the founding Chairman of that department. He has been a guest lecturer at the University of Missouri at Kansas City, Kansas State University, and California State College at Los Angeles.

Professor Levine was the first Editor of *American Studies* and has continued in that post since 1960. His publications include several books, among them the winner of an Anisfield-Wolf Award (*The American Indian Today* with Nancy O. Lurie) and *The Story of American Painting* (with Charles Caffin). He contributed chapters to Vineta Colby's *American Culture in the Sixties* and Hennig Cohen's *The American Culture*. His articles on Art, Culture, Value Theory, and on Herman Melville, Edgar Allan Poe, and on American Indians, have appeared in several journals.

Professor Levine has produced a series of five taped cassette lectures on Edgar Allan Poe for Everett/Edwards, inc., that are included in that publisher's Cassette Curriculum in American literature. He has won numerous academic awards and fellowships, and has been a Fulbright professor four times: to Argentina, Costa Rica (twice), and Mexico. His new, fully annotated edition of the complete short fiction of Poe is now in press.

Contents

Illustrations

Preface

We dodge the hard issues and Edgar Poe is a mighty hard
issue: Vernon Parrington was afraid Poe was un-American and
wouldn't really talk about him; F. O. Matthiessen drummed him
out of the American renaissance. We know the French overrate
him; so, I learned recently, do the Latin Americans. Still, a lot
of Americans read Poe, and there must be something we can say
about him as an artist. Very good things have been said about
his life: we got the facts straight in 1941, and a really fine short
biography came out in 1963.[1] There is also a great deal of good
scholarship devoted to his sources--the works which influenced
him. A few bright but polemic articles, a few perceptive but
fugitive readings of individual stories, three high-powered but
badly outdated Freudian studies and a chapter here and there in
a book really about something else: these things we have. I like
a great many of them; I have tried to do justice to them in
print.[2] But we haven't got any over-all way of looking at Poe,
and bright colleagues who know much more than I do about all
kinds of things come to me to say that they've killed one class
meeting on biography, and one on the Gothic whiz-bang in
"Usher," and now what?

Why has there been no larger "reading" of the stories of
Poe? I think that one reason is the absence of the sort of major

issues--moral, social, theological, for instance--which have attracted so many critics to the work of other nineteenth-century
American authors. Such issues serve as a handle with which to
grasp the works, for example, of Herman Melville.

This book attempts to provide such a handle, to fill, if I
may change my metaphor, what I take to be a gap in the Poe
literature. It is not intended to be either exhaustive or
definitive. The opening chapters utilize certain of Poe's critical
writings, and I should note in my own defense that I am aware
of the shallowness of Poe's theoretical writing on the subject of
beauty. As Yvor Winters observed in a provocative article,[3] Poe
tended to confuse beauty as subject matter with beauty as style
and form. Poe's essays on the topic may well seem superficial,
but he apparently believed what he wrote, and his theory of
beauty seems too convenient a "handle" to his fiction to be
ignored.

Moreover, the fiction seems frequently to transcend the
limitations of the theory from which it presumably sprang.
T. S. Eliot[4] noted that practicing authors often derive their
artistic creeds through a process of rationalization from their
own work. This is probably true in Poe's case, but it makes his
criticism no less useful as an approach to his tales.

- 2 -

I like to think that the approach to Poe which will be
outlined in the first pages of this study will serve to unify the
insights of numerous sensitive critics who have written about
Poe. Consider, for instance, the following passage from a fine
discussion of Poe by W. H. Auden:[5]

> Poe's major stories fall roughly into two groups. The first
> group is concerned with states of willful being, the destructive
> passion of the lonely ego to merge with the ego of another
> (*Ligeia*), the passion of the conscious ego to be objective, to
> discover by pure reason the true relationships which sensory
> appearances and emotions would conceal (*The Purloined Letter*),
> self-destructive states in which the ego and the self are passionate-
> ly hostile (*The Imp of the Perverse*), even the state of chimerical
> passion, that is, the passionate unrest of a self that lacks all
> passion (*The Man of the Crowd*). The horror tales and the tales of
> ratiocination belong together, for the heroes of both exist as
> unitary states--Roderick Usher reasons as little as Auguste Dupin

feels. Personages who are the embodiment of such states cannot, of course, change or vary in intensity either through changes in themselves or their environment. The problem in writing stories of this kind is to prevent the reader from ever being reminded of historical existence, for, if he once thinks of real people whose passions are interrupted by a need for lunch or whose beauty can be temporarily and mildly impaired by the common cold, the intensity and timelessness become immediately comic. Poe is sometimes attacked for the operatic quality of the prose and *décor* in his tales, but they are essential to preserving the illusion. His heroes cannot exist except operatically. Take, for example, the following sentence from *William Wilson*:

> Let it suffice, that among spendthrifts I out-Heroded Herod, and that, giving name to a multitude of novel follies, I added no brief appendix to the long catalogue of vices then usual in the most dissolute university of Europe.

In isolation, as a prose sentence, it is terrible, vague, verbose, and sense at the mercy of a conventional rhetorical rhythm. But dramatically, how right; how well it reveals the William Wilson who narrates the story in his real colors, as the fantastic self who hates and refuses contact with reality. Some of Poe's successors in stories about states of being, D. H. Lawrence for example, have tried to be realistic with fatal results.

In the second group, which includes such tales as *A Descent into the Maelstrom* and *Gordon Pym*, the relation of will to environment is reversed. While in the first group everything that happens is the consequence of a volition upon the freedom of which there are no natural limits, in these stories of pure adventure the hero is as purely passive as the I in dreams; nothing that happens is the result of his personal choice, everything happens *to* him. What the subject feels--interest, excitement, terror--are caused by events over which he has no control whatsoever. The first kind of hero has no history because he refuses to change with time; this kind has none because he cannot change, he can only experience.

I think that there is a way in which the tales of the first and the second of Mr. Auden's groups may be shown to have a great deal in common. The "states of willful being" and the passivity seem to me to be means to an end, and part of a more general scheme. The scheme involves the manner of perception of beauty, and is the subject of my first two chapters.

Poe is one of the easiest of authors to parody. Most of his poems can be utterly demolished by a competent parodist, and his tales are almost as simple to mock; their language is indeed "terrible, vague, verbose." Yet, as Mr. Auden maintains, in context some of these terrible passages function efficiently. This must be because the tale which contains the rhetorical passage has in it elements which induce the reader to accept the theatrics.

Poe's plots and situations, by our standards, are equally unpromising. Summarize a Poe story, and one usually has what sounds like an unlikely framework for a decent piece of fiction. Neither manner nor matter, then, seems, in isolation, to promise very much. And yet these tales have had remarkable staying power. One suspects that not very many of the short stories appearing in current periodicals roughly equivalent to those of Poe's day will still be read a century and a quarter from now.

What saves Poe's best tales? Their sensationalism doubtless has something to do with their survival, but, while that may partially account for their popularity with younger readers, it is not in itself sufficient. Poe had dozens of contemporaries who wrote tales with the same sorts of subject matter. Let us take our hint from the tales of Hawthorne. His, too, is an art which, reduced to its component parts, seems relatively unimpressive. Summarize one of his tales and one usually has merely an unlikely situation. Unlike a Poe situation, of course, most of Hawthorne's involve some moral issue, but their relatively static nature would seem to limit them. Yet one does not feel, in reading Hawthorne stories, that one is reading trifles. Even could one exclude their moral concern, they would be more convincing than summaries would indicate.

The Hawthorne story, which differs from that of Poe in several respects, has one obvious feature in common with it: taken literally, its action is improbable. A man tries to remove his wife's single blemish; he does, but the operation kills her. A man attempts to flee from a haunting double of himself which repeatedly frustrates his evil plans. He kills the double. Each summary, stated thus nakedly, seems stagey; each is, however, the outline of a splendid tale, the first by Hawthorne, the other by Poe. Somehow, each author manages to divert his readers' attention from the artificiality and the improbability. This ability is the quality which Poe and Hawthorne most obviously share. In the text of this study, I generally refer to it as the ability to establish a "margin of credibility." The characteristic tale cannot be taken literally--it is too improbable--and yet it must not seem to the reader fantasy, either. It must hover somewhere between.

These perhaps seem rather mechanical considerations. I might as well admit at the outset that they are. Poe often thought of his tales in mechanical terms. That alone might not justify a mechanical approach to his work; what does justify it is the fact that such an approach is about the only one which can produce evaluative judgments of everything he wrote. Poe's art is in one sense very limited. Elements which are of prime importance in the works of other writers are reduced in Poe to devices, to be used to produce an effect.

I do not wish to imply any hostility toward other methods of approaching Poe. The Freudian approach, for example, can doubtless yield fruitful results; the difficulty is that its ultimate aim is psychoanalysis, not evaluation. It also seems to me that there has been relatively too much criticism of this type focused upon Poe, and all of it which I have read includes a basic misconception: that all of Poe is pretty much the same. Poe's fiction is, in fact, limited in range, but quite varied in approach. I have tried to stress the diversity of his tales. Although my aims are neither biographical nor psychological, I think that this diversity is meaningful for the student of either discipline. The reader might find it useful to attempt to remember his first impression of some of the Poe stories, the things which struck him before he had read enough Poe to begin to see over-all patterns. How different from one another, for example, are even some of the most familiar horror stories. The events are similarly grotesque, perhaps, but the tone of voice in which they are told runs from cool detachment to frenzy. Now, the psychological treatments of Poe deal, on the whole, with the events and the images; they attempt to show that these are the projections of the author's subconscious. They do not treat what we might loosely term the "feel" of the individual tale.

And yet this "feel" is what strikes the reader most forcibly. Poe, at his best, could fuse an improbable plot and high-flown language into a remarkably unified literary imple-ment. I said that Poe's art is limited; it is, because he insisted upon subordinating all else to effect, but within his range, the number of possible effects is limitless, as Poe fully understood. This fact implies, I think, a craftsmanlike control of materials which should be used to qualify any psychological or biographical treatment of his stories.

It is, of course, impossible entirely to avoid making judgments which have other than purely literary connotations, but I have attempted at least to make them in terms of Poe the struggling writer rather than Poe the hopeless psychotic. I do not mean that Poe was not abnormal, but I am not a psychologist, and I would like to stake out my claim in other areas. There is literary ground enough on which to damn Poe when he deserves to be damned without poaching upon the preserve of the scientist. Perhaps the change in emphasis will be refreshing; I certainly hope so. Roderick Usher, after all, does not narrate all of Poe's stories. He does not, in fact, even narrate "The Fall of the House of Usher."

A Postscript

During the three years since this book was completed, my wife and I have been working on a fully-annotated edition of the complete short fiction of Edgar Poe. It's about done now, and should appear within a year. This postscript is by way of a brief summary of things we have learned since I finished *Edgar Poe: Seer and Craftsman.*

The present volume quite deliberately focuses upon the more familiar tales of Poe, and upon only those "minor" works which are close in manner to the familiar tales. It plays down and even tends to underrate the "obscure" and puzzling stories. The job of explicating those obscure tales was back-breaking, but ultimately very rewarding. We were gratified to see how many of the judgements made in this book were borne out by careful investigation of Poe's sources and allusions. We also learned some things we hadn't known.

First: Poe's "minor" prose — the satires, the tales of the Folio Club, and so forth — is often very private. Unless the reader has been following Poe in all of the different magazines for which he wrote, reading just what he was reading, and, in some cases, seeing just the plays and operas he saw, many tales have no apparent meaning. If one has this background filled in, the tales make very good sense: Poe satirizes current fiction, teases literary friends, demolishes enemies, growls about American and British politics, or, often, simply plays with ideas.

Second: The joking, the private snickering-up-the-authorial-sleeve, never stops. It goes on in the "major" prose as well. What I say in this book about "multiple intention" (see pp. 28 ff.) is far truer than I dreamed.

Third: Poe's erudition is impressive. Even though he fakes at times, he knows an enormous amount about contemporary English and continental literature, major and minor; about classical authors, even about non-Western literature. He knows his Bible, too, and some non-Western scripture as well. Two very favorite sources of allusion showed up in dozens of tales: Isaac Disraeli's *Curiosities of Literature* and Carlyle's *Sartor Resartus.* We suspect, despite Poe's steady mockery of Carlyle, that he rather envied him. But these two works do not begin to account for all of the submerged erudition. The man knew much more than we have been led to believe, and his mind danced about, the trivial with the timeless.

Fourth: If the Poe of these "minor" tales reminds one of a twentieth century author, it is, of all people, James Joyce. We can think of no other author so prone to make the real point of his prose a sort of mental ballet of connections, intuitions and whimsical allusions, to write for the sheer fun of constructing a magical web at once absurd and mystical in its interconnectedness.

Mexico City
March, 1972

Prologue

The View from "The Light-House"

Poe scholars are indebted to the late T. O. Mabbott for having uncovered the fragment of an incomplete short story by Poe, "The Light-House." It runs but two pages, is in the sort of journal form Poe used in "Julius Rodman," "The Balloon-Hoax" and other stories, and deals with a narrator, a dog and a lighthouse. From the little we have, we know that the narrator is a nobleman who has been in some sort of difficulty and who has "... a passion for solitude."[1] He assures himself in the journal that the lighthouse is solidly constructed, and yet worries about the raging sea around him. Mabbott suggests that the lighthouse is to be destroyed, and that the dog is to rescue the diary and possibly also the narrator.

Short and unsatisfactory as it is, this fragment of a tale seems strangely typical of Poe's fiction. Even the dog seems familiar. Pets, of course, show up in several Poe stories; there is a fine dog in "Julius Rodman." Indeed, Poe sometimes uses animals to reflect aspects of the personalities of his supersensitive narrators; the murder of the first cat and the treatment of the second in "The Black Cat" are intended to exemplify the narrator's instability. As often in Poe, a common reaction is heightened to a pitch of madness. What carries the reader along is perhaps the commonness of the reaction. Petting a kitten, let's say, he remembers having had the impulse to bash it against a wall. If he is "properly socialized," he has repressed his adolescent confusions between sexuality and violence, though he may remember them, too. The boundaries between affection, love, eroticism and cruelty are socially established--though troublingly ambiguous--but it is not clear that they are psychologically or even physiologically as discrete as we would like them to be. The answer to the old question, "Why do youngsters like Poe?" may be so obvious we don't like to see it. And our discussion of pets in Poe, which was conceived in whimsy, might, pressed to its implications for human personality, end in horror. There is, after all, also Arthur Gordon Pym's dog, which, maddened by starvation, thirst and foul air, nearly kills his master. Poe, in short, had numerous possibilities open to him in "The Light-House."

The story is typical in more important ways as well. There stands the characteristic Poe narrator, the same character who has tempted so many good critics to read "Poe" when he says "I": nervous, bright, aristocratic and isolated. Even with the little we have as evidence, we feel we know a good deal about him--enough to draw comparisons. Hawthorne once put a narrator in a tower from which he watched the world of a New England town pass in review, and that story, "Sights from a Steeple," is hauntingly symbolic of its author's fragile art and his relation with the world outside his attic. Isolated because of his long climb, the author wonders whether it has been worth the effort: "So! I have climbed high, and my reward is small."[2] The man in the steeple never considers acting upon the people below or the natural world he sees; indeed, he is even afraid to look too hard. Beautiful clouds, bright "... as a young man's visions" can only "... be realized in chilliness, obscurity, and tears"; he "... will look upon them no more." The narrator is a sort of Peeping Tom, looking at the town through a "pocket spyglass" and fearful even of his perch: "I love not my station here aloft, in the midst of the tumult I am powerless to direct...." He looks from without, and, seeing the outer appearance, "... can but guess" what human feelings may lie within. In the storm even the sky seems "... gloomy as an author's prospects." "Sights from a Steeple," slight sketch that it is, leaning heavily upon the form which an entry in the notebooks suggests, may be taken to typify Hawthorne's entire creation. The insight is there, but it is tentative, and the artist is almost afraid of it. "The ideas of people in general are not raised higher than the roofs of their houses," says the notebook; "The meeting-house steeple reaches out of their sphere,"[3] and the artist is frightened by the giddy height.

Herman Melville sent Ishmael up a steeple--for, in *Moby Dick*, the masts are called steeples--but the contrast between Ishmael and Hawthorne's timid narrator is strong enough to suggest the difference between Melville's power and Hawthorne's craft. The narrator of "Sights" distrusts the clouds; Ishmael is happy to mingle with them. His perch is far less secure than a steeple, yet he is happiest there. Knowing full well the dangers of a lofty mast in the treacherous sea, he still goes there to speculate. Knowing these two passages, one feels strongly tempted to commit the very sin we have noted in the Poe criticism, for one feels able, in terms of these works, to use the characters as masks, and to understand, for example, why the friendship between the two authors could never be fully satisfactory. The extroverted Ishmael fearlessly facing the ambiguities which, like the ocean winds, drove the *Pequod* onward, could hardly converse for long with the introverted landsman, who though he perhaps felt the same drizzle in his soul, was rendered giddy by a tower on firm land.

Each narrator is an isolato, yet even the nature of the isolation is different. This type of Hawthorne narrator can observe; he uses his pocket spyglass or, like Miles Coverdale, eavesdrops, but he seems too reticent to commit himself emotionally. Ishmael, paradoxically, forms close ties easily. He and Queequeg quickly become brothers, and, when Ahab drives his crew into a frenzy, Ishmael quietly informs his listeners that he, Ishmael, was one of that crew. The paradox lies here: unhappy in a landsman's world, he goes to sea. The Hawthorne isolation is isolation because of inability to establish contact; Melville's is isolation because immersion in the world has shown the world's weaknesses.

And what of Poe's flagpole sitter? As the "aristocrat" unable to utilize his patrimony, he seems analogous in his position with that suggested for Poe by his most reliable biographer, Arthur Hobson Quinn.[4] Like the narrators in Hawthorne and Melville, he is isolated--indeed, he is even farther removed from the world of men--but here the isolation seems to have been imposed as punishment. Yet he says he has "... a passion for solitude." The paradox runs throughout the works of Edgar Poe: his heroes say that they are moody souls who revel in unholy learning and love isolation, yet frequently they resent the loss of power, money or position which the isolation causes. They remind one of the romantic picture of the artist-in-the-garret. This narrator has, as we will see, the usual characteristics of the artist in Poe's fiction. Were the story complete, it would no doubt contain the narrator's attempt to record in sensational terms aspects of some harrowing experience. The unusually acute sensitivity which equips him to perceive beauty in such an experience is just the factor which keeps him from worldly success. That this is the usual complaint of the romantic artist is perhaps another way of saying that Poe has a great deal in common with other romantic artists. But note that in Poe the rejection of society usually does not include the glorification of a kind of bohemian existence. If his narrator is out of touch, he is in the lonely and isolated House of Usher, or tending a lighthouse. If he is to be rewarded, the reward is material success, as in "'Thou Art the Man'" or "The Gold Bug," or public success, as in the Dupin stories. If he is even less able than a Hawthorne character to deal with the outside, he has at the same time a more earnest desire to gain the commonly desired rewards of such contact. Poe might parody lionizing, but Dupin is the lion *par excellence.*

Finally, "The Light-House" can characterize Poe's creative output by its very incompleteness. It never becomes clear what the isolation represents. Poe said, in his preface to the last volume of poetry which he published, that he might have been a fine poet had he been given the time. I think we should read his statement as a frank confession, and not as a conspicuous display of modesty. Poe turned from poetry because he had to, and taught himself the craft of the story teller. The stories are probably more important, but they too are incomplete in terms of what he could have done. Too frequently Poe seems to have lost patience with just those stories which strike the reader as most promising.

He worshipped [Nature] . . . more in her dreary and savage aspects, than in her manifestations of placidity and joy. He stalked through that immense and often terrible wilderness with an evident rapture at his heart which we envy him as we read. He was, indeed, the man *to journey amid all that solemn desolation which he, plainly, so loved to depict. His was the proper spirit to perceive; his the true ability to feel.*
-- "The Journal of Julius Rodman"

Part One
THE AESTHETIC

Chapter I

The "Look" of Beauty

Salem, June 17, 1846

My Dear Sir,--

*I presume the publishers will have sent you a copy of
"Mosses from an Old Manse"--the latest (and probably the last) of
my tales and sketches. I have read your occasional notices of my
productions with great interest,--not so much because your
judgement was, upon the whole, favorable, as because it seemed
to be given in earnest. I care for nothing but the truth; and shall
always much more readily accept a harsh truth, in regard to my
writings, than a sugared falsehood.*

*I confess, however, that I admire you rather as a writer of
tales than as a critic upon them. I might often--and often
do--dissent from your opinions in the latter capacity, but could
never fail to recognize your force and originality in the former.*

Yours very truly,

NATH. HAWTHORNE

"Romanticism was the rebellion of the heart against the
mind." "If The Age of Reason was thesis, then the Romantic
Age was antithesis." If it were only all that simple! The case of

3

Edgar Poe alone is enough to prove that it is not simple. Poe claims that the poetic intuition is literally the source of scientific, moral and religious truth. One side of his aesthetic theory makes him seem the godfather of art-for-art's sake. His biography makes him seem the prototypical romantic artist starving in the garret. Yet we know also of his reputation for firm logic, for ratiocination, if you will, for rigorous analysis. And we know, despite his talk of transcendent inspiration, that he believed in the importance of cool and thoughtful planning, and spoke as much of novel effects, commercially-appealing subjects and the mechanical devices backstage behind a literary work as of supernal inspiration.

Poe, in short, is complicated, and this attempt to understand him is a complicated book. Before we are done, I hope to be able to demonstrate that his interest in popular topics, his love of logic and his passion for craftsmanship are not inconsistent with his seemingly paradoxical concurrent faith in that supernal beauty-in-unity which, as a good high-Romantic, he believed suffused the visible world.

For a start, we'll examine an aspect of Poe's taste. I want to show what it is that he considers beautiful. Then I will discuss how that beauty is perceived, and even try to demonstrate that, though they are many other things as well, most of Poe's tales are about the act of perceiving beauty. Turning to the tales of terror, I will discuss the old and tough question of the depth of Poe's involvement in his more gruesome material, and attempt to show that these tales, too, involve artistic perception.

Horror in Poe, however, also raises the issue of commercialism and the marketable story-type, so the next section of this book is a discussion of the magazine environment in which Poe's fiction appeared. I want to show first that this is in a surprising number of ways a market which responded to popular tastes and interests, and that popular taste and interests strongly influenced Poe. Yet paradoxically, these popular influences were not really a contradiction of his romantic ideas and ideals. The magazine-reading public was interested in phrenology, spiritualism, voyages to the moon, communication after death and Dupin, the brilliantly intuitive detective, but these odd things and others all had implications meaningful to a poet who believed literally in the Romantic world-view in which the psyche of the artist was aware of its unity with the beautiful logic of the universe. So our discussion of the content of the magazines should do more than establish their artistic level; it should suggest some relationships between transcendental philosophy and popular thought, and suggest also a reason, beyond simple economics, and independent of psychoanalysis, for Poe's interest in strange topics.

En route to whatever insights I can provide into the romantic view which saw art, science and even religion as the results of essentially the same human activity, there will be discussion of many of the stories in their own terms. This for two reasons. First, I dislike those one-strong-thesis books, which review an author's work to show that it conforms to a pattern which the critic has noticed. There is such a "pattern" in this book, but, although I think that it is most important, I don't feel that it alone explains Poe. I want to explain some other things as well. Second, I dislike the arbitrary division of literary study into "scholarship" and "criticism," with a set of licensed practitioners of each art producing studies of one sort or the other, but never both. Good scholarship illumines good criticism, and vice-versa. The two are not incompatible. Aesthetic evaluation, close analysis of structure, or other critical techniques will often yield not only insight into worth or meaning, but also into intellectual currents, biography and literary history.

- 1 -

Poe's Working Theory

I am going to ask the reader of this chapter to consider some prose of a very unfashionable sort, high-flown and filled with capitalized words like "Beauty," "Poetic Sentiment" and "Human Aspiration." The quotations are presented largely because they give us a fairly clear impression of Edgar Poe's taste. In each of them he discusses beauty or describes something which he considers beautiful.

Poe's taste is important to us because it determines his critical theory, and we need his theory to get at his works. This is because Poe's fiction does not seem to be organized around the kinds of major problems we expect to find in the "big" nineteenth century literary figures. In lieu of such problems we need some other unifying element.

It is clear, for example, that the critic seating himself before his typewriter, his notes, and an open volume of Hawthorne or Melville begins his labors with advantages which the critic of Poe does not enjoy. Allen Tate says,

> In reading Poe we are not brought up against a large, articulate scheme of experience, such as we see adumbrated in Hawthorne or Melville, which we may partly sever from personal association, both in the writer and in ourselves. Poe surrounds us with Eliot's "wilderness of mirrors," in which we see a subliminal self endlessly repeated....[1]

Shift the angle slightly, and other differences become evident. In writing about Melville, one can begin, if such is one's critical bent, by defining the central issues involved in his major work, and proceed from there to an analysis of his experiments to find suitable matter, form, and techniques to embody them. In Hawthorne, again there are clearly discernible issues--indeed, almost the same issues which troubled Melville--and again the critic has the option of moving from issues to techniques. Working outward from technique or inward from issues, one has at least the convenience of ideological reference points around which to center one's work.

One has a great deal more trouble with Poe. Major issues, as the present book in several places attempts to show, are by no means absent from the writings of Poe, but it would be foolish to maintain that they provide the sort of continuing guide line they do for the works of Hawthorne or Melville. Poe writes a tale of horror, a clever detective story, science fiction, a hymn to beauty, humor we don't "get" unless someone explicates it for us. Common issues hardly seem obvious. In their absence, it would be well to find some other means of effecting an entry into the tales. Such is the purpose of this chapter and the next.

The apparent absence of major issues need not imply that there is no pattern to the stories. Philosophically, they are quite consistent, as a number of students of Poe's critical theory have pointed out.[2] For the moment, though, let's not attack the problem of placing Poe in historical or philosophical context, but rather examine in juxtaposition some of the most obvious elements in his working theory of composition. It should suffice, for the time being, to note that the simple matter of taste, which we are about to discuss, and the subtler issues of philosophy, which we'll get to later, are closely related. A good deal of Poe can be read as a variation on the theme presented with such pomposity in *Eureka*: "In the original unity of the first thing lies the secondary cause of all things, with the germ of their inevitable annihilation."

When one goes to Poe's best-known critical essays, one finds two seemingly contradictory tenets advanced. In "The Philosophy of Composition," Poe, giving as his chief example his poem, "The Raven," suggests that the creation of literature is, on the whole, a rather mechanical business. His statement is so extreme that it has sometimes been taken for parody.

> Most writers--poets in especial--prefer having it understood that they compose by a species of fine frenzy--an ecstatic intuition--and would positively shudder at letting the public take a peep behind the scenes, at the elaborate and vacillating crudities of thought--at the true purposes seized only at the last moment--at the innumerable glimpses of ideas that arrived not at the maturity of full view--at the fully matured fancies discarded as unmanageable--at the painful erasures and interpolations--in a word, at the wheels and pinions--the tackle for scene-shifting--the step-ladders and demon-traps--the cock's feathers, the red paint and the black patches, which, in ninety-nine cases out of the hundred, constitute the properties of the literary *histrio.* [3]

In another essay, "The Poetic Principle," besides attacking didactic poetry, he speaks in almost transcendental terms of "an immortal instinct, deep within the spirit of man," the sense of beauty. Poe says, toward the end of this piece,

> ... while this [Poetic] Principle itself is, strictly and simply, the Human Aspiration for Supernal Beauty, the manifestation of the Principle is always found in an elevating excitement of the Soul--quite independent of that passion which is the intoxication of the Heart--or of that Truth which is the satisfaction of the Reason. [4]

Well then, one might ask, is one to write mechanically, by formula, or should one wait for a bolt of inspiration? The answer, at least as regards Edgar Poe, is "Both." I am going to argue, in Chapter Five, that Poe's fiction is poetic fiction, so perhaps my use of essays on poetry to demonstrate a point about his prose is not entirely arbitrary. But in truth, one could make the same point from his more scattered statements in fugitive essays on fiction: the fine essay on Hawthorne's *Twice-Told Tales* which he published in *Graham's Magazine* in May, 1842, the overlapping "Tale-Writing" in the November 1847 *Godey's Lady's Book* or any of numerous items from reviews or his "Marginalia" also demonstrate that what he said about the craft of composition, about intensity and unity of effect, about brevity, and about supernal inspiration applied to prose as well as poetry. Indeed, in his own case, since his prose was more highly matured than his poetry, and better embodies his best critical thinking, the best fiction seems better illustration of his poetic strictures than his poems.

Contained within the pages of these two essays is an artistic code which is at once pragmatic and romantic. It works terribly well, as we'll see, on Poe's own work. His best stuff seems to follow it; his failures deviate from it. The code is the critic's equivalent of the sweeping problems of Hawthorne or Melville; it is the gateway to the very center of the man's artistic personality.

The philosophies of composition suggested by the two quotations above are not as thoroughly incompatible as they appear. Poe says, in "The Philosophy of Composition,"

> I prefer commencing with the consideration of *effect*. Keeping originality *always* in view--for he is false to himself who ventures to dispense with so obvious and so easily attainable a source of interest--I say to myself, in the first place, "Of the innumerable effects, or impressions, of which the heart, and the intellect, or (more generally) the soul is susceptible, what one shall I, on the present occasion, select? Having chosen a novel, first, and secondly a vivid effect, I consider whether it can be best wrought by incident or tone--whether by ordinary incidents and peculiar tone, or the converse, or by peculiarity both of incident and tone--afterward looking about me (or rather within) for such combinations of event, or tone, as shall best aid me in the construction of the effect. (XIV, 194)

Whether or not Poe insisted upon effect as the first principle of composition because of his own limitations need not concern us for the present. Poe at his best was the master of the short piece, the piece that could indeed be constructed around a single effect, and so it was appropriate, when he came to formulate his critical theory, that he made effect his first main objective. In the essay on *Twice-Told Tales* he put the matter succinctly: a tale should be brief enough to be read at one sitting, so that "During the hour of perusal the soul of the reader is at the writer's control."

One is to concentrate upon effect; one is also to pay attention to popular appeal. The second sentence of that paragraph is essential; one must take into account the interests of one's audience. The last principle presented in the passage is equally practical. Once one has selected the effect, and decided that it will be of interest to the readers, one must decide upon a workable manner in which to present it. Some effects can be made convincing only through very special handling, and at this point Poe reaches the problem discussed in "The Poetic Principle." The preliminary mechanical work is now complete; one must now look "within" "for such combinations ... as shall best aid ... in the construction of the effect."

This is peculiar, is it not? When we think in these terms, we tend to think that inspiration (whatever that is) comes first, followed by the relatively mechanical processes of realization and development. "I have a wonderful idea!" shouts the artist as he leaps from bed at 2 a.m. and races to his desk. The dirty work comes in the morning, when he once again confronts his brilliant idea and begins the task of making of it a convincing work. But Poe claims the reverse, and this is significant. His great strength as an artist, as we shall repeatedly see, lies not in his selection of subjects, but rather in the nature of his realizations. His diagnosis is correct in his own case. If there is such a thing as inspiration, Poe seems to have been more strongly under its influence when he reached the second stage of the process which he describes.

The goal of Poe's ideal artist, and the goal which he set for himself, is beauty, and the highest praise he would have wanted bestowed upon a work of his can be summed up in a single sentence: It creates a beautiful effect. It is here that those capitalized words Poe uses in "The Poetic Principle" become relevant, for the perception of beauty involves, for Poe, "Inspiration" with all its Transcendental overtones.

It is also at this point that the extensive discussions of the philosophical location of the literary edifice which Poe constructed may first be seen in relation to this technical problem. One school of romantic critical theory demands that the artist be part god, and, as numerous scholars have pointed out, Poe understood the perception of beauty in similar terms. Poe believed that beauty is perceived through inspiration; Poe wanted to create fiction which would embody the beauty perceived. Almost every tale he wrote may be regarded as an attempt to embody in fiction the process of that perception. The form which each of the tales took was a function of the nature of the perceptive process. Thus Poe's tales can be classified in terms of that process. It can be said to determine both the personalities of his characters and the manner of their insight.

The act of perception as Poe understood it would look religious to an anthropologist, and the artist would seem to be functioning as a holy man, using his stories to show, through his characters' acts of perception, what the universe is all about. The characters are holy, too, in a sense, but before we get into that, we should have a working idea of the nature of the beauty which their "angelic imaginations" create.

- 2 -

The "Look" of His Beauty

Thus the next step in this discussion of Poe's working theory is an illustration of what appeared to him to be beautiful. Fortunately, this is not as vague a thing as it sounds. Poe's concept of beauty is another link between the seemingly contradictory principles of the two essays under discussion, and he is quite specific, if not especially profound, in the essays and in practice in his works, concerning the nature of beauty.

"The true Poetry," says Poe in that portion of "The Poetic Principle" in which he discusses his conception of beauty, is embodied in

> ... the bright orbs that shine in Heaven--in the volutes of the flower--in the clustering of low shrubberies--in the waving of the grain-fields--in the slanting of tall, Eastern trees--in the blue distance of mountains--in the grouping of clouds--in the twinkling of half-hidden brooks--in the gleaming of silver rivers--in the repose of sequestered lakes--in the star-mirroring depths of lonely wells. (XIV, 290-291)

Earlier in the same essay, he says,

> The Poetic Sentiment ... may develop itself in various modes--in painting, in Sculpture, in Architecture, in the dance--

very especially in Music--and very peculiarly, and with a wide
field, in the composition of the Landscape Garden. (XIV, 274)

Poe followed his own artistic creed in all his good work, but it
shows through most clearly in that series of rather unusual
pieces in which his only concern seemed to have been the
creation of a beautiful effect. Considering the amount of space
he devoted in "The Poetic Principle" to the beauties of nature
and landscape gardening, perhaps a good place to start would be
in "The Domain of Arnheim," or, as it is called in another
version, "The Landscape Garden." This piece tells of the
narrator's enormously wealthy friend, Ellison, and of the vast
landscape garden which he creates. I am going to use Ellison to
represent Poe's ideal artist because he acts precisely according
to the principles laid down by Poe in "The Poetic Principle."
Indeed, the language of "The Landscape Garden" is, in places,
almost identical with that of the essay.

> In the widest and noblest sense he [Ellison] was a poet. He
> comprehended, moreover, the true character, the august aims, the
> supreme majesty and the dignity of the poetic sentiment. (IV,
> 263; VI, 180)

> Ellison became neither musician nor poet; although no man
> lived more profoundly enamored of music and poetry. Under
> other circumstances than those which invested him, it is not
> impossible that he would have become a painter. Sculpture,
> although in its nature rigorously poetical, was too limited in its
> extent and consequences, to have occupied, at any time, much of
> his attention. And I have now mentioned all the provinces in
> which the common understanding of the poetic sentiment has
> declared it capable of expatiating. But Ellison maintained that the
> richest, the truest and most natural, if not altogether the most
> extensive province, had been unaccountably neglected. No
> definition had spoken of the landscape-gardener as of the poet;
> yet it seemed to my friend that the creation of the landscape-
> garden offered to the proper Muse the most magnificent of
> opportunities. Here, indeed, was the fairest field for the display
> of imagination in the endless combining of forms of novel beauty;
> the elements to enter into combination being, by a vast
> superiority, the most glorious which the earth could afford. In
> the multiform and multicolor of the flower and the trees, he
> recognised the most direct and energetic efforts of Nature at
> physical loveliness. And in the direction or concentration of this
> effort--or, more properly, in its adaptation to the eyes which were
> to behold it on earth--he perceived that he should be employing
> the best means--laboring to the greatest advantage--in the fulfill-
> ment, not only of his own destiny as a poet, but of the august

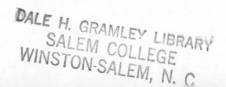

purposes for which the Deity had implanted the poetic sentiment in man. (VI, 181-182)

Poe's list of the various fields in which the poetic sentiment can find expression is very similar to the list in his essay, and, again, the transcendental nature of poetic inspiration is evident. The last sentences of the paragraph above clearly associate the Deity, Nature, and the poet. The language itself suggests something of the nature of Poe's taste. "Endless combining of forms of novel beauty"; "multiform"; "multicolor"; "energetic: these imply that Poe's landscape garden would hardly be pastoral in the usual sense of that placid summer word. Rather, Poe's ideal scene is to be richly ornate, complex, highly colored, and, to repeat a key word, "novel."

The tale concludes with the arrival of the narrator at Arnheim. Once again the special tone of Poe's beauty is evident; his description of the garden fulfills the promise contained in his commentary on Ellison's poetic talent.

> There is a gush of entrancing melody; there is an oppressive sense of strange sweet odor;--there is a dreamlike intermingling to the eye of tall slender Eastern trees--bosky shrubberies--flocks of golden and crimson birds--lily-fringed lakes--meadows of violets, tulips, poppies, hyacinths, and tuberoses--long intertangled lines of silver streamlets--and upspringing confusedly from amid all, a mass of semi-Gothic, semi-Saracenic architecture, sustaining itself by a miracle in mid-air; glittering in the red sunlight with a hundred oriels, minarets, and pinnacles; and seeming the phantom handiwork, cojointly, of the Sylphs, of the Fairies, of the Genii, and of the Gnomes. (VI, 196)

The extent to which Poe's conception of ideal beauty remained constant throughout his various writings can, unfortunately, be best demonstrated by quotation; perhaps one more long passage will be excusable. Just as Ellison's garden can serve as prototype of Poe's dream-like landscapes in other stories, so the ideal room he describes in "The Philosophy of Furniture" seems a model for the fantastic interiors in which Poe set so many of his stories. And, not surprisingly, the interior and the exterior scenes have a good deal in common; even the color schemes are identical--crimson, gold and silver again predominate. (Indeed, it is remarkable how little green Poe's landscape possessed.) Both pieces are without plot. Ellison's fantastic wealth and the discussion of American immaturity in

house-furnishing serve the same purpose: they give Poe an
excuse to describe what he took to be beautiful. The room

... is oblong--some thirty feet in length and twenty-five in breadth
.... It has but one door--by no means a wide one--which is at one
end of the parallelogram, and but two windows, which are at the
other. These latter are large, reaching down to the floor--have
deep recesses--and open on an Italian *veranda*. Their panes are of
crimson-tinted glass, set in rose-wood framings, more massive
than usual. They are curtained within the recess, by a thick silver
tissue adapted to the shape of the window, and hanging loosely in
small volumes. Without the recess are curtains of an exceedingly
rich crimson silk, fringed with a deep network of gold, and lined
with silver tissue, which is the material of the exterior blind.
There are no cornices; but the folds of the whole fabric (which
are sharp rather than massive, and have an airy appearance), issue
from beneath a broad entablature of rich giltwork, which encircles
the room .... The drapery is thrown open also, or closed, by
means of a thick rope of gold loosely enveloping it, and resolving
itself into a knot.... The colors of the curtain and their fringe--the
tints of crimson and gold--appear everywhere in profusion, and
determine the *character* of the room. The carpet--of Saxony
material--is quite half an inch thick, and is of the same crimson
ground, relieved simply by the appearance of a gold cord (like
that festooning the curtains) slightly relieved above the surface of
the *ground*, and thrown upon it in such a manner as to form a
succession of short irregular curves--one occasionally overlaying
the other. The walls are prepared with a glossy paper of a silver
gray tint, spotted with small arabesque devices of a fainter hue of
the prevalent crimson. Many paintings relieve the expanse of the
paper. These are chiefly landscapes of an imaginative cast--such as
the fairy grottoes of Stanfield, or the lake of the Dismal Swamp
of Chapman. There are, nevertheless, three or four female heads,
of an ethereal beauty--portraits in the manner of Sully. The tone
of each picture is warm, but dark. There are no "brilliant
effects." *Repose* speaks in all.... [The frames] have the whole
luster of burnished gold.... Two large low sofas of rosewood and
crimson silk, gold flowered, form the only seats, with the
exception of two light conversation chairs, also of rose-wood.
There is a pianoforte (rose-wood, also), without cover, and
thrown open. An octagonal table, formed altogether of the
richest gold-threaded marble, is placed near one of the sofas. This
is also without cover--the drapery of the curtains has been
thought sufficient. Four large and gorgeous Sevres vases, in which
bloom a profusion of sweet and vivid flowers, occupy the slightly
rounded angles of the room. A tall candelabrum, bearing a small
antique lamp with highly perfumed oil, is standing near the head
of my sleeping friend. [Poe is pretending that the room really
exists, and that as he describes it, his friend is dozing on one of

the sofas.] Some light and graceful hanging shelves, with golden
edges and crimson silk cords and gold tassels, sustain two or three
hundred magnificently bound books. Beyond these things, there
is no furniture, if we except an Argand lamp, with a plain
crimson-tinted ground-glass shade, which depends from the lofty
ceiling by a single slender gold chain, and throws a tranquil but
magical radiance over all. (XIV, 106-109)

When, in the course of this book, tales are discussed in which
Edgar Poe makes use of settings, internal or external, of an
unusually vivid nature--strange, asymmetrical, Gothic--it would
be well to bear in mind these two pieces. If, as Poe repeatedly
says, the business of the artist is neither truth, nor duty, but
rather beauty, then one might expect that the common element
in his best work would be the expression of beauty.

The two essays on the nature of the creative process, "The
Poetic Principle" and "The Philosophy of Composition," taken
together can form the basis for a critical appraisal of Poe's
stories. The former deals with the source and the nature of
inspiration, and the latter with the technical means by which
the beauty one has perceived through this inspiration may be
effectively set down on paper. The two are by no means
incompatible; on the contrary, they offer a rather level-headed
definition of an artist's practical problems. They express for the
writer just about what Edison's famous old saw expresses for
the empirical inventor, assuming, of course, as we will insist
upon assuming, that Poe was artist enough to understand
inspiration, and human enough to perspire.

Poe, then, had a very practical manner of looking at
himself as he did his daily work. This suggests a parallel to the
process by which his heroes perceive beauty. The complex
vision must be conveyed through action. Ellison is his ideal
artist in an ideal situation; he has at hand the means and
material with which to create, and the temperament to
commune--and one might as well use the word--with his
Oversoul. It was suggested that the nature of the perceiving
process can be used to determine the structure of the tales.
Ellison, bountifully endowed, appears in a piece which has, for
all practical purposes, no plot. Other characters have more
difficulty perceiving, and the tales in which they appear can be
said to be organized around the more complex manners in
which their heroes achieve their inspiration. When Allen Tate

speaks of "The Angelic Imagination," he is, in effect, speaking of the process of perception. This is the process of the god-like scientist for whom Poe called in *Eureka*. It is also the process by which Dupin, whom Robert Daniel called "Poe's Detective God,"[5] perceived the complex patterns beneath the details of crime. It can be seen as the reason that Roderick Usher and the unnamed narrators of the horror stories must be mad, or the reason that the Norwegian in "A Descent into the Maelstrom" must be frightened to the point of insanity.

It is possible, then, by tracing this interplay between the manner of perception and the structure of the tales, to define common technical elements and devices throughout Poe's work. And, happily, one can take or leave Poe's own psychological involvement. There is adequate technical reason for madness when madness is present in the tales.

Reading through Poe is a little like humming a tune in a stall shower. Sing any song in any key, and certain notes, always the same, keep booming in your ear. Poe, in his quest for means to embody his peculiar conception of beauty, repeatedly used a fairly fixed set of procedures; these boom in the ear. The booming is a grateful sound, so long as we do not let it obscure the fact that, unlike our man in the shower, perhaps, he knew a lot about progressions, chords and cadences, not to mention modulations to distant keys.

In writing of Melville, one can trace the manner in which he expresses the problems which underlie his work. In writing of Poe, we will trace the manner in which he reveals his conception of beauty. Ahab and the whale are man and the intolerable truths of the universe. The old Norwegian and the Maelstrom are the frightened mind and the awesome beauty and terror of nature.

Chapter II

The Perception of Beauty

The first notice I had of any important change going on in this part of my physical economy was from the reawakening of a state of eye generally incident to childhood, or exalted states of irritability....--In the middle of 1817, I think it was, that this faculty became positively distressing to me; at night, when I lay awake in bed, vast processions passed along in mournful pomp; friezes of never-ending stories, that to my feelings were as sad and solemn as if they were stories drawn from times before Oedipus....

Thomas De Quincey,
*Confessions of an English
Opium-Eater*

Not all of Poe's characters are extremely nervous, acutely sensitive men monomaniacally fascinated by minute details of their surroundings or addicted to liquor or drugs, but enough of them are to tempt critics to attach their characteristics to Poe himself. Indeed, the temptation must be seductively strong, a ripe red apple dangling before the eyes of the reader, for the idea remains alive three decades after Arthur Hobson Quinn showed us that we do not know that Poe was as abnormal as we thought, and four decades after the evidence began coming in

17

that the subject-matter of Poe's tales makes tricky evidence for the biographer and psychoanalyst because so much of it is borrowed from the popular magazine fiction of his day. Of these matters, more in Chapter Four. For now, without intending to debunk, I would like only to suggest another, purely aesthetic, reason for the presence of these hypersensitive characters.

For after all, when one finds in the works of an author a discernible pattern, one has more than one way to account for it. It may certainly be related to elements in the author's personality; indeed, it would be surprising if it were not. But it may also be there for any number of other reasons: perhaps because the author is a hack, and writes by formula; perhaps because the author has repeatedly found it to be a useful convention which makes it easier for him to say what he wants to say; perhaps because it reflects something in his world-view, or his artist's outlook. In Chapter One we noticed a recurrent pattern in Poe's work: a character "perceives" a beautiful vision. A second pattern is that many of Poe's characters--often the narrators--are hypersensitive. In the present chapter I want to point out the connection between these two things. "Poor Eddie"--the phrase is his own--has been psychoanalyzed sufficient times because of these nervous characters; let us try to account for them in a simpler manner.

-1-

Salvation and Terror

"A Descent into the Maelstrom" is a good example of a story dealing with the sort of beauty which Poe seemed to admire, and also a good introduction to the functions of the hypersensitive observer. The narrator and his Norwegian guide climb to a lofty crag overlooking the Maelstrom. No accounts of the whirlpool, says the narrator, can "impart the faintest conception either of the magnificence, or of the horror of the scene--or of the wild bewildering sense of *the novel* which confounds the beholder."[1] The language is significant; we are dealing again with the elements of Poe's beauty--wildness, magnificence, novelty. The narrator's description of the wonder and horror of the spectacle sets the stage for the Norwegian's story. He and his brothers had been fishermen who worked the waters near the whirlpool. In a memorably violent storm, their boat was swept into the Maelstrom itself. One brother was immediately lost, and the other, maddened by fear, perished when the ship, having been sucked into the vortex, was finally destroyed. But the storyteller, having given up all hope of surviving, emerged from his initial horror and bewilderment to a sense of how magnificent "it was to die...in view of so wonderful a manifestation of God's power." (II, 240) Poe's few lines describing the transformation which the fisherman underwent are a key to the story.

> "After a little while I became possessed with the keenest curiosity about the whirl itself. I positively felt a *wish* to explore its depths, even at the sacrifice I was going to make; and my principal grief was that I should never be able to tell my old companions on shore about the mysteries I should see. These, no doubt, were singular fancies to occupy a man's mind in such extremity--and I have often thought since, that the revolutions of the boat around the pool might have rendered me a little lightheaded.["] (II, 240)

As a result of this "unnatural curiosity," he was able to observe enough of the behavior of various objects floating about in the vortex to realize that, by abandoning the ship and clinging to a water cask, he could be saved.

For me, this very fine story has one annoying flaw: the fisherman uses what seems too erudite language. But it takes unusual brilliance, in Poe, to see beauty. One can quite readily divide a great many of his tales into types according to the manner in which the narrator or the protagonist perceives beauty. In the type to which "A Descent into the Maelstrom" belongs, the hero, thrown by the horror of his predicament beyond ordinary despair, becomes abnormally rational and is able to gain brillant insight into the nature of the awful beauty. The insight saves him. The beauty can be natural, as in this story, supernatural, or man-made. Indeed, it does not even have to be beautiful in any normal sense of the word, so long as it demonstrates a sort of Gothic complexity and novelty. What happens to the narrator in "The Pit and the Pendulum," for example, is not very pretty, but it is for him what the whirlpool is for our fisherman.

"The Pit and the Pendulum" should not frighten us away

because of its popularity or its sensationalism, for it provides an excellent review of Poe's techniques. In psychological treatment, it stands somewhere between the Dupin stories, the stories about "expiring ladies," and the "Maelstrom." As in the "Maelstrom," the narrator is in a woefully hopeless situation, and, also as in the "Maelstrom," he saves himself through "the keen, collected calmness of despair." The narrator's progress up through successive levels of consciousness and down through levels of insanity until he achieves the final brilliance of sheer despair is delineated with great detail and with consummate skill. The closest modern counterpart of what Poe here accomplished is perhaps George Orwell's *1984*; Winston Smith's torture also drives him insane, but in his case, the reemergence to a sanity of sorts is controlled by skilled psychologists. Poe's hero has to fend for himself. If his torturers are less methodical than Winston's, they are no less cruel, and far more diabolical.

Poe's story is no doubt sensational in both the psychological and journalistic senses of the word, but it will be remembered that sensationalism was one of the tenets of his critical theory; it was the artist's business to choose an arresting subject. Actually, in "The Pit and the Pendulum" Poe may be said to have followed his own advice carefully. The entire story is designed to produce a single effect, the pattern presented is Gothic in its complexity and horror, and the narrator's solution of it is achieved through use of that fierce insight which, in Poe, always characterizes the perception of beauty. It is necessary for the protagonist to go through all the stages of madness before he can achieve the desperate rationality which will save him, and his monomaniac powers of concentration are, as we shall see later, of the same type which characterize the narrators of tales like "Berenice," "Ligeia," or "Morella." His brilliant solution to the complex pattern is of the same order as that achieved by the Norwegian in the "Maelstrom" or by the detective Dupin in the tales of ratiocination. The story is at once a tale of terror, a beautiful pattern, and a tale of ratiocination. It is richly symbolic. The mind emerges from darkness as the narrator regains consciousness in his dungeon; it slowly becomes acquainted with its environment as he gropes his way around the room in which he is imprisoned; it escapes into insanity as the full details of the situation are revealed. Like Winston Smith at the point of complete breakdown before his mind is to be remodeled, Poe's hero is "an imbecile--an idiot." (V, 80) As in Winston's case again, incidentally, his emergence is prefaced by contact with unspeakable horror--in each case, exposure to rats.

> They pressed--they swarmed upon me in ever accumulating heaps. They writhed upon my throat; their cold lips sought my own; I was half stifled by their thronging pressure; disgust, for which the world has no name, swelled my bosom, and chilled, with a heavy clamminess, my heart. (V,83)

But the passage is nearer to Melville than it is to Orwell. Poe's narrator snaps out of his daze after contact with the seamiest sort of living things; reality returns with the rats. Compare the passage to the following, from the brilliant closing scene of Chapter LCII in *White-Jacket*, in which White-Jacket tumbles from the top-mast of his man-of-war into the sea. As Poe's narrator, at the opening of the tale, fears that he is already in his tomb, so White-Jacket wonders whether he is already dead. Both must be shocked out of their dazed states before they can be saved.

> As I gushed into the sea, a thunder-boom sounded in my ear; my soul seemed flying from my mouth. The feeling of death flooded over me with the billows. The blow from the sea must have turned me, so that I sank almost feet foremost through a soft, seething, foamy lull. Some current seemed to be hurrying me away; in a trance I yielded, and sank deeper down with a glide. Purple and pathless was the deep calm now around me, flecked by summer lightnings in an azure afar. The horrible nausea was gone; the bloody, blind film turned a pale green; I wondered whether I was alive or dead, or still dying. But of a sudden some fashionless form brushed my side--some inert, coiled fish of the sea, the thrill of being alive again tingled through my nerves, and the strong shunning of death shocked me through.[2]

What Poe and Melville are "on to" in these episodes is an important matter indeed: it is nothing less than the great romantic discovery of the psychological connections between death, sexuality and creativity, the discovery which, as Freud freely acknowledged, the artist had made before the scientist. The sexuality is not overt in either the Poe or the Melville passage, though it becomes almost unbearably overt in later Melville, especially in *Pierre*. In the case of Poe, I suppose we must accept the suggestion of Freudian critics that in a prudish age, the idea of death becomes erotically exciting. There is certainly a connection between what happens here in Poe and a high-romantic document such as Whitman's "Out of the Cradle Endlessly Rocking," in which "the outsetting bard," the young boy on the beach by the sea, in contact with death for the first time, feels the connection between it, his poet's mission, and sexual drive (the "sweet hell within," the mated birds, and the pregnant moon).

But I promised not to psychoanalyze Poe, so suffice it to say that in both "A Descent into the Maelstrom" and "The Pit and the Pendulum," the narrator emerges from fear into lucidity, and the lucidity saves him.

The pattern of salvation-after-immersion-in-horror evident in these two stories is common enough in myth, but it also suggests, especially in the case of "Maelstrom," Coleridge's "The Rime of the Ancient Mariner." Numerous commentators have remarked the relationship between Poe and Coleridge, [3] and Poe's considerable debt to his English contemporary, but I have not seen drawn out the rather strong similarity between this tale and the poem. There are notable resemblances. In each, a horrible experience on the sea is related by the lone survivor to a single listener. In each, the survivor has lost his companions and his hope of surviving, to be saved only after a kind of spiritual rebirth.

In the details of its plot, Poe's "Maelstrom" is closer to the French story "Le Maelstrom" cited by Turner than it is to Coleridge. Yet comparison is useful, if only to point up the rather revealing differences in moral emphasis. Poe's hero does, in fact, pray as his ship plunges into the whirlpool, but he does so because he is certain he is about to die: "I muttered a hurried prayer to God, and thought all was over." (II, 241) How unlike the Mariner's

> O happy living things! no tongue
> Their beauty might declare:
> A spring of love gushed from my heart,
> And I blessed them unaware:
> Sure my kind saint took pity on me,
> And I blessed them unaware.
>
> The self-same moment I could pray:
> And from my neck so free
> The albatross fell off, and sank
> Like lead into the sea. (lines 282-291)

Much nearer the tone of the Mariner's awed awakening to the beauty of the sea-creatures about him is what happens to Poe's fisherman *after* the prayer. His heightened sense of wonder and his perception of the beauty around him seem a secularized version of the Mariner's experience, though of course in the works of any romantic author one must be careful of calling "secular" any passage in which nature is seen as beauty. As we shall see in a later chapter, Poe shares with his romantic contemporaries most of their important attitudes about nature and the universe. But it is fair enough to say of the present story that it is far less overtly religious than Coleridge's poem. Salvation comes not through a miracle of God but through the strength of the sailor's awakened--and perhaps inspired--intellect. Or, in terms of the pattern of such perceptions in Poe, the fisherman, in his "madness," perceives the central truths, and is saved.

This, it will be seen, is thoroughly in keeping with the theory of poetry to which Poe subscribed. Like Shelley's legislator-poet, the artist in Poe is the man who can cut through to centrality, and Poe here has made his fisherman an artist. The usual aspects of beauty are present:

> "Never shall I forget the sensation of awe, horror, and admiration with which I gazed about me. The boat appeared to be hanging, as if by magic, midway down, upon the interior surface of a funnel vast in circumference, prodigious in depth, and whose perfectly smooth sides might have been mistaken for ebony, but for the bewildering rapidity with which they spun around, and for the gleaming and ghastly radiance they shot forth, as the rays of the full moon, from that circular rift amid the clouds...streamed in a flood of golden glory along the black walls, and far away down into the inmost recesses of the abyss.["] (II, 242)

Awe, horror, yet also admiration: this would seem central to an understanding of Poe's version of romantic beauty.

In the Coleridge poem, perception of the beauty calls forth the benediction, which releases the soul for salvation. In Poe, perception of the beauty is a sign of heightened sensitivity; the sailor becomes the poet, and the poet can save himself. His acute observations will keep him alive until the beneficial changes in nature which both works have in common (but which here both reader and survivor know will come eventually through natural processes) can occur. The prayer in Poe is irrelevant so far as the hero's survival is concerned.

Carroll D. Laverty has pointed out[4] that in this and other Poe tales everything that happens can be accounted for in scientific terms, and in this tale Poe, as noted in footnote 3, went to the *Encyclopedia Britannica* for his physics. But this does not negate the mystical quality so obvious in the fisherman's long description of the beauties of the whirlpool, nor of course, his assumptions concerning science and inspiration. If we loosely equate this inspiration with the influence of a supernal force--"Oversoul" is again probably our best word-- then it will be seen that the same general elements present in "The Rime of the Ancient Mariner" are present here: awesome nature, an awed personality, and an Oversoul. But the emphasis is totally different.

One reason for the difference is the tone of the Poe story. Except for the paragraphs in which the Norwegian is speaking of the horror and grandeur of the Maelstrom, the tone is deadly cold, so cold that it seriously detracts from the total effect. One might defend it in these terms: Coleridge, dealing with a mystical religious experience, used a ritualistic and mystic language. Poe, dealing with a triumph of human ingenuity and inspiration, used the calm language of reasonable men. But even this is not really convincing, for the deep shock of the experience in itself, without any mystical connotations, should have produced a more emotional narrative.

When the fisherman loses his youngest brother, he says, "'... both our masts went by the boards as if they had been sawed off--the mainmast taking with it my youngest brother, who had lashed himself to it for safety.'" (II, 236) The sentence structure is wrong. Fisherman don't talk this way. One could list other examples of jarringly inappropriate language; the difficulty seems to be that Poe failed to decide what his tone of voice would be. The story's opening is fine in its way; the manly good-nature of the narrator (the one to whom the tale was told) and the fisherman comes across effectively. "'Do you know,'" asks the Norwegian, "'I can scarcely look over this little cliff without getting giddy?'" (II, 225) The narrator turns, in effect, to the reader, and says,

> The "little cliff," upon whose edge he had so carelessly

thrown himself down to rest that the weightier portion of his
body hung over it, while he was only kept from falling by the
tenure of his elbow on its extreme and slippery edge--this "little
cliff" arose, a sheer unobstructed precipice of black shining rock,
some fifteen or sixteen hundred feet from the world of crags
beneath us. Nothing would have tempted me to be within half a
dozen yards of its brink. (II, 226)

But even here, in the story's opening, the fisherman speaks too
much like a lecturer: "'...the six hours of deadly terror which I
then endured have broken me up body and soul.'" (II, 225)

Nor is there any development of tone as the story
progresses, except in terms of excitement; the Norwegian's
language remains scholarly. How he should speak is hinted at in
his reference to the school-teacher who explained to him the
principle which saved him: he should sound like an uneducated
man groping for a language in which to express the details of a
fantastic experience he has undergone.

It is almost as though Poe had intended a parody of
Coleridge, rather than a serious story. The unwilling wedding
guest has become a tourist, and the Mariner a guide. Urgency of
narration is replaced by a laconic manner. Nature is still
awesome, but man and not God brings salvation. At any rate,
the tale achieves nothing like the power it seems to have in
potential, so that at the close, when the Norwegian says of his
tale, "'I now tell it to *you*--and I can scarcely expect you to put
more faith in it than did the merry fishermen of Lofoden'" (II,
247), the reader is tempted to answer, "No, but I might have
believed it if you really sounded like a fisherman." Poe had to
make his fisherman brilliant to make his story work, but the
brilliance makes the character less credible.

This lucidity or brilliance is the technical element which
links the several types of tales, for it can be achieved in several
ways. The Norwegian and the victim of the Inquisition achieve
it through the violent shocks to which they are subjected.
Dupin, the master detective, seems to possess it as an integral
part of his personality. Both "The Pit" and "Maelstrom" have
many of the elements of the tales of terror, but they differ from
them in that in the tale of terror, as that term is used in
this volume, the narrator is able to perceive the awesome
beauty not through his rationality, but rather through his
madness. In each case, however, the act of perception is

intrinsically the same as that of which Ellison, Poe's ideal poet, is capable. There are many different types of poet in Poe.

-2-

Madness, Credibility and the Beautiful Subject

A paraphrase of Poe is liable to sound absurd out of context, but he did say that the most beautiful effect one could create was the effect of beauty itself, and that the subject most appropriate for the production of the effect was the death of a beloved woman. To learn what this effect was, let us turn to stories about dying women to see what there is in them which he might have thought beautiful. "Ligeia" is the best known of this group, but the stories have numerous features in common. For convenience I am going to lump together Poe's entire grisly chorus line under the heading "expiring ladies." I have also heard them called "misty women"; neither title seems suitably grave, but I have been unable to unearth any more solemn. The fact that one has to worry about a name for them--that is, that a group of stories exists, large enough and important enough to require a general category-- suggests again Poe's ties to his times. We are dealing once more with the substitution of death for sex, and in these cases, the sexuality has become more overt. When, years later, Twain made fun of the morbid fascination with death in the Emmeline Grangerford passages in *Huckleberry Finn*, he was parodying something genuinely widespread in nineteenth century culture. In Poe's stories, however, we are given not merely evidence of the sickness, the confusion between sex and death, but also the great discovery which went with it, the realization of the connection between these things and creativity. In every case, the death of the woman is associated with some manner of vision or inspiration. "Berenice," "Eleanora," "Ligeia" and "Morella" are horror stories, like "The Fall of the House of Usher," and like that tale follow Poe's usual pattern for such pieces. We may expect to find a perceiver and a vision.

"Berenice," especially in its ghoulish closing paragraphs, may violate the canons of taste, but it illustrates the pattern very nicely. The narrator is mad, a monomaniac capable of losing himself, due to an extreme heightening of the attentive powers of his mind, in morbid contemplation of the most minute items.

> To muse for long unwearied hours with my attention riveted to some frivolous device on the margin, or in the typography of a book; to become absorbed for the better part of a summer's day, in a quaint shadow falling aslant upon the tapestry, or upon the door; to lose myself for an entire night in watching the steady flame of a lamp, or the embers of a fire; to dream away whole days over the perfume of a flower; to repeat monotonously some common word, until the sound, by dint of frequent repetition, ceased to convey any idea whatever to the mind; to lose all sense of motion or physical existence, by means of absolute bodily quiescence long and obstinately persevered;--such were a few of the most common and least pernicious vagaries induced by a condition of the mental faculties.... (II, 19)

Clark Griffith[5] has defined the situation of such Poe characters as "the inner madness," which enables the characters to perceive "the outer wonders." And so the narrator, Egaeus, becomes fascinated with the teeth of Berenice.

"Eleanora" fits into the same pattern.[6]

> I am come of a race noted for vigor of fancy and ardor of passion. Men have called me mad; but the question is not yet settled, whether madness is or is not the loftiest intelligence-- whether much that is glorious--whether all that is profound--does not spring from diseases of thought--from *moods* of mind exalted at the expense of the general intellect....(IV, 236)

says the narrator at the opening of the story. The outer wonders here are the wonders of the strange valley in which the narrator and his misty Eleanora dwell, wonders akin to those in "The Landscape Garden." The valley becomes even more wondrous in the presence of Eleanora.

> A change fell upon all things. Strange brilliant flowers, star-shaped, burst out upon the trees where no flowers had been known before. The tints of the green carpet deepened; and when, one by one, the white daisies shrank away, there sprang up, in place of them, ten by ten of the ruby-red asphodel. (IV, 239)

There exists a certain ambiguity in the structure of these stories. The narrator is mad; the narrator has seen the wonders. Has he created them himself? A problem of this sort would be of utmost importance in Melville; it is less important in Hawthorne or in Poe. The reader is never sure whether Goodman Brown really saw witches in the forest. As will be demonstrated in this discussion, it makes very little difference

in either Hawthorne or Poe whether or not the vision is real.
Whether or not the whale sheared off Ahab's leg with divine
malice, however, does matter. Melville is dealing not only with
the psychological make-up of his characters, but also with
problems of morals, of theology, and of epistemology. Hawthorne has far more in common with Poe so far as the technical
problems which he faced in his fiction are concerned. Although
the moral concern of Hawthorne is not often present in Poe, the
two have in common a concern for psychology. In many of
their tales, the reader is offered something of a choice, a
"margin of credibility." Because the action of the individual
tale frequently is of the nature of a vision, Poe and Hawthorne
frequently leave open the possibility that that action really did
not occur. The reader can believe in the action, or he can regard
the objects in the tale as parts of the landscape of a troubled
mind. Of course, the emphasis is different; in Hawthorne the
"trouble" involves moral issues. If such issues are present in
Poe, they are usually present as additional portions of the
landscape; Poe is more purely a psychological writer.

In the stories discussed in the present chapter, Poe is
concerned with the progression of minds into madness and with
the beauty which they perceive in their madness. In the passage
quoted above, a change may not really have fallen upon all
things except in the narrator's mind. Again, the old Norwegian
may be lying and may be mad; his hair may have turned white
from old age, and not from the experience of the descent into
the maelstrom; it does not really matter. The critic need only
concern himself with the techniques with which Poe deals with
these minds and the beauty which they perceive.

-3-

"Ligeia": Multiple Intention, Unified Effect

We have no clearer illustration of Poe's taste than the
description of Ligeia, whose beauty has the "radiance of an
opium-dream," and whose beauty Poe uses to establish an
explicitly romantic aesthetic: "...her features were not of that
regular mould which we have been falsely taught to worship in
the classical labors of the heathen." They are, rather, strange,
and Ligeia herself is Poe's "outer wonder." The narrator, true to

form, perceives her in his "heated fancy" (II,249), and says that
the ideal of beauty which she represents is not classic.

Poe surrounds her with darkness. "She came and departed
as a shadow"; (II, 249) her pale and ivory skin is set off by "the
raven-black, the glossy, the luxuriant, and naturally-curling
tresses"; (II, 250) her eyes are orbs of "the most brilliant...
black." (II, 251) She is immensely learned; she has applied her
"fierce energy" (II, 253) to the darkest regions of German
metaphysics. Ligeia dies, and the narrator leaves "the dim and
decaying city by the Rhine." (II, 258) Rowena, his second wife,
is purchased from her parents--a mundane procedure in contrast
to the unworldly elements which surround Ligeia. Where Ligeia
was bathed in darkness, Rowena, as Clark Griffith points out, is
surrounded by gold imagery. She is blond; her family sold her
from "thirst of gold"; the bridal chamber contains "a huge
censer" of gold on a chain of gold, gold candelabra, and golden
tapestry. The figures on the tapestry, however, are of "the most
jetty black," and the bed on which she lies ill is of ebony. (II,
259) The room as a whole reminds one very strongly of the one
described in "The Philosophy of Furniture," or of the sort of
beauty delineated in "The Landscape-Garden." In some cases,
the language is almost identical--for example, the words
"semi-Gothic, semi-Druidical" in "Ligeia," and the words
"semi-Gothic, semi-Saracenic" in "The Landscape-Garden." The
difference is that in "Ligeia" Poe organizes his beauty not only
for its own sake, but also to serve specific symbolic ends. The
return of Ligeia is heralded by the motion of the tapestry and
occurs on the ebony bed. The moment of Ligeia's return itself is
represented by a shadow moving on the golden carpet; when the
transformation is complete, blackness has replaced the gold, and
the tale closes:

> ...there streamed forth, into the rushing atmosphere of the
> chamber, huge masses of long and dishevelled hair; *it was blacker
> than the raven wings of mid-night!* And now slowly opened *the
> eyes* of the figure which stood before me. "Here then, at least," I
> shrieked aloud, "can I never--can I never be mistaken--these are
> the full, and the black, and the wild eyes--of my lost love--of the
> Lady--of the LADY LIGEIA." (II, 268)

"Ligeia" poses numerous special problems, not the least *conclusion*
disconcerting of which is that it is actually difficult to read with
enjoyment. A safe first test of a Poe story is Poe's own--Is it

effective? But who can remember what was the effect of "Ligeia" on first reading? Allen Tate opens his charming and perceptive essay, "Our Cousin, Mr. Poe," with his own childhood memories of Poe; he was fourteen when he first read "Ligeia," and liked it best of Poe's stories. Perhaps I may be permitted the same rights of reminiscence. Since we are shortly going to discuss the reactions of a number of critics to the story, it seems worthwhile to make the effort to recall a naive first reaction. It so happens--and I hope this will not be thought "confessional"--that I remember my own experience in some detail. It might be more accurate to say that I *think* that I remember, for there is always the danger that I am rationalizing. Here, at any rate, is an attempt at listing aspects of that first reaction.

First: the supposed quotation from Glanvill, the references to antiquity, Lord Byron and deep scholarship worked. They produced a feeling that Poe was dealing with dark and mystical people in an unearthly world. I had no reason to question the authority of a man whom I took to be a great writer, and I really did not expect to understand everything I read.

Second: because my ideas of love were vague and colored by the idealized and romanticized accounts which were all my pre-adolescent experience included (I must have read Poe earlier than did Mr. Tate), I was not struck by anything terribly wrong with the relationship depicted. This was all very strange, but that there might be present anything sexually abnormal--I certainly did not know the term--never consciously occurred to me.

Third: I felt that Poe gave away his ending too early for maximum impact at the close. This sounds too sophisticated; say that I resented the fact that Poe did not extract more shock from the disclosure that Rowena had become Ligeia, and that this resentment made the last pages of the tale less effective. Young people expect a few goosepimples from their literature. Yet I liked the ending, and thought the last fragmented sentence fine writing. I do remember very clearly thinking that it was too bad that the last words-- "LADY LIGEIA"--were so conspicuous on the page that one had to read them before one reached them. This, again detracted from the thrill.

This dredging up of memories is intended to point up one quality which makes tales like "Ligeia" so difficult to handle. If my testimony may be taken as evidence, the story can be read with enjoyment by a naive reader. It is not possible to draw a sharp line and say that a reader of "x" maturity is disqualified, although were the attempt made to locate such a line, it might be determined by a factor such as the reader's awareness that there is something shallow in all the conspicuous erudition that Poe parades. Suffice it to say that the majority of readers of "Ligeia" have probably taken it seriously, and that its continuing popularity is a sign of its effectiveness on *some* level. Let's call this response of the naive reader who comes to Poe for entertainment "Reaction A," and see how it compares with other reactions.

"Reaction B" I offer as those points on which most of Poe's critics are agreed. One must be careful and general, for "Ligeia" seems to invite radical readings, but these seem to be safe enough ideas: "Ligeia" is a carefully constructed tale in which Poe, using his operatic stagecraft, displayed his pet devices and preoccupations, yet still maintained at least moderately effective artistic control. There is no general agreement concerning the tale's success, but these elements seem to be present in even the more radical interpretations. It is also thought that "Ligeia" has much in common with Poe's verse (it even contains a sample), and most modern critics would probably agree with T. S. Eliot's comment that only adolescents profitably read Poe's poetry.

One should list Poe's own estimate; let it be "Reaction C." According to the author, this is his best story.

Under "D" let us place the specialized readings. The troubling thing about the more extreme reactions is that they are often the most perceptive. A writer to whom this study is most deeply indebted, Clark Griffith, published an article suggesting that "Ligeia" is intended as satire.[7] Mr. Griffith documents his thesis carefully, and although Edward Davidson tactfully calls it "a stimulating and controversial analysis,"[8] one senses that Griffith is on to something. This writer, for one, almost wishes the idea had not occurred to Griffith, for it throws too much of Poe out of focus.

It is perfectly possible for a tale to be a satire as well as an effective entertainment for those who miss the satirical intent, but, in truth, one has difficulties enough with "Ligeia" without this added analysis. The style, for example, seems to indicate a

serious intention, not satire. The prose of "Ligeia" is overwrought by contemporary standards (once again the reader is
referred to Tate's "Our Cousin, Mr. Poe"), but no more so than
that of numerous other Poe stories; indeed, if anything, it seems
more carefully deployed on these pages than in most of Poe. To
see how peculiar the situation is, let us again use Melville as a
reference point. When one reads the enormously overdone
opening chapters of his *Pierre*, the tone seems so forced--
especially in relation to Melville's usually successful prose--that
one suspects that the author himself does not believe in the
idyllic land he is depicting. The novel bears out the suspicion.
But this is Poe's Sunday-best style. In Tate's words,

> ...no man is going to use so much neo-Gothic, over and over
> again, unless he means business with it; I think that Poe meant
> business. If the Gothic influence had not been to hand, he would
> have invented it, or something equally "unreal," to serve his
> purpose.[9]

Poe could parody the sensation recorders, but one is always
sure, in those stories, that one is reading satire. He seems so
clearly to "mean business" here that Griffith's suggestion
undercuts more than one feels willing to lose. Yet there it
stands, and it is too convincing for comfort.

An argument might be raised that this tale, like certain
other pieces of literature, can be read on several levels, and,
indeed, considering the wide range of opinions concerning what
"Ligeia" means, this seems reasonable. Certainly the tale can be
read by the right reader as a skillfully sustained horror story, in
which a normally unbelievable event becomes credible because
of its environment. It will also stand up as a psychological study
of the narrator's haunted mind, which, after all, is what it
frankly purports to be. Very close to this approach is another:
regarding "Ligeia" as a document in Poe's personal case history.
Considering this list, satire seems rather out of place as another
"level," possibly because our literary experience does not
include works which are at the same time designed for
maximum emotional impact in a limited space, and also satire.

Moreover, using this type of language--"levels"--inevitably
brings to mind that most levelled-at book, *Moby Dick*, and the
honest reader feels compelled to differentiate. It is a very
different thing from saying, "*Moby Dick* can be read by
youngsters as a great seafaring adventure and by adults as a

parable of man's quest for...," to say, "'Ligeia' can be read by youngsters as a horror story and by adults as either a probing into a fear-ridden mind or as a satire." For one thing, "Ligeia" is too short and too obviously aimed at the single strong effect to produce such varied reactions. Besides, we are not sure it can be read by adults at all, except possibly as a psychological study.

The answer to this problem of intention is probably to be found in a peculiarity of Poe's artistic personality. It is this writer's feeling, generally speaking, that when we encounter something in Poe's work which merits explanation, we should look for aesthetic grounds for its presence before we turn to personal grounds. I would counsel looking to several other sources before resorting to Poe's biography. If aesthetic considerations do not explain it, look to philosophy. Poe, as we shall see, wrote from a surprisingly consistent philosophical position. If that doesn't work, try something more mundane-- commercial reasons, for instance. Perhaps Poe put it in because he thought it would sell. But every now and then in Poe one comes to an impasse, and no normal New Critical analysis, no Old Scholarly account of sources and influences, can really do the job. In such cases one flies by the seat of one's pants. One takes one's own feeling for Poe's artistic personality, tries to imagine him writing, and plunges ahead. Let me propose what will doubtless sound like a crazy thesis: every one of the approaches we have mentioned is correct. "Ligeia" *is* a satire. The almost-allegorical contrasts between materialism (gold) and transcendentalism (black) are deliberate; the author knows what he is doing. The aesthetic statement about the sources of creativity is conscious and is intended seriously. The horror effects are also serious in intention, supported by stagecraft as convincing as the author can create.

But if all of these things are true, then what is the total intention of the thing? My impression is that the author doesn't know and neither can we. If we insist on finding comparable works, we must turn to contemporary literature, to *Under the Volcano, The Natural,* to the Theatre of the Absurd, to Kafka, to Nathanael West. There we can find works in which crazy things happen, in which nervous or exhuberant creativity deliberately juxtaposes wildly disparate elements. One cannot really speak of "levels" in the usual sense in such works, because the authors do not keep the levels discrete. Whereas in more conventional works a "level" of allusion (to mythology, let's say) remains beneath the surface, coloring, enriching or commenting upon the "real" action, in these works it and other "levels" penetrate the surface so that the usual sense of reality is shattered. What Poe does is probably less controlled than what happens in most of the works in the genre to which I have alluded, though one cannot be sure of that. But one senses an instability in his compounding of all these elements. He has worked carefully on each, yet they should not all be here together, not if the story is to be understood fully. How can a story which parodies mysticism also present, seriously, the mystic thesis that the human mind is the present source of all creativity and power, that it can literally overcome the apparent physical laws of the universe? It can't, in any normal terms. One needs, as I have suggested, some conception of Poe at work, and my guess is that fitful changes of mood best account for what we have here.

We know some fact about Poe which will account for every element in "Ligeia." The irritation against the New England Transcendentalists is a motive for a satire on mysticism; perhaps there are others. The craftsmanlike pleasure any good artist takes in setting himself hard problems and then solving them can account for his efforts to make the transformation of Rowena into Ligeia sufficiently credible so that the ending of the tale can be effective. The commercial writer's knowledge of his market, of the intellectual climate and of the sensational impact of a fantasy on the deaths of beautiful women can account for much of the choice of subject matter; so can his previous success with similar material. His own taste can account for that, too, for in the essay on how he wrote "The Raven" he claimed that such a subject was the most beautiful which a poet could select. And the mysticism we know from almost all his major work to be a serious belief. The "circle of analogies" of which the narrator speaks in describing Ligeia's eyes is orthodox occultism: to the occultist, reasoning by analogy is not a logical error, for the "linked analogies," to use Melville's phrase, are the key to transcendent truth and unity. All of these things do not "add up," but all of them are demonstrably a part of Poe. We can build a plausible case if we can imagine him perhaps returning to work on this tale in different moods: methodical at times, crafting a credible manner to handle an incredible subject; deeply moved at others by the romantic sweep of the cosmology upon which his tale was built; caught up in the overwrought language he was himself creating; struck by the absurdity of similar ideas in the hands of other writers, and even at times his own.

One needs little in the way of "depth psychology" to conclude that Poe was capable of such fitful shifts in mood or attitude. All are present in his work. All, moreover, are patently visible in his biography, even those portions of it of which we are completely certain. Browse through those of Poe's letters which Arthur Hobson Quinn reprinted in his biography and you will see, I am certain, how deeply Poe could be changed by mood. People are not consistent; they hold contradictory ideas, and moods alter their personalities. Unstable people are even less so, and unstable people in situations of continual stress, as Poe was throughout his career, may be expected to show the rapid transformations in attitude toward a given object which I think are visible in "Ligeia."

Paradoxically, none of this keeps "Ligeia" from succeeding. A reader (as opposed to an analysist) perhaps feels something nervous turning beneath the prose, but the lines Poe has begun are drawn out to their conclusion. I mean "lines" here as in music. A romantic composer spins out a line, the listener hears moods change in it and beneath it, but, though these affect his emotions, the line itself has a kind of logic, and he hears it out, not merely as a way through different moods but as an entity in itself. The moods and emotions cannot be named; music is too abstract an art for that, but the listener and even more the performer feels both the ineffable sequence of their progression and a sort of urgency that the line be completed. Good musicians who love the Baroque and the Classical find themselves coming back to the Romantics, surprised to find how well Brahms, or even Tchaikovsky, structure their emotional works. Readers of surprising sophistication come back to Poe, knowing all about the hokum and the stagecraft, perhaps even knowing about the contradictions in intent, yet moved both by the turbulence beneath the line and by the craftsmanlike spinning of the line itself.

Poe said that good art was unified in effect. But good

romantic work need not be unified in intention. If we can respond to "Ligeia," and sometimes we can, we respond as we do to music.

We don't even need unity of meaning; unity of effect and our interest in seeing the pattern work itself out are enough. By way of illustration, let's examine yet another "radical" treatment of "Ligeia." Speaking of the stories about expiring ladies in general, Roy P. Basler says,

> Even a casual comparison of these stories will reveal not merely the similar theme of obsession but also the dominant concepts which provide the motivation in all three: the power of the psychical over the physical and the power of frustrate love to create an erotic symbolism and mythology in compensation for sensual disappointment.[10]

Basler believes that the struggle to overcome death suggested by the Glanvill quotation is the narrator's, not Ligeia's. Ligeia's own philosophy, he says, is materialistic, as is evidenced by her poem. (Here we must ignore the distinction which Griffith draws between Ligeia and Rowena; he is doubtless right in assuming that Ligeia is surrounded by imagery suggesting German transcendental thought, while Rowena is surrounded by materialistic--gold--things. Basler is quite correct in pointing out that Ligeia says and does very little, and that the poem "The Conqueror Worm" is materialistic. There is no real contradiction; it's just that the two writers are using the word "materialism" differently. Griffith means it in its economic sense; Basler refers to a philosophical position.) The narrator "...resolved to bring her back to life"; this is "...the old story of the madman who knows that he is right and the rest of the world is wrong." (367) Moreover,

> The key to his failure is hinted in the paragraph which reveals his symbolic deification of Ligeia as a sort of personal Venus Aphrodite who personifies the dynamic urge of life itself but who, because of the hero's psychic incapacity, cannot reveal to him the "forbidden knowledge...." (365)

In this reading, Ligeia is passive; "...the hero's approach to power is thwarted by Ligeia's death. Just at the point when triumph seems imminent, ...Ligeia dies...." (366)

Here one has to deal again with that ambiguity which gives to these tales whatever credibility they possess; the strongest asset of the Basler article is that it rests upon the assumption that the mind of the narrator is a diseased mind, and not to be trusted: "...it must be recognized that the hero has murdered Rowena in his maniacal attempt to restore Ligeia to life." (368) Certainly the hero may have done so. There is no evidence in the story to prove that he has not. Consider the drops in Rowena's glass. Basler thinks that after having tortured the girl to the point of death, the narrator now poisons her, though he deludes himself into thinking "...that it [the poison] is distilled from the atmosphere rather than dropped from a bottle held in his hand." Then, "As the body of Rowena writhes in the throes of death, his wish takes complete command of his brain." (369) This reading is completely consistent with the facts of the story, and one must be indebted to Basler for having spelled out accurately the "realistic possibility" which Poe offers us.

But this qualification must be kept in mind: this is the reading which says that Young Goodman Brown saw nothing in the forest. The entire affair was a dream. That is the "realistic possibility" which Hawthorne leaves open to his readers. The secret of both stories is that the authors offer both the fantasy and the explanation for it and refuse to choose. "Ligeia" cannot be given a final reading; the ambivalence must remain or one injures the delicate tissue Poe created. There in the dark forest, Brown may have seen his trusted friends at a black mass. To insist that he saw them or to insist that he saw nothing destroys the story. Hawthorne has made us feel that it does not matter; in "Ligeia" so has Poe. The difference (besides the fact that one tale is concerned with a moral issue, and the other with madness) is that if one must label one side "realistic," in the Hawthorne story it is the possibility of the dream, and in the Poe it is the possibility of the act. As satire, as horror story, as allegory, as philosophical statement, "Ligeia" can be reinterpreted intelligently and continually. No doubt it will continue to be discussed; it is too rich to be a closed case. But while even such "normally-basic" elements as its meaning, intention and plot-line seem to shift, alter, and evade final definition, its effect remains reassuringly constant. Though we are not even sure which character has the "vision," we recognize its characteristics. The tale creates the "beautiful effect."

-4-

Catastrophe as a Beautiful Effect

"The Fall of the House of Usher" is a splendid example of our assumptions that in these near-fantasies of Poe (and Hawthorne), one can not be sure of what is really happening, and that precisely what is happening does not, in the final analysis, make very much difference. Several of the most sensitive readings which "Usher" has received agree about the story's themes, and yet disagree about what happens in it.

Allen Tate, for example, points out that Madeline Usher, when she returns from her tomb, falls over her brother in the traditional vampire embrace.[11] Maurice Beebe, in contrast, thinks that there are clues which indicate that this is, in effect, an act of vengeance; he believes that Usher killed his sister.[12] Yet each critic feels that the story is a fictional embodiment of the philosophical theory adumbrated in *Eureka*. Each sees the progression through "unity—radiation—diffusion—return-to-unity,"[13] a progression which, as we shall see in Chapter Seven, closely matches the assumptions of hermetic philosophy.

Also related to the position of *Eureka* is the "animism" of objects in "Usher." This is pointed out both by Mr. Beebe and by the author of yet another fine reading of the tale, Darrel Abel,[14] but again there is a different interpretation of the details of the action. Mr. Abel is inclined to consider the narrator "Anthropos," a neutral observer who is present as a kind of index of Usher's madness. When Usher shouts, "Madman!" according to this view, he is showing his own insanity. I am inclined to disagree on this point, although I am quite willing to admit that this does not alter the over-all meaning of the tale. Mr. Abel points out that the narrator repeatedly attempts to find rational explanations for the extraordinary events. He says further that when, at the tale's conclusion, the house falls, even "matter-of-fact Anthropos does not suggest any natural explanation; he merely flees 'aghast.'" (185) To this reader, these facts suggest something very different.

I think they show that the narrator, rather than being a neutral observer, is as much in the hands of fear as is Roderick Usher, and that his explanations represent an attempt to maintain his sanity in the face of horror. It is a difficult task;

Usher is a frightening companion, himself "Arabesque" in appearance. By the tale's close, our narrator has despaired of the effort to explain.

The famous opening paragraphs of "Usher," in which the narrator describes the outward appearance of the House of Usher, come through to the reader warped by the narrator's fear. In the course of the story, Madeline, whether one prefers to think of her as a vampire or as the object of an incestuous love (or both, since each is credible), clearly symbolizes the fear of both Usher and the narrator. Madeline, because she "dies" and "returns," has a good deal in common with the "expiring ladies" of other tales of terror. She is a part of the complex vision herself, but her resurrection, unlike that of "Ligeia," has two witnesses.

As we will see repeatedly in discussing Poe's tales, he was, in his good stories, very careful to assign visions only to characters equipped to perceive. In this tale it is the narrator, not Usher, who perceives many of the wild beauties which present themselves. He describes the final storm as follows:

> It was, indeed, a tempestuous yet sternly beautiful night, and one wildly singular in its terror and its beauty. A whirlwind had apparently collected its force in our vicinity; for there were frequent and violent alterations in the direction of the wind; and the exceeding density of the clouds (which hung so low as to press upon the turrets of the house) did not prevent our perceiving the life-like velocity with which they flew careering from all points against each other, without passing away into the distance. I say that even their exceeding density did not prevent our perceiving this--yet we had no glimpse of the moon or stars--nor was there any flashing forth of the lightning. But the under surfaces of the huge masses of agitated vapor, as well as all terrestrial objects immediately around us, were glowing in the unnatural light of a faintly luminous and distinctly visible gaseous exhalation which hung about and enshrouded the mansion. (III, 291)

The key words in the narrator's description are contained in his first sentence: "tempestous," "sternly beautiful," and "wildly singular." These serve to identify this type of beauty in Poe; the sentence could have been used to introduce a description of the maelstrom as well as the storm. The presence of the word "singular" here, as elsewhere in Poe, is evidence of his continuing concern with novelty. Poe narrators are forever explaining that what they have to tell is so unusual and unique that the reader will have to take them at their word. What this means is that Poe, in his search for novel (or "singular") beautiful effects, has found one so novel that it requires an apology.

This narrator, at any rate, reacts to the horror by seeing the wild beauty which is inherent within it. Roderick Usher reacts differently and more violently; in his madness and irrationality he can himself, god-like, create the outward beauty; he writes and composes; he extemporizes fantastic music on his guitar. He is another of those Poe characters whose senses, as a result of madness, become abnormally acute. He cannot bear most sounds, his attention is channeled into monomaniacal interests--his strange books, for instance--and, at the close of the story, he says that he has been able to hear the first faint movements of his sister in her coffin. Moreover, he fully anticipates his own disintegration, so that when Madeline, fear, rises in her shroud to confront him, his collapse seems logical and inevitable. Madeline is not brought back from her vault only for melodramatic effect or because Poe knew that burial alive was a good "commercial" subject; in her confrontation of Roderick Usher is the final traumatic contact of a fear-crazed mind with the object with which its subconscious associates the fear.

> For a moment she remained trembling and reeling to and fro upon the threshold, then, with a low moaning cry, fell heavily inward upon the person of her brother, and in her violent and now final death-agonies, bore him to the floor a corpse, and a victim to the terrors he had anticipated. (III, 296)

"The terrors he had anticipated" destroy Usher, but the narrator is able to flee. In the masterful last paragraph, he turns to see the house collapse. It may well be that he, too, disintegrates. It was he, one recalls, who perceived the horror of the House of Usher at the tale's opening, even before he saw Usher, and his mind, one is constantly reminded in the course of the story, is as terrified as is Usher's. He, not Usher, sleeps directly above the chamber in which Madeline is entombed. His mind keeps an outward appearance of firm rationality, but it too may have a dangerous flaw. Certainly the condition of the House itself is meant to be analogous to the condition of a human mind, but the following passage could hardly refer to Usher's mind, which does *not* possess the outward appearance of sanity, but is, rather, deeply and obviously eroded.

No portion of the masonry had fallen; and there appeared to be a wild inconsistency between its still perfect adaptation of parts, and the crumbling condition of the individual stones. In this there was much that reminded me of the specious tonality of old wood-work which has rotted for long years in some neglected vault, with no disturbance from the breath of the external air. Beyond this indication of extensive decay, however, the fabric gave little token of instability. Perhaps the eye of a scrutinising observer might have discovered a barely perceptible fissure, which, extending from the roof of the building in front, made its way down the wall in a zigzag direction, until it became lost in the sullen waters of the tarn. (III, 276-277)

It could hardly be said of Roderick Usher that he "gave little token of instability"! He is beyond all "putting on a front." It could be said of the narrator. Poe tells us that the "House" stands for both the building and the family line. But two souls collapse with the widening of the once barely discernible fissure which, at the close of the story, splits apart to let through the "wild light" of "the full, setting, and blood-red moon."

This story seems to me less ambiguous in intention than "Ligeia." It is organized around the conception of a universe which is spiritually unified. Wild nature reflects wild history; the crumbling house reflects crumbling humanity; the tarn literally reflects everything, and serves to symbolize the doubling which is at the philosophical center of the tale. Usher rocks back and forth in his seat as his sister totters toward him; we are told they are twins, and that "sympathies of a scarcely intelligible nature had always existed between them." Everyone has heard superstitious stories about mysterious links between twins, but in this story, there are links between all people and all things. Though Freudian readings make sense, one does not really need them. The horror may strike a reader as built out from a core of guilty incest, or merely as built out, like the composition of Munch's "The Scream," from a central nameless shape of terror. What is important is that it is built out, that the story reflects itself, that what happens affects all of the universe--house, Ushers, heavens and narrator--which one sees within its frame.

-5-

Summary

The greatest contribution of the numerous patient studies of Poe's sources has been to demonstrate conclusively that Poe borrowed his gruesome subject matter. Precedents exist for all the Gothic paraphernalia of the horror stories, and there is an increasing body of evidence to show that Poe had access to such predecessors.[15] Poe, once he decided that there was money in short fiction, methodically set out to find out what sort of thing would sell; he even kept a file of back issues of the important magazines. The tale of terror had evolved before Poe wrote his major stories. The explanation one frequently finds in accounts of "the sources of Poe's sources" is that the horror story had grown from one aspect of the sentimental novel: the author of such a novel, in treating a moral problem, set up situations which would evoke an emotional response from his reader. If one drops the moral problem, there remains a story written solely for effect, and, in this tradition of composition, the stronger the effect, the better the story.

Poe not only knew these writers, he parodied them on several occasions. The fact that Poe could produce parodies of this nature would seem to preclude any deep-rooted addiction to horror of the sort which certain of Poe's critics have suggested. For example: it is obvious that "A Predicament," one of the parodies, is written according to the instructions in "How to Write a Blackwood Article," but the instructions would also fit any of the serious horror tales Poe produced. A good deal has been made, to pick an especially morbid case, of Poe's supposed fear of entombment alive, because of the number of stories he wrote dealing with the subject. The subject is, undoubtedly, unpleasant; it is also the sort of thing that is very tempting to amateur psychologists. Yet, whatever psychological traits there may have been in Poe's personality which led him to choose such a subject, it is clear that there were also purely artistic or technical, not to mention financial, reasons for his choice. Poe has "Mr. Blackwood" say, "There was 'The Dead Alive,' a capital thing!--the record of a gentleman's sensations when entombed before the breath was out of his body--full of taste, terror, sentiment, metaphysics, and erudition. You would have sworn that the writer had been brought up in a coffin." (II, 273) Edgar Poe was not brought up in a coffin. However emotionally attached he may have been to the tale of terror, he knew what he was doing when he wrote one, and could see the humor inherent in the process. A few of "Blackwood's" comments are so relevant to Poe's own work that they are worth quoting.

And then there was 'The Man in the Bell'...the history of a young person who goes to sleep under the clapper of a church bell, and is awakened by its tolling for a funeral. The sound drives him mad, and accordingly, pulling out his tablets, he gives a record of his sensations. Should you ever be drowned or hung, be sure and make a note of your sensations--they will be worth to you ten guineas a sheet. (II, 274)

The tone metaphysical is also a good one. If you know any big words this is your chance for them. Talk of the Ionic and Eleatic schools--of Archytas, Gorgias, and Alcmaeon. Say something about subjectivity. (II, 275)

There is no passing muster...without Spanish, Italian, German, Latin, and Greek....Any scrap will answer....(II, 278)

Poe does, in fact, make a good deal of sensations; "The Pit and the Pendulum," for example, comes through to the reader almost entirely in terms of the sensations of the sufferer, as he gradually brings himself back to the rationality which keeps him alive until his rescue.[16] The latter two quotations are even more troubling--or amusing. Poe throws around so much metaphysics and so many Greek quotations in the course of even his best tales that one may be led to doubt his sincerity. A better explanation is that Poe's attitude toward the tale of terror was largely professional. He wrote it because he knew he could write it well, and because he saw within the form an opportunity to fulfill his primary purpose as an artist--the creation of patterned beauty. But when he wanted to, he could satirize it, hence stories like "The Man That Was Used Up" or "Loss of Breath." There may even be elements of satire within the serious horror stories; "Ligeia," as noted, is felt by one critic to be a satire of the same excesses of the Transcendentalists which Poe spoofs in "How to Write a Blackwood Article." But professionalism and detachment need not imply mediocrity, and when Poe was writing seriously--that is, according to the tenets of "The Poetic Principle"--he was both a craftsman and an artist.

It is time to point out, however, that the signs of a

"serious" Poe story are not morbidity, madness, and the Poe-mask narrator. If one had to pick the single assumption which has most damaged critical appraisals of Poe, it would be this: almost all of Poe's best critics have taken for granted that Poe "means business" only when he talks about what are usually taken to be his "great obsessions." This is the source of what might be termed the "Poe-mask fallacy." There is nothing wrong with seeing characters as projections of their creator, providing one keeps open the possibility that balance and detachment might also be involved in the artistic process. *Typee* can not be fully understood unless one knows its relation to Melville's youthful adventure, and the extent to which Redburn and Ishmael are also Melville is considerable. But if one picked, for example, Captain Ahab alone, insisted that he were Melville, and ignored less deeply involved "seekers," one would be greviously distorting Melville, his art, and his relation to his art. If Ahab is a "Melville-mask," so is Ishmael; so are Redburn, Tommo, and even Billy Budd.

Similarly, if one were to view Hawthorne's work as concealed biography, one would gain insight into "Young Goodman Brown," but to say that Brown appears in a serious work and to deny the importance of, let us say, Miles Coverdale, would be to deny one whole side of Hawthorne's personality. The very minor poet Coverdale is not like Ethan Brand either, but that does not mean that *The Blithedale Romance* is not fully as revealing of Hawthorne as is the short story.

Even so astute a critic as Allen Tate has made this type of error when treating Poe; like most Poe critics, he assumes that the only serious Poe is the Poe of the compulsions.[17] Perhaps there should be ground-rules to cover the field: if one is to treat the narrator of any of the tales as a "Poe-mask," one must take into account all the narrators of all the tales. Or, if one assumes that Poe is emotionally involved only in stories which contain elements of horror, one must treat all the stories which deal with horror, including those little-discussed tales in which horror is handled with great detachment. But a far better test of whether or not Poe "meant business" in a tale is the amount of care with which he constructed it.

And this is a point concerning which one might as well be dogmatic. No great art, no good art, was ever produced unconsciously. Even the extreme and seemingly irrational compositions of the late Jackson Pollack were the results of craft. If, as he claimed, he simply "flung" paint at his canvas, we have the testimony of those who saw him work that the "flinging" was carefully premeditated, and that his aim was uncanny. A comparison between Poe and an abstract expressionist painter such as Pollack is not merely arbitrary. Though suspicious of artistic credo and manifesto, the abstract expressionists, or Action Painters, or Tenth Street Painters, or New York painters (to use the overlapping titles which various critics have assigned to different groupings among them) share a concern for the "Great Moment," the wonderfully creative day or hour when everything felt exactly right. They regard the painting as largely a record of the manual gestures of the artist when he was in that condition. There is a species of mysticism at work in such aesthetic thinking; the artist, like earlier mystical artists, feels himself to some extent merely the finger of the gods. The art work itself is supposed to affect the viewer by putting him in contact with whatever it was that moved the artist. Behind these ideas are numerous intellectual forces, and every one of them leads back to nineteenth century romanticism: the interest in oriental religions; the romantic ideals (the most eloquent spokesman of the group, Hans Hofmann, used the old capitalized words "Beauty" and "Inspiration"); the veneration of the sketchy, the unfinished, the intuitive. And, as in Poe, these attitudes are paradoxically felt not inconsistent with a craftsmanlike respect for the materials of one's art. Where Poe spoke of the stage-machinery behind the literary work, these artists cultivate an image of the artist-as-manual-laborer. Although Poe as a good romantic believes in supernal Beauty and Inspiration, he also borrowed consciously from writers whose primary concern was for effect. Indeed, it was he who codified the rules of the craft. He is thus about the last person one should suspect of putting down on paper that which only his compulsions dictated. The line between conscious and unconscious in art is ever a difficult line to draw. This is eminently clear in Poe's theoretical writings; he understood that craft must take up where "inspiration" leaves off (and vice versa), but he could not--nor can we--precisely define the point at which the changeover takes place.

It is a healthy exercise to place oneself imaginatively in the artist's boots, so to speak, in order to consider just this problem. Let us say that we are describing a landscape, and that, for no accountable reason, the idea comes to mind to include in it a detail which might not ordinarily be there--a dead dog will do. The dog has nothing reasonable to do with the tale in which we are to use the landscape, and yet, as we read the passage over, the dog seems strangely "right." We give the page to a friend to read; he reports that the description is very effective: "That dead dog--brrr." Now, how did the dog get there? It "welled up from our unconscious," perhaps, and is hence a justifiable subject for psychoanalytical treatments of our work. Granted, but our inclusion of it in the passage was completely conscious and purposeful. We put it there for effect. Even though it may have come from somewhere too deep in our subconscious for us to understand, we made the clear and careful decision to put it to use because we felt that it would operate efficiently upon our readers.

Moreover, in Poe's work there is seldom justification for saying that a Gothic element did come from so deep a spot; Poe knew too much horrific fiction too well. His contribution was not the creation of the horrors, but the making of them an art form. Further, Poe's horror tales can be shown to hold to a consistent philosophical position. The area of agreement which we noted in the discussions of "Usher," for instance, was that the tale expounds the world-view of *Eureka.* Messrs. Abel and Beebe convincingly demonstrate the extent to which Poe manipulated the *decor* of his tale to carefully premeditated ends. Clearly the material was not running away with the writer. Even in "Ligeia," where we cannot be certain of his intention, or in "A Descent into the Maelstrom," where he failed to achieve a convincing tone, the "lines" are all worked out.

In this chapter we have considered several different types of stories by Poe, each of which includes "horror." Painstaking research by an impressive group of scholars has revealed that each type, indeed, each story, has, in its central horror, clear roots in the fiction of Poe's day, roots so plentiful, in fact, that it is sometimes difficult to decide from which source Poe was borrowing. In each tale, the horror has about it a "look" which is so similar that Poe sometimes duplicated the adjectives he used to describe it. That "look" is also very much like the "look" of what Poe, romanticist that he was, called "beauty."

There is, moreover, a strong sense of pattern to be derived from the group. Poe repeatedly faces the same artistic problem. If he is to produce a strong effect, and if that effect involves presenting a central and Gothically-complex pattern, he must find means to embody that pattern in fiction. Most frequently, he solved his problem by suggesting that the pattern is at least partially the result of the mental condition of the character who perceives it. The outer wonders, to use Mr. Griffith's fine terms once more, become a projection of the inner horror, just as Hawthorne's "outer wonders"--the serpent in the bosom, the witch in the forest--are projections of the moral turmoil within.

Part Two
THE HORROR

Chapter III

Some Context for the Minor Horror Story

An imagination of any power at all will often project its deepest assumptions about life in symbols that duplicate, without the artist's knowledge, certain meanings, the origins of which are sometimes as old as the race.

Allen Tate, "Our Cousin, Mr. Poe"

-1-

The Significance of the Minor Tale

It's hard to say what makes us decide that a portion of an artist's production is "minor." In Poe's case, one surmises, we sometimes make the decision simply on the basis of other people's judgment. One might say that a minor Poe story is one that has not been frequently anthologized, or one that is seldom accorded critical attention. This is, perhaps, largely a matter of audience response, and, in the long run, there may be a kind of rough justice in it. Some very good Poe stories are not too well known. "The Man of the Crowd" and "William Wilson" are certainly less widely read than the best known of the horror stories, even though they are among the very best things that Poe ever did. On the other hand, for the bulk of Poe's writings,

51

the popular judgment seems reasonably just. " 'Thou Art the Man,'" which we are going to discuss in this section, is not a famous story (though just recently someone has based a movie on it), and though it is an extremely interesting piece of evidence for us in our attempt to understand the nature of Poe's creative imagination, its obscurity is probably deserved.

Judgments of this sort, of course, are partially subjective. There is always the danger that we decide that a piece of an author's work is minor simply because it is not characteristic, not his usual sort of thing. This is true enough of " 'Thou Art the Man,'" though it seems to me that we can also provide reasonably objective evidence of aesthetic failure. "Failure" may be too strong a word; the story is entertaining, and, in the sense that it tells us some things about Poe, very interesting. But surely it leaves less strong an impression than much of Poe's fiction, and I suppose that we may fall back upon Poe's own criterion for the success of a story. He said that it should create a strong effect, and this one doesn't. But applying this test is a little unfair, since Poe intended the story to be a satire, and one should probably not expect quite the usual intensity from a satiric piece.

In outline, the plot of " 'Thou Art the Man'" sounds passably promising. An unnamed narrator relates how he pieced together the facts in the murder of Mr. Barnabas Shuttleworthy of Rattleborough. Mr. Shuttleworthy, a prosperous business-man, disappeared while on a trip to a neighboring city. His horse returned riderless and wounded, and a search was instituted. Most assiduous in the detective work was Shuttle-worthy's companion, Charley Goodfellow. As clues were found, it became increasingly evident to the townspeople that Shuttle-worthy had, just before his disappearance, promised to give Goodfellow a case of wine. A note arrived, saying the case was on its way; Goodfellow promptly invited a crowd of cronies to help him enjoy it. The case arrived later in the day. The narrator pried it open,

> ...the top of the box flew suddenly and violently off, and, at the same instant, there sprang up into a sitting position, directly facing the host, the bruised, bloody, and nearly putrid corpse of the murdered Mr. Shuttleworthy himself. It gazed for a few moments fixedly and sorrowfully, with its decaying and lack-lustre eyes, full in the countenance of Mr. Goodfellow; uttered slowly, but clearly and impressively, the words--"Thou art the

Man! " and then falling over the side of the chest as if thoroughly satisfied, stretched out its limbs quiveringly upon the table. (V, 306)

The stunned murderer confessed, and the story closes with the narrator's explanation of his own part in the affair. He had come to distrust "Old Charley," had realized that Charley was leading the searchers astray, and, by searching independently, had discovered the body. He planted it in the box, with a piece of whalebone to cause it to sit up when the box opened, and used ventriloquism to produce the accusation.

Poe's satire in this story has a number of targets. I think the most basic of these is the tale of ratiocination itself. Poe has simply turned the procedures of "la novela policial" upside down. The trustworthy friend is a scoundrel, carefully accumulated evidence is misleading, and the spoiled rake is a good guy. The story, while satirical, does make a thematic statement, essentially the same statement which Poe's more famous detective stories have made: reality is not the way you think it is. But "'Thou Art the Man'" is very different from the Dupin stories. It has dramatic action. In the Dupin stories, the murders are events in the past; the bulk of each story deals with Dupin's reconstruction of events. In "The Mystery of Marie Roget," there is no action at all; Poe quotes "newspaper articles" and lets Dupin explain his reasoning; the murder of poor Marie is seen only at a distance. In this tale, in contrast, the body reappears in the melodramatic scene at Goodfellow's party, and the narrator's description of the events leading up to its appearance seems part of a deliberate attempt to build suspense.

Before discussing the problems posed by the plot, however, let us take a look at some of the other targets of Poe's satire, for these suggest how very revealing the minor work can be. Poe's dislike of Charley Goodfellow is very evident; he does, after all, portray him as a murderer. I think that Poe here intended to deal with what is by now a familiar national type, the seemingly above-board, glad-handing, straightforward, hearty and fun-loving sort whom later satiric writers have often shown us at places like lodge meetings and class reunions. Poe's treatment of this good-time Charley (or is he Robin Goodfellow?) is not so devastating as it could have been, but the source of Poe's trouble is easy enough to diagnose, and Poe's intentions seem reasonably clear. Poe chose to be expository and flippant in handling Charley. He introduces him as follows:

Now, whether it is a marvelous coincidence, or whether it is that
the name itself has an imperceptible effect upon the character, I
have never yet been able to ascertain, but the fact is unquestion-
able, that there never yet was any person named Charles who
was not an open, manly, honest, good-natured and frank-hearted
fellow, with a rich, clear voice, that did you good to hear it, and
an eye that looked you always in the face, as much as to say: "I
have a clear conscience myself, am afraid of no man, and am
altogether above doing a mean action." And thus all the hearty,
careless, "walking gentlemen" of the stage are very certain to be
called Charles.

Now, "Old Charley Goodfellow," although he had been in
Rattleborough not longer than six months or there-abouts, and
although nobody knew anything about him before he came to
settle in the neighborhood, had experienced no difficulty in the
world in making the acquaintance of all the respectable people in
the borough. Not a man of them but would have taken his bare
word for a thousand at any moment; and as for the women, there
is no saying what they would have done to oblige him. And all
this came of his having been christened Charles, and of his
possessing, in consequence, that ingenuous face which is proverbi-
ally the very "best letter of recommendation." (V, 306)

It seems to me that had Poe allowed Charley to speak for
himself more often in the early parts of the story, he might well
have tricked the reader into liking and trusting Charley, and
could thus have increased the impact of his satire while at the
same time maintaining suspense.

It may be that this judgment is a trifle unfair. Perhaps Poe
wanted Charley's unreliability to be evident from the start, so
that only a fool could miss it. The implication would then be
that the people of Rattleborough, and perhaps the unwary
reader as well, were fools. My guess is that the reason is simpler;
I don't think that Poe was very comfortable with his material in
this story, and I think that he made a number of artistic
mistakes.

Mistakes in no sense obscure what the story has to tell us
about Poe's attitudes. There used to be a lot of discussion about
whether or not Poe had any feeling for his American environment. It seems obvious that his effectiveness as an editor
answers the question well enough: at least he knew his
audience. But now and then in his stories there is biographical
evidence of an even more obvious sort, and Charley Goodfellow
is one of those creations which suggest Poe's reactions rather

strongly. The story can be understood with some consistency as a defense of disreputable-seeming young men and an attack upon good-hearted-seeming old ones! One thinks inevitably of Poe's difficulties with his stepfather, his gambling debts at the University of Virginia, his financial difficulties at West Point and his life-long attempts to live down a reputation for bad social behaviour. Too explicit an insistence on any one of these things would distort this story, but one senses that one's guesses about its sources in Poe's personality are not without base.

If artistic errors keep "'Thou Art the Man'" from being an important tale, they fail to hide its themes. The passage quoted above is a mistake structurally, for it comes too early. When Charley's real nature is revealed, the revelation seems anti-climactic. But Poe's intention in it is very clear. Poe fails again to allow Charley to speak his piece convincingly in the passage which follows, but again his intention is unambiguous. When suspicion begins to fall upon young Pennifeather, Goodfellow rises to his defense, and Poe, instead of reproducing Charley's speech, quotes only a bit of it.

> He made a warm and intensely eloquent defence of Mr. Pennifeather, in which he alluded more than once to his own forgiveness of that wild young gentlemen--"the heir of the worthy Mr. Shuttleworthy,"--for the insult which he (the young gentleman) had, no doubt in the heat of passion, thought proper to put on him (Mr. Goodfellow). [Pennifeather, who realized that Charley was parasitically living upon Shuttleworthy's generosity, had quarreled with and struck Charley.] "He forgave him for it," he said, "from the very bottom of his heart; and for himself (Mr. Goodfellow), so far from pushing the suspicious circumstances to extremity, which, he was sorry to say, really *had* arisen against Mr. Pennifeather, he (Mr. Goodfellow) would make every exertion in his power, would employ all the little eloquence in his possession to--to--to--soften down, as much as he could conscientiously do so, the worst features of this really exceedingly perplexing piece of business." (V, 297-298)

He then has his narrator explain,

> Mr. Goodfellow went on for some half hour longer in this strain, very much to the credit of his head and of his heart; but your warm-hearted people are seldom apposite in their observations--they run into all sorts of blunders, *contre-temps* and *mal àpropos-isms*, in the hot-headedness of their zeal to serve a friend--thus, often with the kindest intentions in the worl, doing infinitely more to prejudice his cause than to advance it.

> So in the present instance, it turned out with all the
> eloquence of "Old Charley"; for, although he laboured earnestly
> in behalf of the suspected, yet it so happened, somehow or other,
> that every syllable he uttered of which the direct but unwitting
> tendency was not to exalt the speaker in the good opinion of his
> audience, had the effect to deepen the suspicion already attached
> to the individual whose cause he pleaded, and to arouse against
> him the fury of the mob. (V, 298)

Poe's facetiousness I find irritating. Certainly his bits of
dialogue are unconvincing, and his use of parentheses to
differentiate between the characters is more annoying than
amusing. The reader has seen through Charley Goodfellow from
the start, and rather expects the story to end with Charley's
guilt exposed. But whether or not Poe is artistically successful
in handling Charley, how very angry he seems to be! What all of
this is supposed to say is that popular favorites are vicious
cynics, and that in the world of Rattleborough, people are
foolish enough to be taken in by them.

After Charley has "accidentally" mentioned that Pennifeather is Shuttleworthy's heir, the townspeople jump to the
conclusion that they have found a motive for the crime. Worse,
rumor has it that Shuttleworthy had considered changing his
will in order to disinherit his nephew. Poe has the narrator say,

> But the will being unaltered, while the threat to alter remained
> over the nephew's head, there appears at once the very strongest
> possible inducement for the atrocity: and so concluded, very
> sagaciously, the worthy citizens of the borough of Rattle. (V,
> 300)

Poe had dipped his pen in acid, but somehow corroded his
artistic judgment in the process. To be effective, this kind of
satire must be executed with a straight face, and Poe refuses to
keep one. The word "worthy" does not belong in that last
sentence, and the absurd names serve only to lessen the effect
of the satire. " 'Thou Art the Man' " would more nearly succeed
if more were left unsaid. Perhaps some local joke is involved, for
example, in Poe's decision to call the merchants from whom the
case of wine was to have been ordered, "Hoggs, Frogs, Bogs, &
Co.," but I'm afraid that the modern reader doesn't laugh.

Still, its very lack of subtlety makes " 'Thou Art the Man' "
more clearly significant as a reflection of Poe's social thought. If
the world of Rattleborough reflects some of the more in-
furiating aspects of the world around Poe, it may also be an

early appearance of the universal small town, mocked by Poe
sixty-six years before Clemens' "The Man That Corrupted
Hadleyburg" and a century before *Main Street*. Charley
Goodfellow's hoodwinking of Rattleborough is in the tradition
of the Duke and the Dauphin's theatrical frauds in the towns
along Twain's Mississippi, or for that matter the tradition of
Poe's own stories "Diddling" and "The Business Man," tales
about small-scale swindling. There is an even closer resemblance
between Poe's tale and Twain's *Pudd'nhead Wilson*. Each is set
in a small town, each involves a young rake, each satirizes
human gullibility, each makes use of a "scientific" angle
(ventriloquism in Poe; fingerprinting and palmistry in Twain),
and each, in the last analysis, is also a detective story.

Poe, as we have noted, probably intended to parody the
tale of ratiocination, but for any author, that can be a tough
order. The unravelling of the pattern almost invariably becomes
too much an end in itself; the audience comes to respond not to
the parody but to the conventions of the form which is being
parodied. More modern instances are easy to recall: the various
parodies of the Hollywood western have been too good as
westerns; the claptrap of sex, violence, gadgetry and intrigue in
the James Bond novels has too much appeal in itself for the
satire to remain uppermost in the minds of most readers. But in
these parodies there is really more consistency of tone than in
Poe's story. Perhaps a closer parallel is a work such as Twain's *A
Connecticut Yankee in King Arthur's Court:* Twain put too
many good things into his novel. The reader wonders why, for
example, if the Yankee's values are being satirized, the author
himself is so obviously fascinated with machine guns, tele-
phones and modern industrial administration.

In the sense in which it resembles these works of Twain,
"'Thou Art the Man'" is a bitter story. Our comparison is not
entirely gratuitous, because Poe's failure to produce major
fiction here may have several things in common with Twain's
failure in some of his angrier fiction. I'm not certain that we can
pinpoint all the elements of similarity, but we do sense a kind
of unwillingness on the part of the author to commit himself to
his material. He writes as though he were a trifle afraid to let
the reader see him really involved in his own creation, and so
adopts a tone so heavy in scorn and sarcasm that the result is
not even successful satire. It would be perhaps too strong to call

the results neurotic documents of artistic failure, because neither Twain nor Poe is really an artistic failure. But clearly something of this sort is involved. Or perhaps the failure could better be described as a result of an uncomfortable relationship between the author and his audience. Twain and Poe are most alike when they seem to be saying, "Take me seriously, will you? I'll fix you!" No one subscribes, nowadays, to "ordeal-ism" without at least some reservations, but it is obvious enough that neither Twain nor Poe was thoroughly at home in his art. When this fact is too evident, the art fails, or we get, as in "'Thou Art the Man,'" a minor work.

There are also some elements in "'Thou Art the Man'" which seem themselves uncomfortable in their environment. One wonders, for example, about the intense morbidity in the passage in which the corpse appears. Why did Poe include anything quite that horrible in a satiric tale? Or, for that matter, what is ventriloquism doing in the story? It's possible, of course, that Poe included these things as part of his satire on the form of the detective story; horror and a scientific gimmick are reputable conventions of the genre. But I fail to see the sense in which these elements are being parodied here. The horror scene is not a parody of the horror scene; it is just a horror scene. It is possible that these things are present in the same spirit in which incongruous elements are used in contemporary literature of the Absurd, that the appearance of the corpse is included precisely because of its incongruity in an otherwise sprightly satire. One might argue that since Poe is writing not a minuet, but rather a scherzo, one can expect rough effects. However that may be, an easier and safer conclusion is available. This is simply that since in this story as well as in others, horrific episodes appear in the midst of fiction which is otherwise rather cool in conception, our old conception of Poe as a madman obsessed with the grotesque and diabolical, needs revision. The ghastly corpse of Mr. Shuttleworthy is thus almost wholesome in its effect upon our conception of Poe's character: it is nice to know that Poe can turn horror on and off at will.

-2-

Mr. Higginbotham and Mr. Shuttleworthy

No need to envy the literary scholar of a century from now. However well endowed he may be with automated research aids, however loudly university presses (if there still are such things) may clamor for his prose, there is no need to long for the fit of his boots. Think of the job he will have in trying to recapture the feel of a contemporary novel. How is he to understand the texture, for example, of Rabbit Angstrom's life unless he knows, not only what those records which are played on the program Rabbit listens to in his car sound like, but also the genres to which they belong? Shall we envy him the task of watching video tape after video tape of the Mickey Mouse Club until he comes to the day on which Jimmy speaks the words which set Rabbit off on his quixotic quest? If he is a good reader, of course, there are certain allusions which he will catch and understand, because, presumably, scholars in the next century will still know about such things as mythology, mysticism and the biblical accounts of episodes in Jesus' life. But these alone are not enough. Indeed, many of Updike's readers today are completely unaware of them; they enjoy the book simply in terms of its topical allusions, and there are even some critics who remain blind to the author's larger intentions. No, to understand *Rabbit, Run*, one needs both kinds of allusion. Indeed, the juxtaposition of the trivial and topical upon the eternal and the profound is one of the main points of the thing. As even Rabbit himself understands, he is to some extent really a prophet, a saviour, a mystic.

Poe, mercifully, lived and died before the age of radio and television. Unfortunately, the highly competitive popular press was already in operation, and while I do not want to suggest that the student of Poe has anything like the task which a student of Updike will face a century from now, it is nevertheless true that to get a good feel for Poe's material, one must wade through an awful lot of junk. Topical allusions generally do come clear with effort, and the Poe scholarship is notable for tracking them down. At about the same time that the present book appears, Bobbs-Merrill will bring out a new edition of Poe's fiction; in it my wife and I have tried to run down as many of such allusions as we can, using the work of other scholars and our own ingenuity. The work has been fun, and has taught us much about the texture of life in Poe's day. Even more exciting, at least for this writer, is the occasional discovery that a puzzling story by Poe is not entirely isolated, indeed, that it belongs to a recognizable genre. In the case of the story "'Thou Art the Man,'" we're fortunate enough to have another example of the genre from the hand of a first-rate artist. It is as atypical of its author, Hawthorne, as our tale is of Poe, but the two stories are enough alike to suggest that the two writers are responding to similar conventions in the popular literary world around them. Like the Poe story, "Mr. Higginbotham's Catastrophe" is set in a small town, and like it also, is something of a detective story, although the murder with which it deals never takes place. Moreover, although this similarity is a little harder to demonstrate, I think that each tale is constructed around story-telling conventions of the sort which appear in folklore. The modern "myth critics" have shown us that, in a sense, all fiction is, but I have something smaller and more specific in mind here. Poe seems to be deliberately playing with the reader's expectations. If the reader expects a nice young man and a nasty old one, Poe begins by showing a dissolute rake and a jovial toper. Well and good; we readers carry another set of conventions to handle stories about irresponsible youths. But that's all wrong, too, for now Poe tells us that the youth is not only innocent, but worthy.

We may be quite certain that Poe is consciously playing with expectations which are based on folklore, for in his last paragraph, he gives the gag away by using the formula ending of a "fairy-tale," assuring his readers that Pennifeather, having been released, "inherited the fortune of his uncle, profited by the lessons of experience, turned over a new leaf, and led happily ever afterward a new life." (V, 309)

The Hawthorne story makes use of a device of folk literature even older and more basic than "lived happily ever after," namely, the sequential incident, the device which might be reduced to the formula, "first he met a man and such and such transpired. Then he went along a little way and met another man and so and so transpired...."

Finally, the two stories share the convention of the absurd names. The Poe story, in fact, pokes some fun at this convention. Poe takes time to tell us that Charley must be trustworthy because all people named Charley always are, and then names his innocent character Pennifeather to suggest his insubstantiality and unreliability. The names in the Hawthorne story also turn out to be significant, as we shall shortly see.

Hawthorne's plot reminds one of the "whispering game"

which children play, in which a "secret" is whispered around the circle from player to player, invariably returning to its originator in ludicrously distorted form. Dominicus Pike, an itinerant tobacco peddler and something of a gossip, hears, as he travels toward Kimballton, of the murder of a leading citizen of that town. It is a good story; he embellishes it and retells it to customers and cronies as he travels. Unaccountably he runs into people who insist that the merchant is quite alive, having been seen after the date of the supposed murder; also unaccountably, he meets one person who thinks that he is dead, but places the murder at a time later than the day on which Pike first heard the story. After numerous adventures, he arrives at Kimballton, goes to the orchard where the crime was supposed to have been committed, and finds it in the process of being enacted. He saves Higginbotham and is amply rewarded.

Hawthorne's plot is uncharacteristically mechanical. Three men had plotted the murder. One lost heart before the planned time of its execution. It was he who first told Pike the supposed news; he assumed the crime had been committed in his absence. It was postponed a day, the second ran away before it could take place, and, again, met Pike. The crime was postponed a third time, and the lone remaining assassin was about to murder Higginbotham when Pike arrived on the third day.

The tone and manner of all this is very similar to that of the Poe in places. We have already mentioned the close of Poe's tale; compare it to Hawthorne's final lines.

Poe: I believe there is nothing more to be explained. Mr. Pennifeather was released upon the spot, inherited the fortune of his uncle, profited by the lessons of experience, turned over a new leaf, and led happily ever afterward a new life. (V, 309)

Hawthorne: It only remains to say, that Mr. Higginbotham took the peddler into high favor, sanctioned his addresses to the pretty schoolmistress [Higginbotham's niece] and settled his whole property on their children, allowing themselves the interest. In due time, the old man capped the climax of his favors, by dying a Christian death, in bed, since which melancholy event Dominicus Pike has removed from Kimballton, and established a large tobacco manufactory in my native village.[1]

Significantly, it is harder to tell in the Poe story than in the

Hawthorne what the author is about. I suppose that this is not
an intrinsic fault of the tale itself. What is unsettling is that one
has read too much of Poe; otherwise, one would assume that
some of the stylistic excesses which appear in " "Thou Art the
Man'" are intended as parody. The trouble is that Poe uses these
same devices in his serious fiction.

He certainly gives us a good assortment of melodramatic
styles. There is his "powerful" style ("...he arose, staggered
backward from the table, and fell--dead") (307), his lead-footed
ironic style (as in the description of Charley), and the style of
the Great Logician ("*I* had not forgotten, although the
Rattleburghers *had*, that there was a hole where the ball had
entered the horse, and another where it *went out*"). (308) We
can give Poe the benefit of the doubt and say that these
different styles are present for parodic reasons.

Hawthorne's story is far more consistent in tone, but it too
has comic intent. It is just possible that Hawthorne intended a
parody of a detective story: the manner in which the tobacco
peddler wades through confusion and stumbles upon the
intended murder might be designed as a satire on methodical
and systematic investigations, and the criminals' compounded
botchwork is the exact opposite of the usual diabolical scheme.
Whether or not Hawthorne was making fun of detective stories,
it is clear that "Mr. Higginbotham's Catastrophe" is light stuff.
It reminds one that Hawthorne said that he envied Trollope.
Gentle fun is poked at Pike the gossip; the townspeople are
shown to be gullible; there is a satirical quotation from the
small-town newspaper which publishes an extra announcing,
and enormously romanticizing, the "event." Like Poe's story,
this one also seems a percursor of Twain and Hadleyburg.

Poe, as we noted, treated the murder in his story with
apparent seriousness. There is no murder in "Mr. Higginbotham's Catastrophe"; about the worst thing that happens is
that Pike is run out of town. But Hawthorne is careful not to
allow this to become a tragedy. The mood remains basically
sunny, and reminds one rather of the manner which Hawthorne
assumed to make fun of himself in "Sights from a Steeple." The
sun dries the mud which had been thrown at Pike, and, "Being a
funny rogue, his heart soon cheered up...." (918) Even
Higginbotham's murder, had it occurred, would not have been
too great a tragedy; Pike knew him to be a tight and hard man.

His eventual death, mentioned in the passage above, is hardly treated as a terrible event. Certainly there is nothing which breaks the mood as thoroughly as the scene in the Poe tale in which the corpse sits up to make its accusation.

This is not to say that in this story Hawthorne changes his view of the world. All of his usual assumptions are present here, but they are treated lightly. People are as weak and as prone to sin as usual (if one excepts the minor characters about whom we know nothing, as well as the niece, who is the familiar ideal young lady), but the author seems less concerned with analysis of their weaknesses. The only evil characters present are the three criminals, and two of them flee in terror before the murder; the third Hawthorne properly chooses not to develop.

Some critics have noted what they feel is an obscene streak in Poe. His story "Lionizing," for example, has been discussed in this way. What is said is that there was a popular dirty association between the nose and the penis. "Lionizing" is about the "science" of "Noseology." and can therefore, we are told, be understood as an extended private joke between Poe and those of his readers who are in on the gag. So far as I know no one has ever suggested something comparable on the part of Hawthorne, but it may be there in this story as a part of a quasi-allegorical scheme.

The pear-tree upon which Mr. Higginbotham was to be hanged is a St. Michael's, and Pike runs toward it "...as if old Nick were chasing behind." (920) Michael was the angel given the task of chasing Adam and Eve from Eden, and I suppose that our friend Dominicus (Dominican: *Fratres Praedicatores* or Preaching Friars), as he rushes into the garden and toward the tree might be said to be running from his vain "preaching" (the gossip) and toward a recognition of evil which, in Hawthorne, is always a sign of moral rehabilitation, so that one might be said to be nearer spiritual innocence (paradoxically, Eden) because one no longer thinks oneself innocent. The tree is indeed a tree of knowledge, but one needs the knowledge. This seems, frankly, a somewhat forced reading, for Hawthorne does not insist upon his underlying imagery, and I feel that it is safer to consider his story in more general terms. But one can go even further, and wind up with conclusions which make the story seem enormously wicked. Consider the first paragraph. Pike leaves the Shakers (a celibate sect) and travels toward the

Salmon river (Salmon: a fish of notoriously powerful repro-
ductive urges). He drives a cart with cigars painted on it. (The
cigar, we are told, is attractive to smokers because of its phallic
shape, and is smoked as a conspicuous sign of virility.) He is
beloved of pretty girls on his route, who are "...generally great
performers on pipes." (912) (Pipes, indeed!) Worse, he has a great
"itching" to tell the news. I get an image of him spreading it
around the countryside like a salmon spreading milt over eggs.
In this reading, the marriage after the visit to the tree of
knowledge becomes significant in terms of the folk-interpre-
tation of Genesis, in which the sin is carnal love; the selection of
a pear tree for the hanging becomes important. Pike, one might
say, moves from celibacy through promiscuity to properly
sanctioned sexual activity. We are, of course, pressing this
reading rather far, although, in truth, having said it, one finds
oneself half believing it. Think to what lengths poor Hawthorne
was driven to get something coarse by the Missus! More
seriously, this could be construed to represent a kind of
equivalent, in sexual terms, of Hawthorne's usual moral pattern.
The Shakers would represent about the same thing they
represent in "The Shaker Bridal," and, as in that story, their
self-imposed celibacy would be read as a form of the sin of
pride. The idea appears again in "The Canterbury Pilgrims," in
which it is made perfectly clear that the author's sympathies
and approval go with the couple leaving "cold and passionless
security" for the outside world of "mortal hope and fear."
(1203) Needless to say, in the two latter tales, the concern with
sex is quite explicit. Whether in the first Hawthorne, with his
Yankee Peddler, has given us a kind of travelling salesman, I
leave to the reader to decide.

The fact that the Hawthorne story has in it elements which
suggest issues central to others of his tales, and yet is not
apparently concerned with them, may suggest another obvious
contrast with the Poe story. The reader may or may not feel
that there is an inherent moral problem present in "Mr.
Higginbotham's Catastrophe," but he could hardly say, assuming that it is there, that it gets in the way. The tale is not
typical of Hawthorne in this aspect, and could hardly be
considered a major story regardless of its author, but for what it
is, it is well written, and bears evidence of careful craftsmanship. If the other elements are present, they are in so rudimental

a form that there is never any danger of their spoiling the fun. There is never a sense of slapdash construction; if this is not a great tale, it is at least polished.

Poe's "'Thou Art the Man'" is by no means a piece of sloppy hackwork, but it does seem less sure in its intention. There are other stories by Poe which simply don't work at all for a modern reader. If they are difficult to understand, scholarship can help us to figure them out, at which point I sometimes find them entertaining. I don't think that this is true of Hawthorne's minor pieces, though it is easy enough to think of stories which are clearly trifles compared with his major works. Examination of the popular collections of Hawthorne and Poe quickly demonstrates the contrast. Of the seventy-odd pieces which my wife and I are explicating for our Bobbs-Merrill edition, I count about thirty which can be said to show convincing signs of careful workmanship, or which a reader can enjoy without fairly elaborate notes. The thirty-six listed in Pearson's edition of Hawthorne are all finished jobs, though a few seem unimportant, and a few are rather puzzling in terms of Hawthorne's usual intentions.

It is perfectly true, of course, that Poe was more urgently compelled to produce. One feels strongly, in reading Poe's biography, a steady pressure upon him to get down on paper something printable. Hawthorne's career was no joyous round of fruitful productivity, but clearly he could afford to be more careful than could Poe. He was no man of leisure, writing simply because he wanted to, but certainly the creditors knocked more softly on his door than upon that of the little cottage in Fordham. Hawthorne, for example, may not have been happy in the political appointments he received, but at least he received them; Poe's efforts to secure similar governmental underwriting failed. Since Poe had to live by his pen, and since remuneration was never sufficient, he obviously was unable to exercise the selectivity which would have insured that only his best work appeared before the public.

-3-

Horror and Mr. Pennifeather

The source-studies of Poe are generally designed to tie him to the literary environment in which he operated, but Poe produced enough fiction within a fairly limited set of conventions so that one could actually proceed in the manner of the famous Whump-Bird of Australia, circling round and round with his own works to show repetitions and borrowed elements. Several of the elements which appear in "'Thou Art the Man'" are familiar. The unravelling of the mystery is reminiscent of what one finds in the tales of ratiocination. The scene in which the corpse sits up in its box is borrowed from Poe's horror stories, and, although its cause is explained as Dupin might have explained a ruse he used to solve a crime, it is a return from the dead in the tradition of stories such as "Berenice," "Morella," "Eleanora," and "Ligeia." The ventriloquism is another example of Poe's use of popular fascination with science, and Goodfellow's fraud seems only a more violent version of the frauds outlined in "Diddling."

Pennifeather, too, is a carry-over from other stories, though less readily identifiable. Had he narrated the story himself, he would have been more easily recognizable, and the story would have seemed more characteristic of Poe, for he is another of those moody and unhappy men Poe so often uses to narrate his tales. In this case, he has not run to extremes of depravity; he is, like the young William Wilson, merely a snob and a rake.

This is the character type which psychoanalytical critics of Poe most frequently identify with the author. But such critics invariably select high-keyed horror stories for their analyses. We have already suggested what would happen if one tried to account for Pennifeather in the personal terms of Poe's biography. Pennifeather has a reputation as a rakish young man. Shuttleworthy threatens to disinherit him. Shuttleworthy is killed; but Pennifeather is shown to be loyal, and, given the opportunity provided by the inheritance, becomes a mature and responsible citizen. That works rather well, does it not? Allan fits well as old Shuttleworthy, Poe works well as Pennifeather. If we search the story for autobiographical information, in short, it seems to say that the mistrusted young man longs for an opportunity to show his devotion. Given the chance he needs, he will become respectable. This reading is consistent with the general thesis of Arthur Hobson Quinn's reliable 1941 biography. To push the reasoning one step further, one might speculate more extensively about Poe's famous lack of sympathy with his American environment. One wonders to what extent his frustration really involved a rejection of its values (whatever *those* were, and assuming that there ever was a set of universally-held national values), and to what extent it was simply the result of his inability to command enough capital to enjoy it. A little of both, I should think: certainly Poe disliked many things that he saw about him; certainly also, however, he longed to play the part of an aristocrat, and subscribed to a good deal of nonsense about southern gentlemen. Before we decide that he rejected a value-system, we had better define the value-system we are referring to, and assure ourselves that his values were not, in fact, readily available in the society around him.

There is no point in insisting upon a reading such as this one, because Poe does not treat all characters of the type to which Pennifeather belongs in the same manner. I intend this discussion merely as a counter-balance to those which insist that Poe is Roderick Usher or William Wilson. Pennifeather is, again, much like William Wilson, but Wilson goes to the dogs, while Pennifeather, to mix a metaphor, having sown his wild oats, reforms. But if the presence of a Pennifeather demonstrates that Poe could write about characters who were not madmen, how then do we account for the frequent appearance of the more familiar morbid types? The safest explanation, the one Poe himself would doubtless have liked, is not biographical, but strictly functional. Pennifeather and Wilson are rakes so that they can be fitted into the thematic structures of their respective stories. Wilson commits the old Hawthornian sin of dissociating himself from his fellow men, and is haunted throughout his life by the spectre of his own humanity, the whispering double of himself. Pennifeather's sins are less serious, and his relative innocence is brought into relief by the contrast between him and the evil Goodfellow. Usher and other completely morbid characters are different because they have different functions to perform in the stories in which they appear. They are brilliant monomaniacs because such brilliance and monomania are necessary to perceive the wild and Gothic elements which to Poe represented beauty.

We do not have to believe that Poe was entirely serious when he claimed that he wrote "The Raven" according to the theories of his rather mechanical aesthetic formulae, nor do we have to assume, because we can explain horror and mad characters in aesthetic or structural terms, that these things are biographically meaningless. How mad is an author who uses madness systematically? How central is the horror to an author who uses it satirically? About the worst thing that one can say about the horror scene in "'Thou Art the Man'" is that it seems to have been pasted in to add sensational impact; one certainly does not get the impression that Poe had to put it in because he could write nothing but horror. One the whole, I think that Poe found that if he wanted to write a horror story, the best way to go about it was to have the figure who perceived the horror narrate the tale. This gave him opportunity to alter his language and to alter nature in order to produce the strongest possible effect. This was not his purpose in "'Thou Art the Man,'" and so he did not use the device. One can say, of course, that such an explanation is too much like Poe's own theory for the creation of an effective and unified prose work, and that his theory was probably a rationalization of his own practice. But that by no means negates the validity of the assumption. Poe, as we shall see when we discuss works in which he tried to get away from his usual procedures, was at his best when he stuck fairly close to the pattern which we have illustrated. Every tale which is discussed today as an example of the Poe-mask narrator is a tale in which the narrator is deeply involved in the horror. This is only natural; these are Poe's best tales. But there is horror a-plenty in other stories.

-4-

Opium and Strong Green Tea

A further document of Poe's detachment is "The Oblong Box," which could be called a coolly handled horror story. Poe is dealing with the sort of morbid subject matter one finds in the most emotional of the tales of terror,[2] but he tells it all calmly through his narrator, who, during the story, remains detached from Wyatt's agony. In the emotional horror story, it is usually the "I" character who undergoes the maddening experience, hence the critical temptation to identify the "I" with Poe, suggesting a more-than-expressionistic emotional involvement of the author in his work. In the light of this story, one is tempted instead to conclude that Poe so often used an "I" character primarily because doing so made his stories more effective, that it was a technique consciously adapted to heighten the emotional impact. For the experience which Wyatt undergoes is almost exactly parallel to the experience undergone by the narrator in, say, "Berenice." There is the same consuming love, the same horrid attachment to the body of the beloved after death. But in "The Oblong Box," all this happens to the narrator's friend. The narrator, although grieved to see his friend's discomfiture, suffers, for the bulk of the tale, only boredom and a couple of sleepless nights. He sees the entire episode as an outsider, trying to piece his scattered fragments of observation into some meaningful pattern, much in the manner of a tale of ratiocination. Dupin, one supposes, would have imagined himself within the artist's personality, and, with his combination of intuition, inspiration, and fact-piecing, arrived at the solution. The narrator, however, is not Dupin; his methods are more like those of the Prefect; his solution seems logical, but, to use a favorite Poe word, not sufficiently *outré*.

The narrator's language does not become wild or incoherent at moments of crisis, but rather remains that of an intelligent spectator. Even when telling of his sleepless nights, he uses none of the gasping, overwrought and melodramatic sentences which Poe can assign to narrators who are undergoing nervous and fitful hours. He is curious, like many Poe narrators, but his curiosity is not at all morbid.

> Several circumstances occurred immediately after this fit of Wyatt's which contributed to heighten the curiosity with which I was already possessed. Among other things, this: I had been nervous--drank too much strong green tea, and slept ill at night--in fact, for two nights, I could not be properly said to sleep at all. Now, my stateroom opened into the main cabin....[etc.] (V, 282)

Readers who like to imagine Poe as one of his opium-crazed characters might be taken aback by this narrator, whose nervousness is brought on not by monomania and drugs, but by a healthy curiosity and tea. The fragment of the last sentence was quoted to give some idea of the collected manner in which he narrates. A sentence further down in the same paragraph begins, "Well, during two nights...while I lay awake, I clearly saw...." (V, 282) This is plain narration by an interested commentator; the style remains equally calm and detached even during the passage in which Wyatt jumps overboard.

> ...Mr. Wyatt stood up in the stern-sheets, and coolly demanded of Captain Hardy that the boat should be put back for the purpose of taking in his oblong box!
>
> "Sit down, Mr. Wyatt," replied the Captain, somewhat sternly; "you will capsize us if you do not sit quite still. Our gunwale is almost in the water now."
>
> "The box! " vociferated Mr. Wyatt, still standing--"the box, I say! Captain Hardy, you cannot, you *will* not refuse me. Its weight will be but a trifle--it is nothing--mere nothing. By the mother who bore you--for the love of Heaven--by your hope of salvation, I *implore* you to put back for the box! "
>
> The captain, for a moment, seemed touched by the earnest appeal of the artist, but he regained his stern composure, and merely said:
>
> "Mr. Wyatt, you are *mad*. I cannot listen to you. Sit down, I say, or you will swamp the boat. Stay--hold him--seize him! --he is about to spring overboard! There--I knew it--he is over! " (V, 286)

The passage is, indeed, so calm and clear that it doesn't come off particularly well. The formality of the narrator's language detracts from the excitement. "The boat should be put back for the purpose," "vociferated," and "in fact" are too abstract to be used here. Poe probably realized that subjects like that of this tale were far more effective when handled in the style of the tale of terror; in most cases, he used that style. To be just, however, one must admit that within its limits, "The Oblong Box" works fairly well. It stands in relation to the best of the tales of terror about as *Billy Budd* stands to *Moby Dick*, which is to say, its very control makes it effective. The narrator holds back, never revealing his own emotions until the last paragraph, and the contrast between his coolness and the passion involved in Wyatt's situation adds a telling irony to the tale. The last paragraph is splendidly done; the detachment itself has achieved a tension, and here, at the story's close, the narrator's control finally breaks down. One is given a glimpse into his heart, a momentary realization of how maddening his experience has been.

> My own mistakes arose, naturally enough, through too careless, too inquisitive, and too impulsive a temperament. But of late, it is a rare thing that I sleep soundly at night. There is a countenance which haunts me, turn as I will. There is an hysterical laugh which will forever ring within my ears. (V, 289)

-5-

The Poe-Mask Fallacy

Another example of the danger inherent in reading Poe into his characters is to be found in the tale "Hop-Frog." In this case, the closest parallel in plot is to "The Cask of Amontillado"; each is a tale of vengeance. In each, the wronged party plots the death of a noble antagonist (using the word in its general sense), and in each the plot is fully successful. Further similarities exist; the time chosen for murder in each story is a time of confused celebration--in "Hop-Frog," a royal masquerade; in "The Cask," a carnival. Moreover, both are horror stories. The unfortunate Fortunado is led deep into the catacombs beneath Montresor's family home and walled in alive, while the king and his seven ministers are hoisted above the masquerade ballroom and burned alive.

It is by no means easy to treat stories of this sort seriously. "The Cask of Amontillado" is so well known by schoolchildren, and, in a way, so well adapted to their unrestrained imaginations, that one feels as though one were writing a straight-faced *critique* of some lurid horror comic book. And both stories are so baldly sensational that it seems necessary, somewhere in the discussion, to put a finger in one's collar to relieve the embarrassment. Perhaps it will be sufficient here merely to note that the macabre is still with us as a recognizable *genre*. It is perfectly possible to read into Faulkner's circumlocular method the artistic embarrassment of an author unwilling to spell out baldly the horrors which are often his stories' central actions. Such a reading to some extent distorts Faulkner, and by no means fully accounts for either his style or for his technique of revealing the center by examining sectors of the circumference, but our artistic instincts tell us that there is something at least partially valid in it. This writer's personal attempts to create fiction from real events in a town in Alabama perhaps leave him with a prejudice of that sort in dealing with Faulkner. The stories never progressed beyond the first, thoroughly factual, draft, because he was unable to find a tone of voice in which the events sounded credible. One major reason for Faulkner's success is that he, through "a life's work in the agony and sweat of human spirit," found the tone of voice.

"Tone of voice," of course, is here used as a kind of

subdivision under that technical term used by some critics, "point of view," and it is in the matter of point of view that the two Poe tales most obviously differ. In "The Cask," the offended character tells the story, and it comes through to us warped by his madness. In "Hop-Frog," the reader is not even sure who the narrator is. Apparently he has some connection with the court, for he knows the story in good detail. The event which he relates seems to have happened some time before, because he is unsure of its date. "On some grand state occasion--I forget what..." (VI, 218), he says. The story is set in the past, but, for the narrator, the not-too-distant past. At one point, early in the story, he says, "At the date of my narrative, professing jesters had not entirely gone out of fashion at court." (VI, 216) That would sound like ancient history but for the fact that the story opens, "I never knew any one so keenly alive to a joke as the king was," and the fact that the narrator can speak of the king as "*Our* king." (VI, 217)

As the tale progresses the narrator becomes less noticeable; for all practical purposes, one can regard the latter portion as coming from the lips of an omniscient author. The narrator knows things which only one standing beside the king and his jester at all times would know, and yet, when the scene shifts to the ballroom, he speaks of all the characters, king, jester, Trippetta, ministers and masqueraders, in the third person. The transition is nicely handled; one has merely a general sense that the story is becoming panoramic, that we are seeing the entire room.

Unlike Montresor, Poe's narrator here is thoroughly detached, so much so that early in the tale he can be almost breezy as he digresses to reminisce about the character of court life and the figures in his narrative. And yet "Hop-Frog" conforms to that psychological pattern we have noticed in so many of the stories. As in "The Cask of Amontillado," the "beautiful pattern" is the plotted revenge. And the avenger shows all the characteristics of the brilliant madmen who people so many of Poe's stories. The dwarf's reactions are carefully recorded. The wine he was forced to drink "...excited the poor cripple almost to madness...." (VI, 222) Trippetta, another dwarf in the service of the king, plans the *decor* of the ballroom, but she is advised by the "calmer judgment" (VI, 224) of Hop-Frog. Thus it will be seen that Hop-Frog is another of those Poe characters who are thrown by their madness into an acute and brilliant, if monomaniacal, condition. Hop-Frog, maddened by the king's cruelty, becomes extraordinarily cunning, and lays plans for the grotesque and elaborate murder. Poe emphasizes his almost diabolic coolness in passages like the following. In this, the dwarf, having quaffed a second cup of wine, and having perceived that the forthcoming masquerade will provide an opportunity for vengeance, prepares to outline his suggestion for a costume for the king.

> I cannot tell what was the association of idea,...but *just after* your majesty had struck the girl [Trippetta] and thrown the wine in her face--just *after* your majesty had done this, and while the parrot was making that odd noise outside the window [the noise was the gnashing of the raging Hop-Frog's teeth], there came into my mind a capital diversion. (VI, 222)

No sensitive critic would accuse Poe of having written a great passage there, but even if Hop-Frog's speech seems to us hopelessly operatic, it seems also strangely sincere. For there can be no doubt that Poe was genuinely angry at his king, and it is this righteous wrath which, more than any other single element, point-of-view included, differentiates "Hop-Frog" from "The Cask of Amontillado."

Poe set himself a more difficult task in "Hop-Frog" (1849) than in "The Cask" (1846). The earlier story, in terms of reader response, was intended to produce a shudder of horror. Montresor murders because of an unnamed insult. Hop-Frog murders because he--and Trippetta--have been subjected to insufferable degradation. He is striking out against unbearable tyranny and for the preservation of his integrity as a human being. Poe intends to whip his reader into a fury so intense that he will actually welcome the agonized screams of the burning noblemen.

One might imagine Poe disclosing his plan of action here (as he did for "The Raven" in "The Philosophy of Composition") in some such way as this: 1) Using a casual narrator, open the story almost as though it were an anecdote. The cruelty of the king should come out in sharper contrast because it is alluded to in an offhand manner by a witty and carefully unperceptive storyteller. 2) As an antidote for sentimentality, make the abused central character repulsive--a crippled and deformed dwarf. 3) Even after the narrator's personality has faded away, keep the language in which the tale is related calm. 4) When the final stage of the story is reached, allow Hop-Frog's rage to become evident--let him foam at the mouth, shriek, and gnash his "repulsive" teeth--but simultaneously bring the narrative (that is, all but the dialogue) to its most abstract and general state. In this manner, it will be possible for the story to operate as a kind of parable. Perhaps "fairy-tale" would be as good a term, for this device should make it also possible to utilize the story's timelessness and placelessness.

So in one sense, what the narrator is saying to the reader is, "Once upon a time, when there were still court jesters, and orang-outangs had 'very rarely been seen in any part of the civilized world....'" And the story closes with a paragraph as laconic as the formula "...and lived happily ever after":

> It is supposed that Trippetta, stationed on the roof of the saloon, had been the accomplice of her friend in his fiery revenge, and that, together, they effected their escape to their own country; for neither was seen again. (VI, 228)

It may well be, as earlier suggested, that we have outgrown the ability to enjoy a story of this sort. Writers today who deal with the grotesque and the diabolical are more subtle than popular magazinists of the 1840's. Roald Dahl[3] presents his horrors with the detachment of a far more sophisticated and worldly artistry—though the end product is often an effect of naivete—and Isak Dinesen (Baroness Karen Blixen) is able to create a contemporary never-never land of sexuality and Gothic complexity which is convincing, at its best, despite her readers' better judgment. Perhaps the most fruitful comparison one can make for "Hop-Frog," at last, is not with the work of such creators of private worlds at all, but with the thoroughly ghoulish "Fairy-tales" of the Brothers Grimm. "Hop-Frog" makes the most sense, it seems to me, if it is considered as a turning of the lurid raw materials of a Grimm story to moral purposes. (For the Grimm stories, in the original, are thoroughly amoral, not to say grisly.)

The "fairy-tale" conventions suggest a certain distance between author and material; the author who chooses to use them can be expected to run to extremes regardless of what the material means to him personally. If "Hop-Frog" is subjected to the "Poe-mask" treatment generally accorded to Poe's more famous fictions, it can be read as nothing more horrendous than a protest and a direct plea for understanding. One cannot, as we noted, psychoanalyse Poe through the narrator; he is too peripheral. But it is very easy to operate through "Hop-Frog." His deformity, one could argue, is a disguise behind which Poe can hide. His inability to drink (he begs the King not to force him) matches Poe's, and is an issue on which Poe was very sensitive because of the frequent ugly attacks upon him as a drunken profligate. The persecution of the dwarf might be equated with Poe's difficulties with the powers-that-be and with the self-pity evident in many of his letters. The dwarf's pure and pathetic love for Trippetta fits the pattern, and the venegeance seems no more than adolescent wish-fulfillment. Dreaming of burning one's enemies alive is perhaps not a model way to work out one's aggressions, but it does seem at least humanly understandable. Horrible as the dwarf's vengeance is, it is at least motivated.

My point is that if one applies the techniques of the Poe-mask fallacy to stories other than the ones to which they are usually applied, one can still find horror, but one finds other things as well: clear evidence of artistic detachment from the horror, as in "The Oblong Box" and "'Thou Art the Man'"; moral issues and story-telling conventions to provide context for the horror in "Hop-Frog." Our peaceful friends and neighbors gnash their teeth like Hop-Frog over matters as minor as the incompetence of a TV repairman or a stubborn leak in the roof, and dream of deaths more horrible than burning for the faceless clerks of the I.R.S.

Chapter IV

Horror, Beauty and Involvement

> *I made the night tempestuous, first, to account for the Raven's seeking admission, and secondly, for the effect of contrast with the (physical) serenity within the chamber.*
> --The Philosophy of Composition

-1-

The Structure of the Horror Tale

The process of perception which can be shown to determine the structure of the Poe tale has recognizable stages. As one moves from story to story, one repeatedly encounters passages which perform, in terms of that process, similar functions. Usually it is necessary for one character to be abnormally sensitive, and so the passage which delineates the mental state of Roderick Usher is similar to related passages in "The Tell-Tale Heart," "The Black Cat," or the stories about expiring ladies, and has a good deal in common with all passages which serve like purposes, even in stories which do not deal with horror. Ellison and Usher, artist and madman, have numerous qualities in common.

77

Those portions of the tales which inform the reader of the nervous and intense state of mind which will make the perception possible serve both psychological and textural functions. Psychologically, they either sketch the personality of Poe's ideal artist, or they suggest the madness and the fact that what is to be related will be seen through the medium of a distorted intelligence. Structurally, they frequently give Poe a comfortable margin of credibility, since his reader always has the option of considering the events of the tale not "real" events, but rather the maddened visions of a maniac.

It would be well, perhaps, to find a name for the type of art to which stories utilizing this process belong. Patrick Quinn, noting the sharper-than-life manner in which the horror is frequently presented, uses the term Surrealism.[1] The label would make some sense for Poe even were his art in no way surrealistic, simply because there is a clear intellectual tradition running from Poe to the twentieth century school of art called Surrealism. As a label for his works themselves, it fits certain stories very well, but seems somewhat too narrow for many. A surrealist painting uses the techniques of realism to produce a dream-like image. To state the matter in oversimplified terms, the picture is more haunting because, though its subject seems irrational, the recognizable objects portrayed are painted with extreme clarity and sharp definition. If final meaning is as ambiguous as a dream, the objects contained by the frame are strikingly familiar and meticulously delineated.

Such an analogy is valuable for many of Poe's stories. Certainly, for instance, one reason that "The Man of the Crowd" is so compelling is the fact that the image of the city is so sharp. As suggested in my discussion of that tale (in Chapter IX), the final meaning is totally ambiguous; indeed, had Poe been more specific, he doubtless would have weakened the effect of the story. But however sharp, the portrait of the city is, of course, selective. The reader gradually becomes aware that Poe is placing more emphasis upon certain aspects of the crowd that passes his narrator.

However, precisely because Surrealism does imply this super-real sharpness, it may be too limited a term to apply to Poe's work as a whole, particularly to those tales which present the dream-like total effect, but not the clarity of individual elements which must, by definition, be present in Surrealism.

A more general term might be more universally useful; perhaps expressionism, if carefully qualified, would be acceptable. I take it to signify a creative process in which "outside reality" is presented only after it has been distorted or intensified by the imagination of the artist. This is, of course, a matter of degree, since by this definition all art would be expressionistic. The artist must select, and the manner of selection used by even the most disinterested "realist" artist obviously must reflect his imaginative personality. Nevertheless, it is usually sufficiently clear what is meant by the term. An art critic who says that a school of German and Scandanavian artists early in the present century produced an expressionistic art would be clearly understood. He might also say that the specific movement known as Surrealism could be considered as falling under the more general heading of expressionism. Historically, of course, the expressionistic tendencies of the Germans were, in fact, related to the birth of Surrealism as a school.

It is generally recognized that classificatory terms of this type, when applied to literature, must usually be used in a relative sense. Expressionism, so used, is a handy term. One could, for example, explain the difference between certain of the naturalists and certain realists in terms of degree of expressionism. Thus it would be fair to say that Stephen Crane's vision had in it more of expressionism than did that of William Dean Howells. Crane, indeed, of all the naturalists, is probably the one most deserving the appellation "expressionist," for in his work even aspects of the natural world could be twisted and distorted. Nature is selectively filtered through a strong-patterned mind, and the sun emerges as a wafer pasted in the sky, or colors come to be equated with emotions.

Thus, in very general terms, one could say that to the extent that Poe's fictive world is a world of distortion, Poe is an expressionist. But because Poe subscribed to a romantic theory of inspiration, he added another step. In Poe one cannot merely say that the distortion is present because it reflects the author's selectively prejudiced view of reality. One can say that of most naturalists despite their theoretical insistence upon "scientific" objectivity. Their distortion is frequently revealed as a bias toward the more seamy aspects of life, and it implies a philosophy.[2] If Dreiser, for example, distorts his fictional world by over-emphasizing the sense of animalistic struggle, it is because he writes from what he considers to be an insight into the way the world works.

But in Poe the distortion is used to mirror the state of mind of the perceiver. At times, of course, there is no "perceiver" in the piece, but then there is no plot, and we are dealing with a sketch of the nature of "The Philosophy of Furniture." In such pieces it is probably reasonable to call Poe the perceiver. But usually there is a perceiving character in the tale, and Poe distorts or overemphasizes only as his character does. This is the extra step.

In Poe's hands this basic situation produced a surprising variety of structural possibilities. A character or the narrator could be mad, and thus perceive, or he could have the unusual insight necessary as a natural gift, as Ellison does. In either case, the resulting tales would have those related sections which we earlier mentioned—a section to introduce the character's sensitivity, a section to show what he perceived. But there was a further possibility. The statement of madness or sensitivity could be omitted, and appear not as a device to make the story possible, but rather as the subject of the tale.

This I take to be the central fact in a piece such as "The Cask of Amontillado." One is impressed, even after a casual reading, by the fact that this tale has a remarkable economy even for Poe. That economy can be explained at least partially by the fact that the tale opens, in effect, in medias res. In sharp contrast with "Hop-Frog," "The Cask" has no passage to tell the reader that the narrator is mad; the entire story does that. The tale opens with Montresor's cryptic statements concerning his grudge against Fortunato; there is only the slightest hint of any peculiarity in Montresor's make-up.

> The thousand injuries of Fortunato I had borne as best I could, but when he ventured upon insult, I vowed revenge. You, who so well know the nature of my soul, will not suppose, however, that I gave utterance to a threat. (VI, 167)

The nature of his soul is the tale's subject, but at this point one dimly entertains ideas concerning aristocratic pride, not madness. It is this aspect which Poe develops; the reader must on his own become aware that the pride is a rationalization of madness.

This is one of those Poe tales which invites radical

readings. Needless to say, the Freudians have a field day. They are doubtless correct in assuming that such a tale, with its descent deep into catacombs and a walling-in-alive, is psychologically revealing, and the nature of their findings seems sufficiently obvious from a mere mention of these elements not to require summary. It is interesting to note, however, that in some of the other critical reactions one again encounters the paradoxical situation we noted earlier in discussing "Usher," namely, that there is general agreement concerning the "meaning" of the tale even though the critics disagree in the matter of just what is happening. I take this as another illustration of Poe's practice of providing himself with a "margin of credibility."/The reader has considerable choice in deciding just which facts are to be believed, and his choice does not alter the meaning, for he understands that what is being seen is seen through the tinted glasses of insanity.

One critic, for example, thinks that the real crime of Fortunato, in Montresor's eyes, is being a Mason, and that the story is "an elaborate ritual."

> From the outset he [Montresor] conceives of Fortunato's death as an "immolation," a sacrificial act in which Montresor himself assumes a perverted priestly function. The vaults and the wine become sacramental properties which give a blasphemous significance to the ritual murder. And Fortunato, besides being the snake in Montresor's family arms, takes on all the qualities of a serpent, traditional religious symbol of evil. His immolation enables Montresor to accomplish a fitting act of revenge, complete even to the benediction.[3]

A second has developed this ritualistic idea, and feels that Poe unconsciously created a mythic situation. "The tale has a strong flavour of a profane rite, a sort of Black Mass."[4] When Fortunato says, "For the love of God," he is in a "quasi crucified" position. Other parallels which this writer, Donald Pearce, suggests are "temptation by appeal to Pride," betrayal before a holiday, a "place of skulls" or Golgotha, and mockery at the very close of life. Mr. Pearce concludes,

> Obviously Poe's story is not a systematic symbolization of these things; we are not in the presence of Hawthornean allegory. The elements of scriptural parody wind throughout the tale demoniacally, as the mottled striations in a slab of black marble, suggesting powerful but indeterminate patterns that have a mythic feel. (449)

Mr. Pearce has chosen his words carefully. "Mythic feel" is exactly right, and really suggests a great deal concerning the nature of Poe's imagination. We have elsewhere noted that in certain pieces Poe consciously wrote in a quasi-biblical style, or an intentionally archaic style. Here is an example from a well-known passage, the last lines of *The Narrative of A. Gordon Pym*. Note in particular the use of conjunctions at the opening of each sentence:

> And now we rushed into the embraces of the cataract, where a chasm threw itself open to receive us. But there arose in our pathway a shrouded human figure, very far larger in its proportions than any dweller among men. And the hue of the skin of the figure was of the perfect whiteness of the snow. (III, 242)

Poe probably had no clear idea of exactly what all this might suggest, but the use of language is completely conscious. He knew that the figure was to appear as in a dream or vision, and wanted his passage to have a mystical air. Similarly, in the colloquies, he tried to achieve a prophetic air.

It is not unfair to suggest that most of the cases in which Poe assumed such a language are examples of what might be called myth as color. This is not to say that the visions themselves were not legitimately myth-like; Poe loved the feel of subjects which could not be fully understood and which yet seemed to have a kind of power in them. He had, in common with his age, a mythic imagination; he was, for example, happiest with the past when it was a ghostly past. It is not too surprising that he should have turned out a space-filling article on Stonehenge, or that *Pym* should have in it an extended passage of what might with justice be termed archeological science-fiction. (A reader familiar with recent criticism will note that we are not using "myth" in the very broad sense in which "myth-critics" now understand it. We mean less "myth=fable= story," than "myth=old belief.")

The reader may remember a very minor Poe story called "The Sphinx," in which the narrator, in a peculiar state of mind, frightens himself terribly by mistaking a tiny insect close to his eye for a nightmarish monster crawling over a hill. The tale is in a sense a hoax, though there is really very little possibility that the reader will be fooled: the joke (if joke it is) is on the narrator. Poe did not handle his subject very effectively, and the tale seems a rather tepid combination of ratiocination (the narrator and his friend figure out what must have happened) and horror (the narrator has his vision only because the accidental appearance of the insect coincides with his own unusual mental state), but "The Sphinx" is nevertheless revealing. Poe thought about subjects which could haunt or frighten him, and frequently tried to embody them in his fiction. This is, obviously, a fiction of effect; the irrational fear of such things is used coloristically to heighten effect, and the author is usually only incidentally concerned with the possible meaning of the horror.

There is thus a danger of reading too much into such matters in Poe. A practicing author can sense when he has produced something that has about it a haunting quality, and he probably knows that part of the effect is due to the fact that the reason for the reaction is not fully understood. Of course, there really may be "something there"; in Poe's work especially a critic is justified in utilizing psychological theory in an attempt to discover why Poe considered certain subjects "moving." What must always be kept in mind, however, is that Poe considered it his business to exploit such subjects, and that, to a good extent, he thought of his tales in terms of his readers' reactions. He hoped to play upon his audience as upon an organ, and he thought he had a sense of those subjects which could evoke the right response. I think that we would do well to be skeptical of myth-smiths who try to make more of this. Ritual murder is an occurrence so old and so common in myth that it is impossible that Poe had never encountered it, but his use of it here in "The Cask of Amontillado" might not be conscious. The chances are that he liked the feel of it, knew it would sell magazines, and played it by ear. /

In "The Sphinx," the character is confronted with sensory evidence for which he cannot, for the moment, account; he reacts in fear. But the nature of the images which his mind brought up in that moment of dread cannot be accurately listed. Poe has his narrator say, of the sound which the "monster" produced,

> . . . it struck upon my nerves like a knell, and as the monster disappeared at the foot of the hill, I fell at once, fainting, to the floor.
>
> Upon recovering, my first impulse of course was, to inform

my friend of what I had seen and heard—and I can scarcely
explain what feeling of repugnance it was, which, in the end,
operated to prevent me. (VI, 241)

Poe, in short, has no answers either. But some of his narrator's
statements earlier in the tale give at least vague clues. All this
happened during a cholera epidemic in New York; he, like the
noblemen in "The Masque of the Red Death," had retired from
the city for a sort of vacation. News of the deaths of friends had
thrown him into a "condition of abnormal gloom." (VI, 238-
239) Also mentioned are books he had been reading, which
"were of a character to force into germination whatever seeds
of hereditary superstition lay latent" (VI, 239) within him. He
talks also of his interest in omens. Poe has, in short, arranged
the furniture of his character's imagination at the time of the
shock, but he cares to go no further. These are vague and
general things, and their power is enhanced just because they
are not further understood. Indeed, the death's-head which the
narrator sees upon the monster is probably too specific an
element; the effect would have been enhanced had he merely
seen some cryptic shape which stirred vague but less exact
feelings of dread.

And it is only in such vague and general terms that one can
speak of myth in Poe's work. The situation is superficially
paradoxical. On the one hand, one cannot say that what Poe is
doing is unconscious; in most cases, he very obviously knew
what he is about. When he used archaic language, or, as in "The
Sphinx," specifically said that his character had omens on his
mind, he knew full well what he was doing. On the other hand,
I am convinced that he seldom had any specific notion of just
what unconscious associations in the minds of his readers he
might be evoking, or what deep-rooted traits in his own he
might be reflecting. Psychoanalysis is justified in tracing this
latter possibility, but only when the numerous qualifications
and ambiguities involved are taken into account.

Part of Poe's gift lay in his ability to imagine the sorts of
things which might be prominent in the minds of characters in
disturbed mental states, or in that strange borderland between
sleep and awakedness with which all children, I suppose, spend
hours experimenting, the time in which one can make one's
eyes, for instance, play queer tricks. Romantic artists were fond
of telling us that children are closer to the great truths than are

adults; they said that they hoped that they could retain or recapture certain childlike traits which would aid them in the perception of beauty. Certainly one of the things they had in mind was what they remembered of the convincing fancies to which children are subject during their long periods in, as their parents say, "a daze." I would guess that Poe as an adult allowed himself to pass a good deal of time in such a state. I would guess further that one of the important sources of "The Sphinx" was nothing more than such a state of mind.

Now, one can believe that what children see and artists try to see is really there, that there are great truths to be perceived in trance-like states. We'll talk about that possibility later, because it was obviously an idea attractive to Poe. But the mystical alternative is not offered in "The Sphinx"; for the present purposes, it should be read simply as a variation on the usual pattern of the disordered mind and the outer wonder; the narrator is moody, and the bug becomes a monster. The tale deviates from the usual because the usual ambiguity is wiped out at the end. There can be no question as to whether or not the narrator saw a monster; the "margin of credibility" never becomes relevant. He saw a bug.

It is characteristic of these tales of perception that, in story after story, there are passages which perform the same function. "The Sphinx" differs from the ordinary pattern in that, although both the "inner madness" passage and the "outer wonder" passage are present, the ambiguity which they usually produce (did it, or did it not really happen?) is erased at the close by a (not-very-convincing) rational explanation. "The Cask of Amontillado" deviates in the opposite direction. The outer wonder is the evil plot itself; the inner madness is that of the tale's controlling intelligence. As a result, the issue of whether or not this really happened is never raised within the tale. The economy thus can partially be accounted for in terms of the "missing" sections. There is no abstract discussion of mental states, no offering of a choice to the reader, no instance of the familiar Hawthornean words "might have been."

-2-

Into the Catacombs

Matching the fearful economy is a fearful symmetry. The author of another of the radical readings of the tale points out

that the action is framed by a pair of repetitions;[6] at the
opening, Fortunato repeats Montresor's word "Amontillado!"
At the close, the situations are reversed:

"For the love of God, Montresor!"
"Yes," I said, "for the love of God!" (VI, 175)

Indeed, there is a great deal of mocking repetition in the last
pages of "The Cask of Amontillado." Montresor sets the tone
when Fortunato asks if he is a Mason. ("A mason.") The game
continues after Fortunato is chained. ("The Amontillado!"
"True...the Amontillado.") When Fortunato screams, Montresor
screams louder. When Fortunato tries to laugh the entire affair
off as a prank, and says "Let us be gone," the narrator says,
"Yes,...let us be gone." (VI, 172-175) Finally comes the
blasphemous mockery, "For the love of God!"

Repetition is, of course, an obvious characteristic of rituals
of any type. A ritualistic language is frequently a language
heavy in repetition, and a religious ritual derives a good deal of
its emotional power from the repeated use of formulas. Because
this tale succeeds in evoking a "mythic feel," even writers
primarily concerned with analysis of technique have been
moved to seek underlying meanings; certainly the ritualistic
nature of these repetitive passages helps create the sense that
there is something deeper than catacombs present. It will,
however, be noted that the repetitions here, though they
perform a somewhat similar function, are of a different sort
than those in the last sentences of *Pym*, or in the colloquies.
There Poe purposefully used a formulaic language to create a
prophetic tone; here Poe uses repetition for dramatic effect, but
the effect is also ritualistic.

Since, in this discussion we have dealt with terms--myth
and ritual--which to some degree overlap, it would perhaps be
well to differentiate, or at least attempt to define the nature of
the interrelationship. In a useful discussion of the subject,
Austin Warren wrote, "For many writers, myth is the common
denominator between poetry and religion....Religious myth is
the large-scale authorization of poetic metaphor."[7] This is
relevant for Poe, for he shared the then-current notions
concerning the connection between the ideal artist and his
source of inspiration; his ideal artist was a kind of god, and
practiced god-like creation. But clearly Montresor is not the
ideal artist. What he created is a murder plot. Yet that plot has

the characteristic "look" of the beautiful creations in Poe: it is complex, it is ornate, it is *bizarre*. It will, in short, "take" all those terms which Poe uses to characterize ideal beauty, or those terms with which Dupin characterizes the beautiful patterns which he unravels. Mr. Felheim, in the passage quoted above, says that Montresor "assumes a perverted priestly function." In terms of the usual pattern of the Poe story, such a judgment seems just, although it might be better to use a stronger word than "priest." Poe's ideal poet-creator plays god; Montresor, too, plays god, and were the story more overtly concerned with moral issues, one might even be able to say that god-playing is his sin.

"The Cask of Amontillado" closes with these words: "For the half of a century no mortal has disturbed them [the pile of bones.] *In pace requiescat!* " (VI, 175) One critic has suggested that they contain the final irony of the tale. "...The half-century during which Montresor has kept the secret to himself is Fortunado's retribution,"8 and the Latin benediction now, after fifty years, when Montresor has told the tale, applies to both murderer and victim. Were the story more concerned with moral judgments, such an element would have been more prominently displayed. It is by no means impossible for the idea to have occurred to Poe. It is present in Coleridge's "Ancient Mariner" and, as we have seen, it is a strong possibility in Poe's "Maelstrom." But as that tale is, in the last analysis, less concerned with its own inherent moral problems than with the perception of the wild beauties of the whirlpool, so this tale is less concerned with the moral issue which the crime implies than with the elaborate and grotesque manner in which Montresor has devised it.

"The Cask of Amontillado" clearly cannot be called a moral study, for on the whole it ignores its own moral situation. Can it really be called myth? Let us quote again from the Warren essay.

> In the seventeenth and eighteenth centuries...the term [myth] had commonly a pejorative connotation: a myth was a fiction--scientifically or historically untrue. But already in the *Scienza Nuova* of Vico, the emphasis has shifted to what, since the German Romanticists, Coleridge, Emerson, and Nietzsche, has become gradually dominant--the conception of "myth" as, like poetry, a kind of truth or equivalent of truth, not as a competitor to historic or scientific truth but a supplement. (180)

The suggested equation between myth and poetry implies a conception of the artist which Poe would have liked, and the resultant conclusion regarding the function of the creative process in relation to science suggests Poe's reasoning in *Eureka*. This is just the sort of intellectual heritage which Poe shared with his Transcendental contemporaries, and suggests a useful tie to the present. To the romantics' enthusiasm for myth we owe more than a little of our own intellectual trappings. It was they who rediscovered what has been true in all cultures but our own, and in our own, too, in all but most recent ages: that the functions of art and religion are not separate, that art is magic, that the distinctions which we, as western rationalists, make between science, magic, religion and art are unknown in other more traditional world-views. I discussed Poe's part in this rediscovery in a piece called "In the Mystical Moist Night-Air"[9] in which I tried to demonstrate how such an occult world-view may be traced from Poe and his contemporaries into numerous modern artists. But for the Poe of "The Cask," just how relevant is the equation? We have the following facts: 1) The tale is ritualistic, and has the "feel" of myth; 2) Poe elsewhere consciously tried to sound prophetic; 3) Poe believed in a god-like artist; and 4) this tale is closely related to the tales in which such an artist demonstrates his power.

"Historically," Mr. Warren says, "myth follows and is correlative to ritual; it is 'the spoken part of ritual; the story which the ritual enacts.'" (180) What story does the ritual which Montresor performs enact? To be too specific in answering is to distort the tale. As the passage from Donald Pearce's article suggests, there are elements here which are reminiscent of the Passion, but as he points out, they are not used consciously and systematically. Besides, the Passion story obviously does not have about it the emphasis upon diabolism which is so prominent in "The Cask of Amontillado." It is essential to the meaning of the Crucifixion that it be perpetrated by men who know not what they do. Montresor eminently knows what he is about, except in the sense that a man mad enough to murder may be criminally insane.

Perhaps reader reaction may again be of service. What is the most immediate reaction to this story? Obviously: What fantastic cruelty! Montresor gloats over the details of his victim's sufferings. He is happy that Fortunato is now sober, so that he can realize the full horror of his own situation: ⌐

> I had scarcely laid the first tier of the masonry when I discovered that the intoxication of Fortunato had in a great measure worn off. The earliest indication I had of this was a low moaning cry from the depth of the recess. It was *not* the cry of a drunken man. There was then a long and obstinate silence. I laid the second tier, and the third, and the fourth; and then I heard the furious vibrations of the chain. The noise lasted for several minutes, during which, that I might hearken to it with the more satisfaction, I ceased my labours and sat down upon the bones. (VI, 173-174)

At the close of the tale Montresor even teases the reader with the possibility that he may be contrite, only to shatter violently any such idea in the next phrase: "My heart grew sick--on account of the dampness of the catacombs."

I do not think that it is the demonstrable parallels with known beliefs that give to the tale its "mythic feel." Had Poe placed a clearly identifiable crucifix in his subterranean Golgotha, the effect would have been less startling than it is./

Imagine for the moment that Poe had gone back over one of the horror tales which have all the usual "parts," and eliminated everything but the central, grotesque horror. "The Black Cat" will do nicely. Strike from this tale first the passages toward the beginning in which the narrator tells of his moodiness, his alcoholism, and his perversity, and then eliminate the passages at the close in which he betrays himself and his madness to the police. The parallel to "The Cask" will not yet be close, because this tale will still contain evidence of its narrator's development--or rather degeneration--toward the state of mind which enables him to commit the outrages. But if one could freeze the action at one section, one could create something closely resembling the other tale. Start with the murder of the narrator's wife, and go as far as the passage in which he gloats calmly as the police search the house. This is still not quite the same thing, for this was an unpremeditated crime, and Montresor claims that he was in full control, but it is close enough for some important similarities to become evident. Physical resemblances abound--the walling-up, the cellar, the ghoulish satisfaction with the deed well done, the calmness. Now were *this* amplified to the pitch of "The Cask of Amontillado"; were all the emphasis of the tale concentrated on the details of the horror, and all extraneous comments eliminated, one would have another "Cask." The tale would still be about madness, but the reader's reaction would change. As the story stands, the prime reaction is, What a madman! It would become, What fantastic cruelty!

"The Cask of Amontillado" should be regarded as a slice of a horror story. Earlier in this discussion I suggested that the best term to use as a label for the bulk of Poe's work is expressionism, for that implies a selective distortion. It was mentioned that Surrealism in art bears an historical relationship to expressionism. These two stories exemplify the distinctions between the two terms. "The Cask" is one of Poe's most selective and distorted visions. But its stage properties are not sharp and Surrealistic. They are sketchy and impressionistic, if anything. In contrast, "The Black Cat," for all the high-strung horror of its central action, contains some surprisingly familiar objects. The narrator of "The Black Cat" tells the reader a good deal about his biography; there is at least a superficially satisfactory account of how he came to be what he is, and, even at the height of his triumph, Poe lets him condemn himself with the statement, "The guilt of my dark deed disturbed me but little." (V, 154) The moral judgment which that implies is a part of the tale's backdrop of normalcy. The narrator is married; he lives in a house; he keeps pets. "The Black Cat" is enacted by a madman in a normal world. "The Cask" is enacted by demons on the plains of Mars.[10]

James Thurber has written a short story which may be thought of as a parody of "The Cask of Amontillado." The comparison is so far-fetched that it can serve to emphasize the enormous distortion of Poe's tale. The hero of "The Catbird Seat" is a quiet clerk of notoriously regular habits; Montresor is proud, moody, of noble family. Thurber's setting is thoroughly work-a-day; Poe's, a wild carnival in an exotic city. Montresor tells us that Fortunato has, in effect, convicted himself, and that he will be the executioner; "Ditto," says Mr. Martin, "for Mrs. Barrows." And, in a textural detail, contrast Mr. Martin's attitude towards the bottle of Scotch with the nobleman's toward the wines he collects. The Thurber tale obviously derives much of its humor from the incongruity of an act of vengeance enacted by the mildest and most timid of men and placed in the homeliest of settings.

Poe, like Hawthorne, seems to have been worried by just

this type of incongruity. Both men operated best with plots which would not seem credible in normal surroundings, and each had to devise techniques which could provide his readers with a margin of credibility. But in the case of "The Cask of Amontillado," Poe threw out the usual cautious procedures, and attempted to hold his tale together with nothing but its own sustained tone of terror.[11]

As the *Pequod* rushes to its doom at the close of *Moby Dick*, Stubb develops a ravenous desire for cherries. The image is so totally irrelevant to the place and the situation that its effectiveness can only be explained by reference to Melville's sure sense of the appropriate irrational image which will evoke the maximum response. There is a good deal of that type of imagery in "The Cask of Amontillado." Montresor's jest, the terribly incongruous passage in which he shows that he is a "Mason" by producing the trowel with which he plans to entomb Fortunato, is one example. With all due respect for the writer who suggested that being a Mason was Fortunato's sin, and that the tale is, in a sense organized about that passage, one must point out that these lines are present for the same reasons that Stubb wants cherries. The macabre joke succeeds because it is incongruous.

The bells on Fortunato's cap are a similar irrational, incongruous detail. Jingling bells on a clown's cap on the head of a sick man descending winding stairs through dark catacombs to his death!

There are two sorts of images in the story. One type might be called stage-setting. Poe controls it well--indeed, masterfully--but its appearances are obvious enough. It relates to the popular assumptions regarding the nobility, and to the operatic *decor* of Poe's scenery. The second is this irrational imagery. In only one sense can it be called mythic, and that is the sense in which our subconscious throws up, in times of extreme stress, flashes of light from deep fires. Of the shadows which they cast are myths made. Poe had the temperament to see the shadows march, and the craftsmanship to set them down.

Having begun atop a lighthouse, we have now descended into the catacombs. There is nothing more horrible in Poe than what we have just discussed, and it seems worth the trouble to ask what the horror means. The picture is by no means simple; let us review.

1. Poe's minor contemporaries used horror all the time; horror was a marketable product in the periodicals for which they and Poe wrote.

2. Poe's major contemporaries, as we shall see in the next chapter, used horror at least as tellingly as did Poe.

3. Through the device of the inspired madman, Poe found a way to relate horror to his aesthetic scheme. The horror stories are not atypical works; their structure and their philosophy are drawn directly from his general aesthetic. This suggests that the author is in control of the horror, and not vice-versa.

4. So does the fact that not all of the horror stories show great intensity. Some are positively cool in tone.

5. Even when most intense, as in "The Cask of Amontillado," they reveal structure and artistic control. The intense story has too many close relatives to seem the wild outburst of an insane author. We noted that its structure can be considered the result of a careful paring-down of the usual structure of Poe's tales of terror. The procedure suggests craftsmanship, not madness. To change the image to something more appropriate, one might say that that's high-proof stuff in "The Cask," but that it was distilled from the same mash as a lot of the other liquors in Poe's locker.[12]

Accuracy, precision, careful qualification, even a salutary dose of timidity! We know so much about Poe; we should use it. Poe draws adolescent readers and screwball criticism. Well, he is odd, and he is fascinating, and we know that the horror must mean something for his personality. But to ignore all we know of the context of his work is to pare down scholarship and criticism as he pared down the horror story, cutting away the context until nothing remains but shrieks and groans. What is left is exciting, but it smells of the catacombs. It makes a good second-feature at the drive-in, but a rotten academic book.

Part Three
THE ENVIRONMENT

Chapter V

The Magazine Environment

As I am well aware that your course of reading lies entirely out of the track of our lighter literature,...I take it for granted that none of the papers in question have met your eye....Variety has been one of my chief aims.

Poe to Professor Charles Anthon, 1844

"Lighter literature," the excerpts from Poe's letter to Professor Anthon seem to suggest, is somehow less respectable than some other kind. Whether Poe really felt as apologetic as all that about his own work is doubtful, but it is clear enough that he felt some apology necessary for being the kind of writer he was. That kind is a "magazinist," and in the present chapter I would like to discuss the meaning of that status in Poe's day. We will want to know, first, what the magazines were like, and second, what influence their character might have had on Poe's fiction.

- 1 -

Quality and Subject Matter

What, then, were the magazines like? The question itself implies an oversimplification, because they were not all alike in

95

purpose, in originality, in contents, or in quality. The sporting magazines, which were to play such an important role in the Yankee and Southwestern humor traditions, were already in evidence in this period, and I am sorry to report that one can waste afternoons in the microfilm room reading accounts of horse races and cricket matches. The ladies' magazines and the gift books were aimed at a different market, as were a surprising number of specialized journals dealing with all manner of arts, interests, professions, and trades. We will, of course, concern ourselves primarily with literary magazines, but it is worth noting before we pass on to them that the functions of other magazines were by no means so clearly defined as one would expect today. One must not be too surprised to find sketches, short stories, poems, or even occasional reviews of belles-lettres in magazines whose mastheads suggest much more specialized concerns. The effect, until the surprise wears off, is rather like what one might feel in encountering an irrelevant short story in the pages of *Casket and Sunnyside*, the trade magazine which morticians read. The reverse is also true. One finds, that is, in the pages of what we think of as literary magazines items which one would expect to appear in far more specialized and technical journals. *Casket and Sunnyside* does not run new short stories by Bernard Malamud, but *Atkinson's Casket* did run items such as the following:

> *Tic Doloreux.*--The French Scientific Journals say that M. Magendie continues to obtain the happiest results from the application of electricity in affectations of the senses, particularly in that acute disease termed the doloreaux. He causes the electric current to pass over the nerves by means of needles of platina, placed at greater or lesser intervals. In some instances a single application is said to have been sufficient; and, in one case of dreadful suffering, in which the patient had long been forced, from the pain of speaking, to express his desire by writing, six applications to the nerve entirely removed a malady of three years [sic] duration. (XIV, 5 [May, 1838] 235)

Atkinson's Casket would seem to have been a commodious receptacle indeed. It is the magazine which later became *Graham's*; at this stage in its career, it bore the descriptive subtitle, *Or Gems of Literature, Wit and Sentiment*. It would be difficult to determine under which of these three headings material of the sort which we have just examined was supposed to fall.

Finding such miscellaneous material in older periodicals to some extent indicates simply that they were less slick, specialized and professional than magazines of our own day, but it also suggests that the "levels" of audience were even less sharply defined than they are today. We think that *The Atlantic* or one of our "reviews" operates on a level different than, say, the late *Saturday Evening Post*, even though the *Post*, especially in its last years, demonstrated some intellectual courage. But in Poe's time, even this much contrast was not always apparent. Thus a literary magazine might be expected to function also as a popular magazine, especially when the "odd" item, as in our example, carried implications which might be imaginatively stimulating. The real capacity of "the senses" was, after all, a matter of great concern to the romantic artist, who followed such news the way a writer for *Analog* follows investigations of E.S.P., or the way many of our serious writers and philosophers have followed such fields as physics and psychology.

Moreover, even today one should be rather suspicious of any too sharp division of the arts in any field into "levels." We have, I think, taken Ortega y Gasset too seriously; and our critics, with terms such as "high-," "middle-," and "low-brow," tend to overclassify a situation more fluid and dynamic than they think. Instead of "middle-brow" or "mid-cult," for instance, I prefer the neutral word "standard," which for me implies craftsmanlike commercial work. I prefer it because writers who use other terms assume that the middle range represents only watered-down versions of what comes above. I am quite certain that in many cases this is not true, indeed, that much elite art grows from standard, and not vice-versa. Edgar Poe seems an exceptionally good case of a gifted artist working in a genre which we would now call standard, comparable to such twentieth century phenomena as commercial magazine fiction, commercial art, or standard music. Even today these levels are not very sharply defined. Both the artists and members of their audience move quite freely from one level to another. Witness Isaac Singer, whose fiction appears in the reviews and quarterlies, but also in *Playboy* and a Yiddish newspaper. In Poe's time, "levels" were hardly defined at all. But in truth, never in the histories of the arts in America has there been really clear stratification: a surprising number of Action Painters, to pick a notoriously "elite" or avant-garde group, began in commercial art; Faulkner, Hemingway, Porter and others wrote for commercial magazines; Charles Burchfield designed wallpaper; Winslow Homer was a magazine illustrator; Dreiser picked up his infamous prose style from the popular periodicals for which he wrote and which he edited. If art merely "filters downward," becoming dilute in the process, then good art is impossible in a democracy. Obviously it is not impossible; obviously certain arts and artists move in the opposite direction. This is generally how new "elite" art forms come into existence; a gifted practioner working in a new commercial medium sees the artistic possibilities. From the commercial cinema came the motion picture of artistic value; from the popular magazine came the short story.

This is not to say that "levels" of art are meaningless, or even that practitioners of the magazine craft in Poe's day were not concerned about their relatively lowly status. Quite the contrary. The matter of levels was obviously of some importance to editors. Many of the literary magazines of the period were as mercenary in their intentions as our commercial magazines, but they were also as self-consciously arty as the little magazines. They were, moreover, highly nervous about the quality of their contents: one repeatedly finds protestations of high artistic purpose and of contempt for all the junk in competing periodicals. These are sure signs of editorial insecurity.

Indeed, if I were pressed to name a type of twentieth century magazine comparable in general editorial nervousness to those of Poe's day, I would turn neither to literary nor to commercial magazines, but rather those produced in situations which make the editors unsure of whether what they are doing is artistically worthwhile. I would suggest that the science fiction magazines, with their endless self-conscious editorial worrying-out-loud about whether science fiction is really an art form, are very closely comparable in this way to the magazines of Poe's day. Even the best fiction in the magazines of the period was so frequently sensational in subject matter, so frequently topical in its response to new scientific developments, that even were there no problem of audience (and clearly there was), the editors would have had good reason for being a little nervous. I say this in spite of the fact that the better of these magazines published work by distinguished authors.

This nervousness, in fact, shows up in even the better magazines. Since, like all Poe specialists, I am down on the Reverend Rufus Griswold, Poe's literary executor, I was delighted to find that during his editorship, *Graham's Magazine* showed as much evidence of editorial insecurity as did any of the other magazines with which Poe was editorially connected.[1]

This number is considerable; Poe's involvement in the magazine world is deep indeed. His more important editorial posts can be summarized quickly. From 1835 until January of 1837 he was the editor of the *Southern Literary Messenger*; from 1839 until June of 1840, he was an editor of *Burton's Gentlemen's Magazine*. From April, 1841, until May of 1842 he was editor of *Graham's Magazine*. He was with the *New York Mirror* from 1844 to 1845, and from 1845 until its demise in January of 1846, he was the editor of the *Broadway Journal*; during the last few months of its existence he was also that magazine's proprietor. But Poe's editorial career alone is insufficient to suggest how deeply he was immersed in the magazines. His work shows up in a simply stupendous number of magazines of all sorts, including, occasionally, those not primarily devoted to literature. He was in the *Gentlemen's Magazine*, the *Saturday Museum, The Casket*, which later became *Atkinson's Casket* (and, with the change of names, saw fit to reprint the same Poe poem which it had run under its old name.)[2] When it changed its name once again to become *Graham's Magazine*, Poe, of course, was present again. He was also in the *Boston Miscellany*, Lowell's *Pioneer*, the *American Museum of Science, Literature and the Arts*, Sartain's *Union Magazine*, and William W. Snowden's *Ladies' Companion*, not to mention the *North American*, or *Weekly Journal, Flag of Our Union, The Missionary Memorial, The Baltimore Saturday Visiter, The Saturday Evening Post*, John Neal's *Yankee* (or, *Yankee and Boston Literary Gazette*, or *New-England Galaxie*), the *Dollar Magazine* and many others.[3] Suffice it to say that, "In those days," as Frank Luther Mott put it, "one could start a paper on faith and a hundred-dollar bill,"[4] though of course starting a magazine and building a successful magazine were two completely different things, and founding a magazine of some enduring quality was just as clearly yet a third.

Still, it will not do to snicker at all but the most distinguished periodicals. One can find, in Robert Frost's phrase, "mind" at work somewhere in the most unlikely pages. I was struck, for example, by the accuracy of a review in the *Ladies' Magazine* of 1830 of Poe's early volume (1829) *Al Aaraaf*. The reviewer writes,

> A part [of these poems] are exceedingly boyish, feeble, and altogether deficient in the common characteristics of poetry; but then we have parts, and parts too of considerable length, which remind us of no less a poet than Shelly [sic]. The author, who appears to be very young, is evidently a fine genius; but he wants judgement, experience, tact.[5]

Years later, when Poe read the title poem of that same volume to a Boston audience, he himself made comments about its quality which very nearly match those of this early reviewer. One would almost guess that her words had stuck in his mind.[6]

These magazines, which differed in so many ways, differed even in their attitude toward original material. Some, like *Graham's*, seemed to have tried conscientiously to obtain good new stuff, and to have paid well for it. Others, such as Nathaniel Parker Willis' aptly-named *Corsair*, lived entirely because American copyright laws permitted literary piracy.[7] In between lay a large number which ran some original work and surrounded it with reprints of various types. The borrowed material runs the gamut from entire novels stolen outright and rushed into print to beat competitors to the punch, to little exerpts from other magazines reprinted because they are funny, surprising, quaint, exotic, or, one often suspects, merely because they serve to fill up space. In many magazines, these are acknowledged in an apparently ethical manner, but one wonders about the ethics of a magazine with, say, a single original piece and two hundred fifty or so acknowledged but certainly unpaid-for exerpts. Perhaps a sampling of the contents of a totally unexceptional volume of an equally unexceptional magazine will give some sense of the feel of this material: Achievements of Young Men...Anecdote of the New Pope. Adventures in Hungary... Coleridge at School...(the) Dog "Cassius"... Jenny Lind. Anecodote of the Lost Dauphin...Marriage by Proxy...Military Jokes...Old Lady with a Balance at her Banker's. Old Irish Banker...Singular Will. Story of the Pope's Childhood...The Ventriloquist.[8] The same volume contains "A Random Chapter of Melville's Forthcoming Work 'Omoo,'"[9] and it is striking how close this portion of Melville's second novel feels to the magazine prose around it. One is reminded that Melville, too, was something of a magazinist, and had, like Poe, though less extensively, to deal with magazinists' politics.[10]

But my main reason for mentioning this matter of originality is to suggest a context for Poe's own adventures in un-originality: the disgraceful "Longfellow War," in which he accused the poet of plagiarism, and his own piracy in "The Journal of Julius Rodman," of which more in Chapter IX. Like a great many other of the peculiarities of Poe's art and his career, the matter of plagiarism stands out less garishly against the background of magazine journalism than it does against that of general literary history.

There are some points worth making about the physical appearance of these magazines as well. Those which may be regarded as the precursors of such modern showpiece publications as *Horizon* were fairly generous in such matters as the amount of white space with which they surrounded their columns, but in general far less attention was paid to matters of design and composition than in our own magazines, all of which are, to a greater or lesser degree, the grandchildren of cubism. The chapter of *Omoo* which I mentioned above begins in the middle of a column on the left hand page of a two-column magazine, and runs out where it stops. But I suppose the greatest typographical outrage was the Mammoth (or "Leviathan") Weekly, another of the phenomena spawned by the copyright situation. Such magazines stole from Dickens, Bulwer, Captain Marryat, and other established authors. Sometimes the editors hired men to race out to intercept incoming ships in order to obtain copies of the newest novels before competitors, and printed them on elephantine pages several feet high and wider than a man's arms could stretch.[11] I am happy to report that Rufus Griswold, that scoundrel, was a partner in one of these nefarious periodicals.

This is not to imply that the editors were not concerned with the physical beauty of their journals. On the contrary, there is as much editorial chatter about the beautiful cuts which they intend to run as there is about the superlatively good fiction which they claim they are about to present in a future number. Poe, for example, repeatedly made known his preference for simple wood cuts. Fashion plates made popular covers, and cuts of any sort apparently were quite effective in selling issues. A popular technique was to begin an issue with a striking illustration, accompanied by an article, sketch or poem written for the occasion. These poems or sketches are generally unsigned; one usually assumes they are the work of the editor. The sketches especially interest me, for coming as they do in response to the cuts, they are unusually pure examples of the stylistic taste of the magazines. They are, so to speak, written to order, and reflect very directly the editors' idea of what elegant writing should be. It is a little embarassing to say so, but one has to acknowledge that their bombastic rhetorical devices and clichés are very close to those in Poe's own production. Here is one from *Graham's Magazine* which I think is by Griswold himself. I have had it reproduced so that you can read it in the original type and format:

GRAHAM'S MAGAZINE.

Vol. XXI.   PHILADELPHIA: JULY, 1842.   No. 1.

THE POLISH MOTHER.

It was a gorgeous bridal. The old hall of the palace was lit up with a thousand lights, and crowded with all the wealth, beauty and rank of Poland. The apartment blazed with the jewels of its occupants. Princes with their proud dames, high officers of state, nobles whose domains vied in extent with kingdoms, and lordly beauties beneath whose gaze all bent in adoration, had gathered at that magnificent festival to do honor to the bridal of the fair daughter of their host. And loveliest among the lovely was the bride. Tall and majestic in every movement, with a queenly brow, and a face such as might have been that of the mother of the gods, she moved the theme of every admiring tongue. Nor less remarkable was her husband. Warsaw beheld no noble tread her palaces more lordly in his bearing than the Count Restchifky. The fire of a hundred warrior ancestors burned in his eye. The fame of his high lineage, of his extended possessions, of his feats in arms, followed his footsteps wherever he went. In manly beauty the court of Poland had no rival to the count, in majestic loveliness the realm furnished no equal to his bride. And now, as they stood together in that proud old hall, surrounded by all that was noble and beautiful in the land, the peerless beauty of the countess and the princely bearing of her husband shone pre-eminent. Never had Warsaw seen such a festival. All that the most boundless wealth and all that a taste the most fastidious could do to add to the splendor of the occasion had been done, and the guests, one and all, bore testimony to the success of the princely entertainer. The air was laden with incense, flowers bloomed around, unseen music filled the hall with harmony, and statues and carvings of rare device met the eye at every turn. If Aladdin had been there he would not have asked that his enchanted palace should excel in magnificence the one before him. No visionary, in his wildest dream, could imagine aught more beautiful. And through this unrivalled hall the count and his bride moved, conscious that all

this splendor was evoked for their honor, feeling that not a heart in all the vast assembly but envied their exalted lot. At every step congratulations met them until they turned away sick with adulation. What wonder that the rose grew still deeper on the cheek of the bride, that her eyes flashed with brighter brilliancy, or that her step became more queenly? Could aught mortal wholly resist the intoxication of that hour? . . . .

Years had elapsed. That fair young bride had become a mother; but time had passed over her without destroying one lineament of her majestic beauty. But the scene had changed from that through which she moved on her bridal night. There were no longer around her wealth and splendor and beauty, the flattery of the proud, the envy of the fair. She sat alone—alone with her two children, one a lovely girl of sixteen, and the other a smiling boy whose birth three years before had thrilled her husband's heart with ecstasy, filled a province with rejoicings. But now that husband was away from her, that province lay smoking around her. Her own proud home, where since her marriage she had spent the happiest hours of her life, had been sacked and given to the flames, and she now sat leaning against a shattered parapet, with her face buried in her hands, and the bitter tear of a mother's anguish rolling down her cheeks. At her feet, leaning on her for succor, and clasping her hand, sat her daughter; while her boy, too young as yet to be conscious of the misery around him, smiled as he played with the jewelled cross depending from his mother's neck. A broken sword, a dismounted cannon, the shattered staff of a lance, at the feet of the group, betokened that the vassals of the count had not yielded up her house to rapine without a deadly struggle; and indeed, of the hundreds of hearts which beat there, but the day before, only those of the mother and her two children had escaped captivity or death. Part of the palace was yet in flames, while, on the plain beyond, a village threw its lurid conflagration across the sky.

1

Desolation and despair sat enthroned around. Who that had seen that mother on her bridal night, could have foretold that her after life would reveal a scene like this?

The Polish war for independence had broken out. Among the foremost of the patriotic band which periled all for their country, was the Count Restchifky. His sword had been unsheathed at the outbreak of the conflict, his fortune had been poured the first into the coffers of the state. From his own estates he had raised and equipped as gallant a band as ever followed lord to the tented field. And for a short space the war seemed to prosper. But then came the reverse. From every quarter the haughty Catharine poured her countless legions, headed by the fierce Suwarrow, into Poland, and smoking fields and slaughtered armies soon told that the day of hope for that ill-fated land was over. Yet a few noble spirits, among whom the count was foremost, still held out for their country, fighting every foot of ground, and though retreating before the overwhelming forces of the foe, compelling him to purchase every rood of land he gained by the lives of hundreds of his venal followers. It was at this period, and while the count was far from his home, that his palace had been attacked, and given to the flames. Afar from succor, unconscious whether or not her husband yet lived, and trembling for the lives of her offspring amid the desolation which surrounded them, what wonder that even the proud heart of the countess gave way, and that she wept in utter agony over her ruined country and her dismantled home!

"Oh! mother," said the daughter, "if we only knew where father was, or if he yet lived, we might still be happy. Wealth is nothing to us, for will we not still love each other? Dry your tears, dear mother, for something tells me that father lives and will yet rejoin us."

At these words of comfort, more soothing because coming from a quarter so unexpected, the mother looked up, and, drawing her daughter to her bosom, kissed her, saying,

"You are right, my child. We will hope for the best. And if your father has indeed fallen, and we are alone in the world, I will remember that I have you to comfort me, and strive—to—be happy," and, in despite of her effort to be calm, the tears gushed into her eyes at the bare thought of the possible loss of her husband.

"But see, mother," suddenly exclaimed the daughter, "see the cloud of dust across the plain—can it betoken the return of the foe?" and she drew close to her mother's side.

The mother gazed with eager eyes across the plain, and her cheek paled as she thought she distinguished the banner of Russia borne in the advance.

"It is, it is as I feared," said the daughter, "they come to carry us into captivity. Oh! let us hide from their sight—there are secret recesses in the ruins yet where we might defy scrutiny."

"No," said the mother, all the spirit of her race rising in her at this crisis, "no, my daughter, it would not become us, like base-born churls, thus to

fly from a foe. The wife and children of Count Restchifky will meet his enemies on his own hearth-stone, all dismantled though it be."

With these words she clasped her babe closer to her bosom, and sat down again behind the parapet to await, as the daughter of a hundred princes should await, the approach of her murderers; and although perhaps her cheek was a hue paler, the lofty glance of her eye quailed not. Her daughter sank to her feet and buried her face in her mother's robe. But after a few minutes she regained courage, and looked timidly out across the plain. At the first glance she started and said eagerly,

"But see, mother, can they really be enemies? They wave their banners as if to us—they increase their speed—surely, surely that gallant horseman in the advance is my own dear father."

A moment the mother gazed eagerly on the approaching horseman, but a moment only. The eye of the wife saw that her husband was indeed there, and, with a glad cry, she clasped her children in her arms and burst into a flood of joyful tears. She was still weeping when the count, dismounting from his charger, rushed forward and clasped her in his arms.

"Thank God!" he ejaculated, "you at least are left to me. I had feared to find you no more. May the lightning of heaven blast the cravens who could thus desolate the home of a woman."

"My husband, oh! my husband!" was all that the wife could say.

"Father, dear father, you are safe—oh! we shall yet be happy," said the daughter as she clung to her restored parent.

The father kissed and re-kissed them all, and for once his stern nature was moved to tears, but they were tears of joy.

His story was soon told. Finding that all hope of saving his country was over, and eager to learn the fate of those he had left at home, he had cut his way through the enemy with a few gallant followers. As he drew near the vicinity of his palace, he had heard strange rumors of the sacking of his home, and on every side his own eyes beheld the ravages of the foe. Torn with a thousand fears respecting the fate of those he loved better than life, he had pressed madly on, and when the blackened and smoking walls of his palace had risen before him in the distance he had almost given way to despair. But, at length, his eager eye caught sight of a group amid the ruins, and his heart told him that those he loved remained yet to cheer his ruined fortunes.

No pen can do justice to the feelings of gratitude which throbbed in the bosom of that father as he pressed his wife and children successively to his heart. His plans were soon laid. He had, by remittances to England on the outbreak of the war, provided his family against want, and thither they now bent their steps. Over his ruined country he shed many a tear, but, at such times, the smiles of his wife and children were ever ready to cheer his despondency; and as he gazed on his lovely family he felt that there was much yet in this world to bid him be happy.

There is nothing in Poe, I hope, quite so bad as "The Polish Mother," but the similarities between its rhetoric and his are sufficiently strong to suggest at least a familial resemblance. Poe is much better than hacks like Griswold, and far more capable of building poetic effects out of this prose, but it is essentially the same prose. A favorite rhythmic device is the very short sentence to open a paragraph in which something spectacular is to be described. Griswold writes, "It was a gorgeous bridal," then goes on to suggest its glitter. In Poe's "The Masque of the Red Death," the description of the famous masquerade begins with a comparable sentence: "It was a voluptuous scene, that masquerade." One doesn't want to make too much of such matters; writers in other periods and different *genres* have used short sentences in comparable situations. Still, the special theatrical quality of this prose does come through, and to account for it one can only list characteristics, however inadequate any group of them is to reproduce the flavor. The sentence beginning with "and," used at the close of a lengthy description to provide a cadence, often following a long, periodically-organized sentence, or at the end of a paragraph is another such device, evident here in "The Polish Mother" and easy to find in Poe: "And loveliest among the lovely was the bride." My copy of "The Masque of the Red Death" is still open; an example is readily in view: "And the whole seizure, progress, and termination of the disease were the incidents of half an hour."

Griswold's descriptions here are more general than are Poe's in "The Masque," but though Poe was capable of selecting a few concrete details to "fix" an entire scene or incident, he too sometimes manipulated generalities for effect. The business in "The Polish Mother" about Catherine pouring "countless legions" into Poland, where these "venal followers" are slaughtered by Polish patriots (on page 2, paragraph 1 of the reproduction) is comparable to Poe's use of Gottingen as a "dissolute" university in "Mystification" or the similar device in "William Wilson" in which he exploits the reader's stock ideas of a number of places. In each case, easy popular generalizations about peoples or places are used to intensify an effect, though to be fair to Poe, the examples from his work are in no sense ugly. Griswold's evident satisfaction that a goodly number of "venal followers" were killed *is* ugly, though heaven knows there are far uglier passages one could glean from other tales of idealistic political propaganda.

One could, I think, go on to show countless ways in which Poe's prose is like popular magazine prose. I'll mention one other device evident in "The Polish Mother" and then stop: the use of an easy negative and a generality in place of an affirmative description. Griswold writes, "No pen can do justice to the feelings of gratitude...." No pen can tell how many times Poe used that cheap trick, either, and I hope no graduate student spends no year to find out. "The Masque of the Red Death" offers another example: "No pestilence had ever been so fatal, or so hideous."

- 2 -

Illustrations

The illustration (Figure One) for which Griswold provided this sketch is convincing proof that we are dealing with what I have called "standard art." As we noted above, the division of arts into "levels" is largely a modern invention, but Poe's complaints about steel engravings show his awareness that too slick a product was objectionable. This cut, engraved by E. G. Dunnel, from a painting by E. T. Peatis, is very slick indeed, as polished, especially in the central portion, as the engraving on a dollar bill. It is as filled with cliches as the prose which accompanies it: the stock eyes, the meticulous rendering of textures, the saccharine smile of the child are long-established conventions.

It has been suggested to me that if one can equate the "level" of a type of graphic art with that of a type of literary art, one ought to be able also to find comparable reflections in each not only of the overt characteristics of the art of an age and a "level" but also some of the less obvious implications which underlie them. Poe's contemporaries are sensational and sentimental; Poe himself generally avoids sentimentality, though he is certainly sensational. There is a comparable range in the visual material which appeared at the time, and the elite art compares to the standard about as Poe compares to less distinguished writers: the subject matter is similar, but the approach less sentimental and less hackneyed.

Figure One

Now the subject matter of prose and picture is easy enough to compare. Exotic places were obviously sure-fire; Melville's *Typee* and *Omoo* were best-sellers. Many, many lesser examples of tales and essays about faraway places appeared in the magazines, and with them almost as many cuts of exotic harbors, cities and islands. Poe's "The Journal of Julius Rodman" and his *Pym* are other things as well, but certainly they are a part of this literature. But what visual equivalent can we find in the cuts for the covert sexuality, let's say, of much of Poe's work and the "standard" fiction from which it developed? I'm afraid that I can offer only very tentative suggestions.

In an age in which it is not permissable to treat sex, we are told, death is used as a substitute. Fair enough; fascination with death appears in visual and literary art on all levels. There is cannibalism in Poe's *Pym*; there is obvious sensual fascination with violence in the elite paintings of Géricault. In both arts there are "standard" equivalents. "The Polish Mother" will do for one example; the characteristic *Blackwood* article which Poe parodies for another; the popular panoramic paintings of terrible battles and disasters for a third. Significantly, on elite and standard levels these tendencies appear with especial force in the works of Americans. The first great sensational and violent romantic painting, "Brook Watson and the Shark," was the work not of Géricault but of the American John Singleton Copley decades before "The Raft of the Medusa" or "The Death of Sardanapolus." The travelling panoramic painting was popular in England and on the continent, but had its greatest currency in the United States.

It may be that this type of equivalence can be demonstrated on a more subtle level as well, though here our conclusions must be much more tentative. Poe's ladies expire in wedding gowns on bridal beds. So do some ladies in sentimental cuts. But I wonder whether a comparable though far less overt kind of substitution cannot be found in the treatment of "healthy" women as well.

The sixteen-year-old daughter in "The Polish Mother" has a ridiculously tiny foot. I would guess that, to borrow Flexner's language, it would be recognized as a sex symbol by any African anthropologist visiting this country. To some extent we can trace the history of this sort of fetishism, if that is what it really is. Like the stock eyes and sweet smiles, tiny feet and tiny hands show up in various places before our period. In the work of the "little masters," the conversation-piece school in England late in the eighteenth century (men like Arthur Davis or Benjamin Wilson, or the Americans Charles W. Peale or Matthew Pratt), such things seem to be used as flattering conventions, comparable to tiny waists, big behinds and other matters which have, in one age or another, seemed especially attractive. Concern with the hands goes back well before our period. In eighteenth century portraiture, art criticism tells us, there was a vocabulary of hand gestures, which colonial portraitists sophisticated enough to have heard about it did their best to imitate. But I do not think that anyone has noted the extent to which, in paintings of attractive women in which it is not permissible to show legs, how really morbid this fascination with the foot or hand becomes. This is a very different thing than what one finds in the best work of Copley, who paints hands as accurately as he can, and whose hands reflect character as honestly as do his faces, but it was certainly present in the work of lesser men who painted hands never attached to human wrist (see Figure Two) in much the same spirit in which adolescent boys scrawl psychologically revealing (though anatomically preposterous) interpretations of female anatomy on men's room walls.

Examples of such distortion in Poe's day are easy enough to find. Cut Number 3 is from *Graham's Magazine.*[12] More than the stylization one might expect in a fashion illustration is present here. The tiny feet peeping out so slyly from beneath those dresses share qualities with those of Charles Addams' heroines, who also tend to come to a point at the bottom, and are about as wholesome; while the hands, especially those of the first and third women from the left, are not only too small even for the deformed child, but distorted in a way which makes one decidedly uncomfortable. The next two women are holding hands, and I like neither the grip nor their location.

Even stronger in anatomical distortion and sexuality is cut Number 4. This one gives one some clues to the rules of the craft. Apparently by averting a face, one gets license to show a breast.[13] Cut Number 5, finally, is a very sexy engraving indeed, "The Rajpoontnee Bride."[14] In this case the exotic setting and the bride's foreignness apparently give the illustrator even more license. The string of pearls is intended to draw

Figure Two
Anonymous portrait of Mrs. Van Alstyne - 1721
(Used by permission of The New York Historical Society)

Figure Three

Figure Four

Figure Five

attention to cleavage which runs fully to the waist. The girl is shown in a manner emphasizing her exotic profile, her softness and a very sexy, albeit less distorted, hand.

We are dealing with a fairly subtle matter, and should be careful not to make more of it than the facts merit. Any art form on any level develops countless little conventions and procedures. There is, I think, a relationship between the covert or overt eroticism of these illustrations and comparable fetishism in Poe's writing. What is present in the art work seems to be of the same flavor as what is pointed out by Freudian critics of Poe from Marie Bonaparte and Joseph Wood Krutch to David M. Rein. But in both cut and prose, there is so much that is convention, there are so many artistic decisions based on precedent, that we should be cautious in our use of psychoanalytical techniques. Our own age is breast-happy, we are told, and there is supposed to be plenty of sexual voltage in the big-bosomed girls in the *Playboy* fold-outs. But how much voltage is there in, let's say, the ample breast which a commercial artist routinely puts into his drawings of a blouse in his illustration for an advertisement of a clothing sale? There is some, I am sure, but clearly much less. We know nothing at all from the drawing about the artist's sex-life. The artist may be satyr, a homosexual, a clean-cut youngster or an elderly woman, but given the assignment of making the blouse look attractive by draping it on a female torso, any commercial artist might respond in pretty much the same way. The artist may, in point of fact, be "experiencing" his work very strongly as he draws; the breast-lines he puts in may carry great erotic force for him. But he may be feeling nothing at all except the scratching of his pen or the buzzing of his air-brush. When matters of convention are involved, there is no way to determine the degree of personal involvement.

And I think that this is as true in fiction which is produced in "standard" genres as it is of visual art. When the craftsman-like popular writer describes an attractive woman, he may be lusting for her or he may simply be doing his job. More likely, he is somewhere in between: making her attractive to himself because he responds to the same things which others in his culture admire. Elite writers are not immune to conventions which affect standard writers. Hemingway's women are a variation on the "new woman" whom James also studied, but she was present in the standard art of both periods as well. Hawthorne's ladies fall into categories--"blonde virgins" and "dark temptresses," I think one critic called them--which are solidly established in the popular fiction of his day. This fact in no way lessens the artist's stature, nor does it necessarily demonstrate great detachment. There is sexual energy in those dark women of Hawthorne, and those writers who think that he was both fascinated and a little frightened by them are probably right. Similarly, Hemingway's good and "true" girls undoubtedly tell us things about Papa, sometimes, notably in the case of Renata in *Across the River and Into the Trees*, a little more than we want to know. But whatever Renata tells the psychoanalyst about Hemingway, she looks like a *New Yorker* ad; whatever Hester or Zenobia tell us about Hawthorne, they look like cuts in *Godey's*. The meaning of all this for Poe is clear enough: what we think we see in his fiction is probably really there. But much of it is cliché and convention. If we pull him out of his context we lose all sense of perspective. We need New Critical analyses; we need also Old Scholarly *etudes d' ambience*.

- 3 -

Music

The *Broadway Journal*, the magazine with which Poe had his closest connection, ran just two volumes, from January 4, 1845, to January 3, 1846. Poe was the proprietor as well as editor during the last months of its publication. The magazine's brief history makes it easy enough to read through from beginning to end. In doing so I noticed an odd fact: though it was a money-loser, one gets the distinct impression that most of what cash it took in came because of the efforts of its active music reviewer. The number of advertisements for piano sheet music and music stores increases steadily throughout its history (and interestingly, there is "puffing" of advertizers' products in the editorial columns--a piano factory is described and praised; a new music book is lauded at length, each in the same number in which ads appear for them). Henry C. Watson, the music editor, seems in no way a distinguished critic, but his coverage of musical events of all sorts apparently attracted a certain

following. He writes magazine-ese of the same level as that of
Griswold and other .240 hitters, but I found it difficult to fix
the "level" of the musical events which he was reviewing except
through cross-checking the general descriptions of concert life
of the times in John Tasker Howard's *Our American Music*.[15] It
is fair to say, I think, that these concerts were far more mixed
in level and quality than those which one would expect a music
critic to cover today, but I think the evidence too weak to
conclude that the music reviews represent yet another example
of "standard" art in the environment of Poe's fiction.

The *Broadway Journal* concerned itself largely with music,
but did not run any. Several magazines of the day did, however,
and here there can be no ambiguity about the "level" of art
represented. The music is "lady music," designed for home
performance by moderately accomplished readers. Here are two
examples which I have selected from *Graham's*. I picked
Graham's because a learned reader of my discussion of this
problem of the "level" of art represented in *Graham's* objected
strenuously to my saying that much of the magazine's content
was standard. He is quite correct in pointing out that *Graham's*
printed some very good things by well-known writers.[16] My
point is merely that as an environment, *Graham's* is closer to a
popular magazine or, in some ways, even a pulp magazine than
it is to a contemporary literary magazine. That's not necessarily
bad, it seems to me; I think that contact with an established
standard literary market is a good thing for many elite writers,
though of course it is regretable that the market in Poe's day
was so corrupt. But the pressure of standard-level material
seems undeniable. Should the sample of Griswold's elegant
prose be unconvincing, I assume with some confidence that the
"lady music" reproduced in Figures Six and Seven will do the
job. The composers are not named, but the editor tells us that
each piece was written expressly for *Graham's*. I have had
recordings made of these pieces, and would be happy to lend
them to anyone who would like to hear what the musical part
of the magazine environment sounds like. The first piece has
some slight musical merit; a pianist of any imagination at all
can, with a little *rubato*, make it sound rather charming. The
second, I fear, is pretty dreary stuff however you play it, but it
is typical "lady music." Anyone unwilling to admit that the
sentimental sketches, exotic tales, creations of fourth-rate

THE ZANONI GALLOP.

COMPOSED FOR GRAHAM'S MAGAZINE.

Figure Six   From *Graham's*, **XXI, 102**

SEPTEMBER WALTZ.

COMPOSED FOR GRAHAM'S MAGAZINE.

Figure Seven   *Ibid.*, 151

female poets, and pious bilge of the flavor of "The Polish Mother" with which the editors of *Graham's* filled their pages is not high art should be convinced by the music which was its fitting accompaniment. *Graham's*, indeed, was one of the very best of the magazines, and is a magnificent document of the tastes and values of an era. But the presence of an occasional piece by a household poet or Brahmin essayist only serves to demonstrate that these writers, like Poe, are fairly close to the standard art of their day.

I mention this very peripheral matter of music only because it seems an unusually efficient method of indicating the "level" of the magazines. Had we space, photo-reproductions of a few dozen items of the sort illustrated by "The Polish Mother" would do the same job. I am not claiming that Poe hummed these tunes as he wrote his stories. Still, it is worth mentioning that the connection between music and the magazines in this period is by no means slight. John Hewitt, for instance, the song composer, was also a magazinist and editor, who having once offended Poe with an unsympathetic review of *Al Aaraaf*, offended him once again by beating him out in a poetry contest. Hewitt was the editor of the paper which awarded the prize, and Poe was angry enough about the incident to engage Hewitt in a fistfight on the street.[17]

- 4 -

Summary

How then did the magazine environment influence Poe's work? In quite a number of ways, and so profoundly that it is fair to say that Poe's art as we have it could not have existed without the magazines. Since we are going to expand on points made in this chapter in many of the discussions of individual stories in the chapters which follow, let's, for the sake of brevity, use a list instead of an extensive summary.

1. As we noted in the concluding section of Chapter One, over the past forty years an impressive number of source studies demonstrated most conclusively that Poe's subject matter is the one element in his fiction which is clearly not original. We are told that there is a model for nearly every type of story which he produced. It seems

safe to say that the magazines gave him his material.

2. Poe's systematic check list of saleable story-types and his total familiarity with the magazine-as-market suggest that even the genres which he brought to the magazine, for the first time were designed to capitalize on what he knew of audience and medium. For example: scholars have found some likely sources for his detective stories, but, as we shall see in our discussion of those tales, the sources were in book, and not magazine form. Poe is called the inventor of the modern detective story. What this means is that he found a way to turn the material to magazine purposes. He invented a genre, but he invented it in response to very specific knowledge of the medium in which it was to run. It seems significant that he had a very hard time getting his stories printed in book form: publishers had a hard time selling collections of short stories. This is true even today; friends who write fiction tell me that it is almost impossible to get stories placed anywhere but in magazines. Publishers generally will issue volumes of short stories by a single author only if the author is very well known. Even then they would rather have novels. I am less angry on this score with publishers in Poe's day than are most students of Poe; I think they knew their market. Poe's fiction was created for magazines, and belonged there. The magazine helped determine the characteristics of the genres which Poe originated.

3. As our samples of music, illustrations and prose should have demonstrated, the level of the magazines, while very mixed, was generally "standard," and not "elite." Poe's achievement, again, was to create art forms out of the materials of a commercial and sometimes even hack medium.

4. Some of Poe's work is ineffective today because of its topicality. The key to his topicality is the magazine and work of the magazinists. Three good studies provide a guide to that world (Sidney P. Moss' *Poe's Literary Battles*, Perry Miller's *The Raven and the Whale* and Michael Allen's *Poe and the British Magazine Tradition*),[18] but even the most careful scholars have not yet found out what all of his tales are about.

5. Moss' study describes the abuses of the publishing business in Poe's day, the literary puffing which Poe fought so valiantly, but to which he occasionally succumbed himself; also the back-scratching and the back-stabbing. Knowledge of the magazines and their practices gives insight into the terrible pressure under which Poe, improvident and impecunious, worked in his long struggle to make a little money and to fill up the empty columns with copy. And that pressure explains several things in his work: first, the sloppiness of an unpolished story now and then. Second, the characteristic truculence, the willingness to take on a literary battle, or even at times, to pick a fight. Third, less important, the textual variations in much of his work. When pressed for copy, he would re-run material previously published elsewhere, generally editing it in the process.

6. The magazines gave him his style. He was more skillful at handling the clichés of "magazineze" that were his competitors, but clearly spoke the language.

7. The magazines influenced his aesthetic theories. Poe's criticism, as we have seen, is as notorious for its inconsistency as for its brilliance, but it is clear enough that he placed unusual emphasis upon intensity of effect. He said so both in his essays on poetry and in those on fiction (his review of Hawthorne's *Twice Told Tales* is an especially good example); he preferred works which could be read at one exciting sitting. Every sensitive critic has wondered to what extent Poe's praise of brevity and intensity was rationalized after the fact. My feeling is that two factors were involved. First, his romantic aesthetics, with its steady emphasis on perception and intuition, is consistent with what he did in his work. Since he thought that rich, ornate and complex patterns were beautiful, it's fair to say that his tales were fictionalized embodiments of his aesthetics. But on the other hand, Poe was a magazinist, and magazinists are conditioned to produce pieces of a certain length as predictably as professors are to talk for fifty minutes. One of the sources of his aesthetics of

intensity (not the sole source, certainly) was the magazine habit.

8. Yet another characteristic of Poe's writing which is at least in part attributable to his immersion in the magazines in his predisposition toward the outré, and, for that matter, the occult. One certainly does not want to use any phrase quite so strong as "these magazines caused...," because there are other good reasons for their presence in Poe's work. Poe's understanding of inspiration is magical and occult, and the visions of his "perceivers" seem generally rather *bizarre*. Yet this theoretical framework could be derived from random samplings of the magazines almost as readily as it could from the Virginia Edition of Poe's *Works*. The heavy emphasis upon exoticism, extraordinary happenings and inexplicable phenomena in the journals of the early nineteenth century makes an oddly unwholesome diet. Feed too long on that kind of material and the result is liable to be, if not an unrealistic notion of what the world is like, at least an unusual concern with topics far removed from the everyday course of a work-a-day life.

Edward Wagenknecht, in his admirable and informal biography of Poe, says that if Poe is sick, so is his whole age.[19] Strange topics in the magazines must reflect strange interests in the era. But magazines, like any medium of mass communication, not only reflect; they also propagate.

Chapter VI

The Influence of the
Magazines on the Fiction

Henry Adams was the first in an infinite series to discover and admit to himself that he really did not care whether truth was, or was not, true. He did not even care that it should be proved true, unless the process were new and amusing. He was a Darwinian for fun.

The Education of Henry Adams

- 1 -

Poe's Moon-Shot

Poe's first astronaut is a bellows-repairman fallen on hard times. He figures in what must be one of the queerest works from the desk of a major author. The story in which he appears opens, as nearly as I can make out, as a sort of double-satire: Arthur Hobson Quinn said that Poe intends to burlesque "romantic, scientific tales of journeys to the moon"[1]; he also seems to have a political point to make. Hans Pfaall, mender of bellows in Rotterdam, says that he was ruined by the "effects of liberty and long speeches and radicalism, and all that sort of thing"; perhaps Poe, whose politics were, among other things, a

123

pseudo-aristocratic amalgam of southern attitudes and personal nervousness, intended a general sneer at liberalism. The tale begins as a dunce-cap shaped balloon constructed of dirty Rotterdam newspapers descends from the sky above the city. The mob watching its approach frightens off the occupant, an earless dwarf, but not before he drops a long message from Pfaall. Early in it, Pfaall says that bellows-mending petered out because people could fan their fires with newspapers, and because people were too busy reading about revolutions and keeping up with "the march of intellect and the spirit of the age." The tale thus seems to open as a satire on the popular prints and upon a political spirit which Poe did not like. To my knowledge, nothing more specific is intended; I am not aware of any published explication of these opening paragraphs.

Poe also seems to want to poke fun at learned institutions. The tale is, as he says, a hoax, yet it is obviously not intended to fool readers--the opening is too deliberately preposterous. The officers of the "States' College of Astronomers" of Rotterdam are fooled; they are also given foolish names ("Von Underduk" and "Rubadub"). But, again, if Poe has anything more specific in mind, it escapes me. It may be that this is all he intended, or it may be that we have lost the exact topical referents. In a general sense, we know what he is up to, however, because the periodicals of his day were, as we have noted, simply filled with factual, fictional and speculative articles, tales and fantasies written in response to the intense interest in exoticism, science, and exploration. Whatever else it is, "The Unparalleled Adventure of One Hans Pfaall" is a reaction to the environment of the periodicals of the day. Poe starts out, at least, to make fun of it.

In doing so, he was of course parodying his own material. Since most of the subject-matter of his fiction was drawn from the magazines, one is tempted to assume that his attitude toward his work must have been simply calculating. "Uncle Don," the famous radio personality, lost his children's radio program because, at the end of one of his broadcasts, he remarked, before what he thought was a dead microphone, something to the effect of "I guess that'll hold the little bastards for another day." Can we imagine Poe saying something similar as he rose from his desk after writing, let's say, "The Tell-Tale Heart"? Yes, perhaps we can, but that does not make him a sort of literary Machiavelli. Though he called them "little bastards," "Uncle Don" may very well have genuinely loved children; what he said on that fateful day was for the benefit of the people in the studio, all of whom may fully have understood that those were the words of a warm-hearted man joking, and making fun only of himself. Poe, similarly, may have cracked wise about an apparently serious story; we know for a fact that he wrote parodies of his own most compelling work. But we would not be treating the case with sufficient precision if we therefore regarded Poe's habit of capitalizing on popular interests as simply a matter of professional cynicism. "The Unparalleled Adventures of One Hans Pfaall" is not an especially successful tale, but its very faults suggest that Poe was imaginatively committed to his material. There is a contradiction here; Poe spoke of his systematic methods of selecting subjects and parodied his own commercial attitudes, yet used the same subjects in his most serious work. But there are many contradictions in Poe. They are part of the man, and sometimes, when they are seen in the context of his career and its setting, they seem less like contradictions than like varied reactions to the same problems. We noted in our first chapter the seeming critical contradiction between those of Poe's critical pronouncements which say that the creation of art is a matter of supernal inspiration and those which say that it is a matter of cool craftsmanship. If a close friend had pointed that out to Poe, one imagines that he would have agreed that he had contradicted himself, and then said, in justifiable self-defence, "But really, aren't both true?" In the present matter, it seems to this reader that Poe had the detachment to see the comic implications in the stereotyped subject-matter of the popular literature of his day, but that, as a child of his times, he simultaneously responded to the very same material. Contemporary social critics have given us fine analyses of the sources of our value-systems, and, having read their books, we see that some of the sources are absurd. Yet we go on responding to certain characteristics of cars, clothing, and countless other things around us because they and we *are* part of our culture. Poe, similarly, could understand and yet respond; he was a bright man, but brightness and insight do not preclude response.

Indeed, Poe said as much in an article on Richard Adams Locke in *Godey's Lady's Book* for October, 1846. Reading a book on astronomy, Poe writes, "excited my fancy, and I longed to give free rein to it...." He goes on to tell how he came to write "Hans Pfaall," and then says that Locke's "Moon-Hoax," in his penny daily *The New York Sun* was not influenced by the Poe story (Poe's "Balloon-Hoax," about a transatlantic balloon flight, came out in the *Sun* in 1844; "Hans Pfaall" and Locke's hoax date from 1835). But Poe's article stresses the enormous popular excitement surrounding such topics, everyone's desire to believe, and his own pleasure at working with such materials. The Locke hoax, Poe says, is important in the history of journalism. It "made" the penny press.

What happens in "Hans Pfaall" illustrates this response with considerable clarity. As we have seen, Poe evidently intended the tale to be a farce, yet once the diary of the adventure begins, the satirical tone is dropped like one of his hero's sand-bags. For most of the remainder of the tale, Poe gives every evidence of being fascinated by his subject. The entries in Hans Pfaall's log are interesting and well written. Hans takes with him, on his ascent, several animals, and keeps careful check on their reactions to the high altitude; he observes the appearance of the earth as he floats higher; he is excited one day by beholding "the singular phenomenon of the sun rising while nearly the whole visible surface of the earth continues to be involved in darkness." (II, 87) He also reacts with courage and ingenuity to a number of perilous situations, and even invents a water-driven alarm clock to solve a problem he had not anticipated in planning his trip.

Since Poe, as we noted, could not have intended to hoax his readers, and since this interesting central portion of his tale seems essentially unrelated to the facetious opening and conclusion, I can only assume that Poe was enjoying inventing what we would today call science fiction. The contrast between the tone of the opening and conclusion, and the tone of the diary portion in the center, is striking. Here is a sample entry from Hans' log:

"April 6th. Was surprised at finding the rim of ice at a very moderate distance, and an immense field of the same material stretching away off to the horizon in the north. It was evident that if the balloon held its present course, it would soon arrive above the Frozen Ocean, and I had now little doubt of seeing the Pole. During the whole of the day I continued to near the ice.

Towards night the limits of my horizon very suddenly and materially increased, owing undoubtedly to the earth's form being that of an oblate spheroid, and my arriving above the flattened regions in the vicinity of the Artic circle. When darkness at length overtook me, I went to bed in great anxiety, fearing to pass over the object of so much curiosity when I should have no opportunity of observing it.["] (II, 87)

This is a mighty interesting business; the reader is almost as curious as Hans to see what the Pole looks like from aloft. Poe is playing here with an old belief which in his day had gained new currency--the idea that the earth is open at the poles. When Hans actually drifts over the pole, Poe decides not to risk a guess. The entry for April 7 dodges the issue through an ancient storyteller's device: the ship passes over the pole, "but, alas!" says Hans, "I had now ascended to so vast a distance, that nothing could with accuracy be discerned."

Contrast the tone of Hans' journal with that of this description of the dwarf taken from early in the tale:

He could not have been more than two feet in height....The body of the little man was more than proportionally broad, giving to his entire figure a rotundity highly absurd....His hands were enormously large. His hair was gray, and collected into a *queue* behind. His nose was prodigiously long, crooked, and inflammatory...of ears of any kind there was not a semblance to be discovered upon any portion of his head. This odd little gentleman was dressed in a loose surtout of sky-blue satin, with tight breeches to match, fastened with silver buckles at the knees. His vest was of some bright yellow material; a white taffety cap was set jauntily on one side of his head; and, to complete his equipment, a blood-red silk handkerchief enveloped his throat, and fell down, in a dainty manner, upon his bosom, in a fantastic bow-knot of supereminent dimensions. (II, 45-46)

A modern reader seldom understands how one is supposed to respond to humor of this sort, though he knows perfectly well how to respond to the central portion of the story. This is simply because the genre of adventure is still with us, while this particular tradition of humor has died out. There are models for both tones in the magazines, but in mixing the two, Poe destroyed the unity of his piece.

I can hazard a guess at why he sandwiched his adventure story between two pieces of farce. The dwarf is supposed to be an inhabitant of the moon, but we are told at the end that he looks too much like a disreputable dwarf who disappeared from a nearby city. Pfaall's adventure is made out to be a fraud and a hoax; he escaped from his bad situation in Rotterdam, murdered his three most annoying creditors and made fools of the savants of the College of Astronomy. The central adventure, then, is hidden behind several layers of hoax and fraud. Poe probably had in mind the problem of credibility; he could invent any kind of adventure if the adventure was to turn out to be unreal. But the pattern is not sufficiently consistent for that explanation to be totally satisfactory. For one thing, part of Pfaall's diary must be "true"-- the three creditors *are* missing. For another, Poe works very hard at making the adventures described in the journal *themselves* as credible as possible. Third, he found those adventures personally attractive, and returned to them in another story, this time without the farcical "frame" around them. So credibility cannot be his only reason for the "frame." My guess is that he found his own interest in the adventure a little embarrassing, and did what he could to cloak his enthusiasm in absurdity.

Poe does not seem to have had the storytelling knack one senses in the books of many authors of works of adventure. One notices how often throughout his career when he deals with adventure materials he retreats to the device of a log or diary. "The Facts in the Case of M. Valdemar" comes, we are told, from an observor's notes; *Pym* is largely taken from a log; "The Journal of Julius Rodman" is, as the title says, a journal, and so on. Often Poe hides himself behind several layers of narration, so that the story comes to us at second- or third-hand. In the present story, even the diary form itself provides a device for indicating that Pfaall's narration is a fraud: the trip to the moon begins on April Fool's Day.

But if Poe's disguise of his intent is elaborate, it is by no means successful or even consistent. We have to believe parts of what happens, however much he mocks other parts. Pfaall's observations of the behavior of a cat and kittens, for instance, seem "sincere"; Hans says that his heart goes with them when they are accidentally lost. We also have to believe that the creditors are dead; the murder "really" happened. But obviously even in these two "real" events, we are dealing with different flavors of reality, just as we are dealing with two different Hans.

There is no point in spelling out all of the inconsistencies in this tale; it's not that important a story. What is important is the demonstration it affords of Poe's response to the popular materials which he set out to parody. It is an early story, first published, under the title "Hans Pfaall, a Tale" in 1835. Nine years later the material still looked valuable to him, and he used it again in the tale now called "The Balloon-Hoax."

Indeed, even the early story, for all its silliness, gives plenty of evidence of deep imaginative involvement. While Poe copies much of the scientific and technical data from such sources as Rees' *Cyclopedia* and John F. W. Herschel's *A Treatise on Astronomy*,[2] when Hans describes his daydreams about the beauties and terrors of the moon, he uses images which come from very deep in Poe's imagination, as Burton Pollin shows in his essay "Poe and the River."[3]

In "The Balloon-Hoax," Poe solved the problem of unity by cutting away the satirical "frame" and dealing only with the adventure. Instead of inventing an inconsistent character who hoaxed the inhabitants of a far-off city (and yet who "really" had at least a portion of the adventure which he describes), Poe was now able to be the hoaxer himself, and to fool New Yorkers, for he published the hoax as a news story in a special "extra" edition of a newspaper. The new scheme also enabled him to commit himself to the material as fully as he wished without embarrassment, for the more convincing he made the adventure, the better the hoax. I feel, in other words, that the hoaxing was not his sole motive for producing the story. The material itself was attractive to him. With his solid understanding of the light-fiction trade, he was perfectly competent to turn out characteristic trade items. Yet this must have seemed trivial stuff for a man who professed dedication to the high seriousness of his artist's calling. Still...it was fascinating. Perhaps one could indulge, yet demonstrate one's detachment by hiding oneself in some manner: letting a character show the enthusiasm, and then mocking the character, for example, or writing an occasional parody of the genre. Such an explanation accounts also for some of his other puzzling behavior--why, for instance, he produced both horror stories and parodies of horror stories, both detective stories and parodies of detective stories, both tales of adventure and parodies of tales of adventure. His behavior is inconsistent and erratic, perhaps, but not inexplicable.

It would be fun, I think, to devote a chapter to a discussion of the science in the two flying stories.[4] It seems wiser to spare the reader more interested in Poe-as-artist than Poe-as-scientist the texture of such a discussion and to present instead impressions of what the conclusions might be. I am indebted to Professor Donald Fleming of Harvard for a good course of readings in the history of science in America, and think it safe to report that Poe on the whole does very well. He makes a few mistakes, especially in "Hans Pfaall," but generally shows himself not merely well-read in then-contemporary science and invention, but also genuinely inventive himself. The contraption his adventurers fly in "The Balloon-Hoax" is, basically, of sound conception: it is much like a modern dirigible. His idea of propelling it with a spring-driven motor is naive, perhaps, but the idea of combining a lighter-than-air vehicle with propeller drive is, as we know, practical; so, moreover, is his notion that one could utilize air currents for long-distance flights. What is important for us in all this is, very briefly, that Poe was very much in touch with scientific developments, both "pure" and "applied," and that his imagination was thoroughly involved.

The device of the hoax, as we noted, enabled him to share that involvement more freely in the later story, but even there he gives us enthusiasm only third-hand. The "story" is a newspaper article; the "reporter" says that he is quoting from entries in a log, and the log is the work of two passengers in the voyage across the Atlantic. (Poe lowered his sights a bit from his moon-shot of 1835, partially because he wanted his hoax to succeed; the transatlantic flight was more credible than a space voyage. Another reason, I think, is that he was [correctly] unsure of a key feature of the earlier tale: he claimed that the atmosphere extended outward, albeit in rarified form, into space; there would be, Hans had argued, enough air so that a manually-operated pump could condense a breathable atmosphere. It is interesting to note that the point was of some philosophical importance to Poe. In the apocalyptic tales he claims that any human act has consequences throughout the universe. He means this spiritually, but also, he insists, physically. So he needed a medium to carry the "influence" of human action, and decided that space is by no means empty.) One of the passengers for the most part describes the events of the voyage; the second tacks on, at the close of each day's entry, a more emotional response. His words, I think, have a ring of sincerity:

> The last nine hours have been unquestionably the most exciting of my life. I can conceive nothing more sublimating than the strange peril and novelty of an adventure such as this. May God grant that we succeed! I ask not success for mere safety to my insignificant person, but for the sake of human knowledge and--for the vastness of the triumph. And yet the feat is only so evidently feasible that the sole wonder is why men have scrupled to attempt it before. One single gale such as now befriends us--let such a tempest whirl forward a balloon for four or five days (these gales often last longer) and the voyager will be easily borne, in that period, from coast to coast. In view of such a gale the broad Atlantic becomes a mere lake. I am more struck, just now, with the supreme silence which reigns in the sea beneath us, notwithstanding its agitation, than with any other phenomenon presenting itself. The waters give up no voice to the heavens. The immense flaming ocean writhes and is tortured uncomplainingly. The mountainous surges suggest the idea of innumerable dumb gigantic fiends struggling in impotent agony. In a night such as this is to me, a man *lives*--lives a whole century of ordinary life--nor would I forgo this rapturous delight for that of a whole century of ordinary existence. (V, 236)

The excitement seems genuine, and, significantly, one cause of the exhilaration is a vision of natural beauty consistent with Poe's taste and aesthetics. Ainsworth, the "author" of this passage, is evidently of a more artistic temperament than Mr. Mason, the other diarist. We are told that he is the author of a well-known book; Poe uses several real people in the tale. In his state of high excitement, and in his exceedingly "novel" situation, he perceives a nature which is wild, sublime, almost grotesque ("...dumb gigantic fiends struggling in impotent agony") and paradoxical in its silence. Poe is going farther than the mere credibility of his hoax demands; one suspects that the enthusiasm is his own. The fact that it is hidden under so many layers of disguise would seem to bear this out.

Though that view of nature is perhaps somewhat unwholesome to a reader with tastes different from Poe's, it seems to this reader somehow reassuringly refreshing. Poe has in his ear, I think, a passage from Scripture:

> The waters lift up their voices, O Lord,
> The mighty waters, breakers of the sea;

Yet above the voices of the waters
Thou, O Lord, art mighty on high.

Poe's waters "give up no voice to the heavens," but the silence itself is awesome. The psalm, of course, says nothing about fiends torturing the ocean; what we have in Poe is a recasting of a powerful Biblical image in the mould of his own imagination. It is worth noting, parenthetically, that if Poe had the psalm consciously in mind, the rest of it is consistent with his world-view in only certain aspects: Poe says, in *Eureka*, that he believes in an original unity, but he also says there and in the apocalyptic tales that the earth shall end--the "germ" of its destruction was contained in the original unity. The psalm, in contrast, opens,

The Lord reigneth; He is robed in majesty;
The Lord is robed; He hath girded Himself
    with strength;
Now is the world established; it shall not
    be moved.
Thy throne is established of old;
Thou art from everlasting.

Though one of these stories has to do with a voyage to the moon, and the other with a flight across the ocean, though one is a hoax and the other a satiric account of a hoax, and though one is far more successful than the other, one may be sure that Poe had the first in mind when he wrote the second. Mr. Ainsworth writes in the log, "Mem.: at 25,000 feet elevation... the sea does not seem convex (as one might suppose) but absolutely and most unequivocally *concave*." Poe appends a footnote, presumably by the "reporter," which reads,

Note--Mr. Ainsworth has not attempted to account for this phenomenon, which, however, is quite susceptible of explanation. A line dropped from an elevation of 25,000 feet, perpendicularly to the surface of the earth (or sea), would form the perpendicular of a right-angled triangle, of which the base would extend from the right angle to the horizon, and the hypothenuse from the horizon to the balloon. But the 25,000 feet of altitude is little or nothing, in comparison with the extent of the prospect. In other words, the base and hypothenuse of the supposed triangle would be so long, when compared with the perpendicular, that the two former may be regarded as nearly parallel. In this manner the horizon of the aeronaut would appear to be *on a level* with the car. But, as the point immediately beneath him seems, and is, at a great distance below him, it seems, of course, also, at a great distance below the horizon. Hence the impression of concavity; and this impression must remain, until the elevation shall bear so great a proportion to the extent of prospect, that the apparent parrallelism of the base and the hypothenuse disappears--when the earth's real convexity must become apparent.[5]

If their general similarity of situation were not enough to establish the connection between the two tales, this passage would be sufficient, for it appeared almost verbatim in "Hans Pfaall." Taken together, the flying stories illustrate very well the complex nature of Poe's relation to the magazine environment. He was immersed in it, yet critical of it; capable of satirizing it, yet indebted to it for his material; cynical of its enthusiasms, yet interested in them himself. Embarrassed by his own response, he strove to mask his involvement, but recognizing the appeal of the subjects, he returned to them again and again.

-2-

An Arresting Subject

M. Magendie, we were told in *Atkinson's Casket*, applied electricity to the senses, and an American literary magazine saw fit to report the fact. Everyone, presumably, was interested in such matters. Poe must have thought so, for he built numerous stories upon comparable tidbits of popular scientific speculation. We have already discussed the critical temptation to conclude that because Poe responded to such popular interests, the fiction which he produced must be hackwork. If the intrusion of the marketplace automatically makes a writer a hack, then it is. But in truth, although the stories which are under discussion in this chapter happen not to be among Poe's most distinguished, they are so much of a piece with his best work, both in technique and philosophy, that it might be more accurate to say that Poe is responding to popular interests not merely in order to sell stories or to increase circulations of magazines, and not merely because he himself shares the popular interests, but also because he felt that the implications of these topics of popular speculation were artistically and philosophically important.

In "A Tale of the Ragged Mountains" Poe is obviously capitalizing upon popular interest in mesmerism and in the nature of the nervous system in general. It should not surprise us too much to find his hero, Mr. Bedloe, telling us that some of the strange changes and sensations which he underwent felt to him like electrical shocks. One can quickly reconstruct the train of thought. On the one hand, mesmerism, or as we now call it, hypnotism, was mystifying, and highly suggestive; one wondered whether some force did not literally flow from the mind of the hypnotist to that of his subject. On the other hand, there was the fact, known for centuries, that electricity could produce responses in the physical systems of man or animals. It is but a brief step from the twitching of the frog's leg to the work of M. Magendie. Electricity was suitably ineffable to seem a possible medium for some manner of telepathic thought control, and given these facts one has practically all of the plot machinery of Poe's story. Practically all, but not quite all, because there are philosophical implications here which deeply interested Poe and which deeply interested the intellectual community of his day. Poe's story includes a hint that some manner of mystical forces are at work in the universe.

We need the plot, first, to set this in perspective. Poe's story is about a man whose illness is being treated by a doctor who is a disciple of Mesmer. The patient, Bedloe, has been mesmerized so frequently that the doctor can induce hypnosis very easily. Bedloe, on one of his customary walks in the mountains, has a vision so compelling that he is certain that he is really experiencing its events, which culminate in his death. The vision ends; he returns to his senses and his home, and tells the narrator and the doctor what has happened. The doctor explains that Bedloe has, in his vision, experienced the final adventures of a close friend of the doctor's, whose last, fatal, exploit the doctor was transcribing at the time that Bedloe, miles away, had his vision.

Shortly thereafter Bedloe dies when, by mistake, a "poisonous sangsue" (a beast Poe invented for the story) is used as a leech in a bleeding operation. The newspaper account of his death misspells his name ("Bedlo"), and the narrator closes the tale musing on the fact that the young man killed in the "original" of the vision, the doctor's friend, was named Oldeb, or Bedlo reversed.

At first reading, the tricky coincidences of the ending of this story strike one as being no more than a simple lapse of artistic judgment on the part of an author who could not resist the temptation to be a little clever. In the light of Poe's philosophical outlook, however, we should face the possibility that Poe wanted us to think seriously that there might be some mysterious connection between Oldeb and Bedlo. The implications of Mesmerism were quasi-mystical, and if the speculation about electricity strikes us as merely scientific, we must remember that in Poe's way of looking at the world, there was no real conflict between a scientific outlook and a mystical outlook. Mysticism, as we shall see in the next chapter, Poe felt to be literally true, and, moreover, founded upon *physical* fact. All substance is ultimately one substance; all time is one time; all things are interconnected and influence one another. To Poe, who like so many of his contemporaries was impressed with the mystical and transcendental implications of early romanicism, electricity must have seemed a logical candidate for the force which literally and physically made such interconnection scientifically possible.

As we have seen in discussing Poe's aesthetic, beauty can be perceived in his work basically by either of two types of person. First, there is the artist, naturally endowed with the ability to experience the insights; second, there is the character who becomes sensitive through some sort of intense emotional or physical strain. Bedloe is clearly one of the latter. He is given to us as the familiar emaciated, high-strung person whose constitution is sufficiently disordered and whose senses are sufficiently heightened to enable him to perceive the "beautiful pattern." Bedloe is "tall," "thin," "stooped," "emaciated," of "bloodless" complexion and indeterminate age, has "wildly uneven" teeth, a melancholy smile, and "abnormally large" eyes, which at "moments of excitement...grew bright to a degree almost inconceivable; seeming to emit luminous rays." (V, 163-164) The indeterminate age is interesting; Poe says the same thing of a character in his story "Mystification." His reason for using it here is, I think, to hint faintly to us that Bedloe is in some manner, if not Oldeb's reincarnation, then at least the bearer of his soul. The narrator clearly dates the story for us (1845). The battle in which Oldeb lost his life took place in 1780. If all of this seems a trifle more than the reader can be expected to digest so early in the story, it is perhaps a sign, as I have suggested, that this is not a thoroughly successful tale, but

Poe's intention to portray Bedloe as another of his perceivers is clear enough:

> The temperament of Bedloe was, in the highest degree, sensitive, excitable, enthusiastic. His imagination was singularly vigorous and creative; and no doubt it derived additional force from the habitual use of morphine, which he swallowed in great quantities, and without which he would have found it impossible to exist. (II, 166)

As a perceiver, Bedloe runs true to form. The descriptive passages which appear just before and during the vision in this story are very much like those in Poe's tales of ideal beauty, "The Landscape Garden" and "The Philosophy of Furniture."

> "In the quivering of a leaf--in the hue of a blade of grass--in the shape of a trefoil--in the humming of a bee--in the gleaming of a dew-drop--in the breathing of the wind--in the faint odors that come from the forest--there came a whole universe of suggestion --a gay and motley train of rhapsodical and immethodical thought." (V, 167)

Compare this to the quotation from "The Poetic Principle" in the first chapter of this book, beginning "...the bright orbs that shine in Heaven," or the quotation from "The Domain of Arnheim" in the same chapter, beginning "There is a gush of entrancing melody." Consider also the character of the beauty presented in Poe's description of the city (Benares) in Bedloe's vision:

> "The streets seemed innumerable, and crossed each other irregularly in all directions, but were rather long winding alleys than streets, and absolutely swarmed with inhabitants. The houses were wildly picturesque. On every hand was a wilderness of balconies, of verandahs, of minarets, of shrines, and fantas-tically carved oriels. Bazaars abounded; and there were displayed rich wares in infinite variety and profusion--silks, muslins, the most dazzling cutlery, the most magnificent jewels and gems. Besides these things, were seen, on all sides, banners and palanquins, litters with stately dames close veiled, elephants gorgeously caparisoned, idols grotesquely hewn, drums, banners, and gongs, spears, silver and gilded maces." (V, 169-170)

Bedloe has a vision which conforms to Poe's explanations of the nature of ideal beauty. He sees it under physical conditions (drugs, high nervous tension, bodily debilitation) similar to those we associate with hallucination, but which in other cultures are associated with mystical perception. And the fact that the vision is the experience of a second man, relayed through the mind of a third, suggests that the beauty is in fact a truth which lies at the heart of the universe. Beauty and truth, the romantics are forever trying to explain to us, are one. Poe dramatizes their unity.

Before we claim that "A Tale of the Ragged Mountains" is simply an enactment of occult philosophy, we should note that it is other things as well. One might argue, for instance, that the occultism is simply a device, one among others present in the tale, to enable Poe to create the beautiful effect. Bedloe's illness would then seem simply another part of the author's scheme to lend some credibility to the proceedings. Certainly the structure of the piece lends support to this reading, for like many other stories, "Ragged Mountains" can be seen as a problem in preparing the reader to accept an abnormal act of perception on the part of a character. It is in this sense a hoax, but I feel that one should go easy on that word in Poe. Many of his stories and both of his novels pretend to be fact, and present some manner of documentation to establish verisimilitude. Sometimes he seriously tried to fool readers; at other times, he was merely using an ancient story-teller's convention. Hawthorne's *The Scarlet Letter* pretends to be fact; the narrator claims to have held the "A" to his own chest. Yet it would be absurd to call the novel just a hoax because of that. It is a hoax only in that it is a fiction. Poe used the convention with unusual frequency, it is true, and may have harbored some hope of fooling somebody every time he used it. He would sometimes pretend to be surprised if someone took his story seriously. But on the whole it makes more sense to treat most of Poe's hoaxing as a literary device designed to encourage the reader into a "willing suspension of disbelief." If the suspension became permanent, well and good; more fun for the author.

Poe works hard at the problem of credibility. Of strange hypnotic phenomena such as the one he is to describe, his narrator says, "It is only now, in the year 1845, when similar miracles are witnessed daily by thousands, that I dare venture to record this apparent impossibility as a matter of serious fact." (V, 165) One might call that, in the pithy *patois* of my undergraduates, a snow-job, were it not for the fact that Poe is quite right; the periodicals of his day were simply filled with accounts of such things. We tend to think of belief in what is now called "extra-sensory perception" as suspect, though it is still being debated today, and one frequently sees accusations that respectable scientists are ignoring the findings of Professor J. B. Rhine at Duke University. In Poe's time, there was rather more confidence among intellectuals in such phenomena, and Poe capitalizes upon it skillfully to maintain credibility. The "scientific" comments are well-organized; he moves from fact (mesmerism or hypnotism) through speculation (E.S.P.) to fantasy (the mystic psychic link between Bedloe and Oldeb).

Similarly, Poe does what he can, through Bedloe's illness and drug addiction on the one hand, and through weather and setting on the other, to give himself a margin of credibility. Bedloe goes out for his walk on a "dim, warm, misty day" in Indian summer, fails to return on time, and, when he belatedly arrives in the evening, relates his experience. Poe beclouds the scene. Bedloe had discovered a new gorge, and says, "'...it is by no means impossible that I was indeed the first adventurer--the very first and sole adventurer who had ever pentrated its recesses.'" He continues,

> "The thick and peculiar mist, or smoke, which distinguishes the Indian summer, and which now hung heavily over all objects, served, no doubt, to deepen the vague impressions which those objects created. So dense was this pleasant fog that I could at no times see more than a dozen yards of the path before me. This path was excessively sinuous, and as the sun could not be seen, I soon lost all idea of the direction in which I journeyed. In the meantime the morphine had its customary effect--that of enduing all the external world with an intensity of interest. (II, 167)

By this point it has become more than a little difficult for the reader to see clearly. Anything that happens will be sufficiently misty to seem uncertain. Poe now introduces a further ambiguity by having Bedloe say,

> "I remembered...strange stories told about these Ragged Hills, and of the uncouth and fierce races of men who tenanted their groves and caverns. A thousand vague fancies oppressed and disconserted me--fancies the more distressing because vague." (II, 168)

Poe was here using a device reminiscent of Irving's in "Rip Van Winkle"; indeed, he may have selected the mountains of Virginia for much the same reason that Irving chose the Catskills: because he thought they offered a setting in which the author could "get away" with more than he could in more prosaic places. This hint of folklore suggests a line of development which might have been of use to Poe had he lived long enough to further extend his art. It also suggests that he, like Hawthorne and other contemporaries, was worried by the problem of creating romance in a matter-of-fact new country.

It is at this point, after scientific reassurances, the hint of "strange stories" and "fierce races," illness and drugs, that Poe feels he has his readers ready for Bedloe's vision. Poe covers his transition with fog--there is mention of the hazy atmosphere even within the vision--and then, as it were, raises his curtain on the new scene. Bedloe says, "'While I listened in an extremity of astonishment which I need not attempt to describe [he hears voices], a strong and brief gust of wind bore off the incumbent fog as if by the wand of an enchanter.'" (V, 169)

Perhaps I am being too kind to Poe in what is admittedly not a very important story, but I think that all of this is very nice. He is doing a very craftsmanlike job and it is pleasant to see him work out his scheme. Part of the pleasurable response may be the result of simple familiarity with the form, for a story such as this one uses so many tried-and-true conventions that it can safely be regarded as an example of formal art. The play of expectation against surprise is an important part of any formal art. Unless one is familiar enough with eighteenth century concert music, for instance, to know what to expect next in a given musical situation, one misses the fun in a Haydn symphony when the composer's whimsey turns the music in an unexpected direction. So firmly established are the themes and modes of commercial fiction forms that authors can play with clichés and stock procedures and expect an audience to know what they are about.

Is it contradictory to say that the *raison d'etre* of a story is its enactment of an aesthetic and philosophical thesis, and that the story is also satisfying because it is pleasurable to see its mechanics work themselves out? I think not. It is our question which is illogical, for it assumes that a work of fiction need be just one thing. Actually, the question does not exhaust the possibilities; the story is the enactment of an aesthetic, a study in expectation and surprise and other things as well. It is, for instance, a science-fiction story. It is also a psychological story, for it is, after all, about a mental state: sickness and morphine have made Bedloe an unreliable witness. The vision which he reports may be the product of his own mind; it may be, as the story claims, the result of a psychic transmission of some sort from the doctor's mind to his; moreover, both his vision and the doctor's manuscript may be reflections of a larger spiritual fact, if we are to believe the elaborate coincidences surrounding his death.

Those coincidences seem to this reader a bit hard to swallow. Oldeb, for example, was killed by an arrow in the temple. The arrow was "'...made to imitate the body of a creeping serpent, and...[was]...long and black, with a poisonous barb.'" (V, 172) The "poisonous sangsue" which kills Bedloe "'... by its writhing or vermicular motions...resemble[s]...a snake.'" (V, 176) It is applied to Bedloe's temple. So elaborate a coincidence probably weakens the story. Poe wants to suggest some sort of psychic tie between the two; the reader tends to wriggle or make vermicular motions in his seat.

It should be noted, however, that this sort of mechanical cleverness in Poe has frequently been praised by his admirers. The pages of some of the critical magazines are dotted with articles pointing out the merits of Poe's machinery, or minor defects in some cog or wheel. Poe doubtless invited this approach with his pose as The Great Logician, but such a caliper approach seems to this reader a petty sort of hobby. Using it, one can discuss Poe at great length without ever evaluating the pieces in which the machinery operates. Poe was concerned with consistency and credibility, but only as means to an artistic end or to show off his pretended erudition.

Philosophically, the coincidences of the ending are consistent; Poe is hinting that there is "something Out There." The more successful he is in the hoaxing aspects of his story--the more likely, that is, that we are to believe all this--the better his chances of making us believe that there are mysterious ties between men, things and times. One can also justify the coincidences in formal terms. "A Tale of the Ragged Mountains" belongs to a recognizable *genre*: we have seen these devices before. For want of a better name, one might call the genre "formal tall tale" ("formal" to distinguish it from the folk-tale genre of "tall tales"). Its conventions are familiar to any reader of fiction because it has been around for ages: credibility is maintained by references and testimony (science, the narrator, the doctor, the newspaper account of Bedloe's death), and/or by removing the action to some isolated locale (the Ragged Mountains) or period, and, at the close, the most important single piece of evidence, usually the person who had the extraordinary experience, is neatly eliminated in an ironic manner. For the piling-on of documentary evidence that what is to follow is true, one thinks of Defoe's "True Relation of the Apparition of Mrs. Veal" and other eighteenth century pieces which deal with the near-incredible. The journalistic background of Defoe's work is relevant for Poe, too, for both authors utilized journalistic techniques to deal with true material which seemed fantastic, and fictitious material which they wished to present as true. Defoe's reasons for using the documentation seem more pressing than Poe's, but the devices are similar. Poe used "real" newspaper material in "Maelzel's Chess Player" and in his detective fiction; he published his fictional "Balloon-Hoax" as a special "Extra" edition of a newspaper. But even when the hoaxing was less marked, when it was merely a literary device used as a crutch to credibility, one feels the force of the genre. We mentioned that Hawthorne often borrowed its procedures, notably in *The Scarlet Letter;* it is also present in Melville, where large chunks of *Moby Dick* reassure us that whales have destroyed ships, that captains have hunted specific whales, and so forth; it is with us today in popular and serious fiction; its devices are sufficiently well known to invite successful parody.[6] Clearly the form has a kind of life of its own. We concede today that popular or standard media can generate procedures which, though cliches in themselves, can be artfully manipulated by a genuinely creative artist. Whatever else "A Tale of the Ragged Mountains" is (and it is a number of other things), it is also an exercise in the manipulation of familiar storytelling devices.

Indeed, Poe is so foxy in his treatment of the other purposes of the story that one wants to come back to simple facts about the plotline to explain the basic nature of this story. How seriously are we to take the mystical implications? In some of Poe's fiction, one feels that the answer is, "Very seriously"; in this story, one is less sure. Does Poe really intend to fool anyone with his documentation? One suspects not; he just wants us to believe enough to suspend disbelief. Is the vision of Benares the real point? Well, it bears all the marks of the beautiful visions in Poe, but seems less central than in many other pieces. The structure itself, despite the flaws of over-elaboration, seems for once the most memorable thing we have. Everything in "A Tale of the Ragged Mountains" we have seen before--mystic and puzzling experience, documentation, devices to retain credibility. Poe's accomplishment is, in his terms, in having found the "combinations within" to produce the desired effect. If Poe produced his story from what Yvor Winters called a "...theory of Beauty...not fully understood"[7] (that is, a theory in which beauty is subject, not manner), then it is at least clear that his practice showed far more understanding of the nature of the "beautiful effect" than did his theory, for this tale has considerable merit, more than would have been the case were the story's structure in fact a mere excuse for presenting the beautiful scene.

-3-

Putrefaction as a Commodity

In the memorable Chapter XVIII of *The House of the Seven Gables*, Nathaniel Hawthorne, whom we consider a rather reserved author, stomps a taunting and savage dance of triumph and vengeance around the lifeless body of a character he hates and has killed.

> And there we see a fly--one of your common houseflies, such as are always buzzing on the windowpane--which has smelt out Governor Pyncheon, and alights, now on his forehead, now on his chin, and now, Heaven help us! is creeping over the bridge of his nose, towards the would be chief-magistrate's wide open eyes! Canst thou not brush the fly away? Art thou too sluggish? Thou man, that hadst so many busy projects yesterday? Art thou too weak, that wast so powerful? Not brush away a fly? [8]

The passage crackles with nervous energy; Hawthorne's treatment of Judge Pyncheon is almost hysterical. Perhaps a fly in the open eye of a corpse is less horrible than some things in Poe's work, but the horror seems more intensely felt. Emily Dickinson claimed that she could weigh and balance pain; I know of no way to measure horror. But I would certainly be somewhat skeptical of its importance in the work of an impecunious author operating in a fiction market in which, as he himself said in "How to Write a Blackwood Article," horrible experiences are worth ten guineas a page. With his commercial magazinist's awareness of public taste Poe might have produced horror while stifling a yawn. Undoubtedly he did not; the horror must be psychologically significant. But we have no way of saying *how* significant. Arthur Hobson Quinn's *Edgar Allan Poe: A Critical Biography* settled that matter for us in 1941 by demonstrating that most of the most unsavory things we thought we knew about Poe were, if not false, at least unprovable: Griswold's smear campaign had been successful in convincing posterity that Poe was a drunkard, a dope addict, a pervert and a scoundrel, but after a century Griswold was unmasked. The trouble was that Quinn could not demonstrate that Poe was *not* abnormal. The best he could do with the available evidence was to demonstrate that we could not prove that Poe *was* abnormal. The stand for us to take in the light of Quinn's work is that which we would take in dealing with the work of any other author: see what's there, and account for it as sensibly as possible.

Horror is there in "The Facts in the Case of M. Valdemar," and we can account for it in at least three ways: in terms of Poe's artistic purpose, in terms of literary influences upon him, and in terms of his biography. That is the proper order (though of course the categories overlap to some extent), and that is the order in which critics would probably have operated over the years had not the myth of Poe's career destroyed their sense of proportion.

Artistic purpose first. We are safe, for a start, if we take Poe at his word when he says that the aim of short fiction is memorable effect. If he is a "magazinist" and a writer of "lighter literature," it seems fair enough to discuss some of his stories in the terms in which one discusses such material. These terms are mechanical; there is no reason to dodge that fact. If we refuse to look at the mechanical side of Poe, we miss a great deal. A commercial writer wants an "arresting" (Poe's word again) subject. Hypnotism was exciting a good deal of popular curiosity. The mesmerists' apparent ability to transcend the usual physical laws raised all manner of speculation, for they did seem to have tapped some hidden source of power which was going to force a re-thinking of nothing less than the constitution of the universe. We have all seen staged demonstrations of the sort which so intrigued Poe's contemporaries. It *is* remarkable that the frail girl under hypnosis, her neck and feet on wooden horses, can support the weight of three grown men on her abdomen; it is remarkable that the warmly-dressed man in the overheated auditorium believes that he is freezing and shivers as he wraps more clothing around him. And, though medical and psychological use of hypnosis has turned out to be surprisingly hazardous and tricky, the subject is still sufficiently appealing so that research in this area is covered far more faithfully in the popular press than research in many other areas of at least equal importance. For our age, all this is fascinating, but, though we do not yet understand it fully, it is also a trifle old-hat. It was new in Poe's time.

It is worth saying also that although we properly think of our own time as a period of revolutionary scientific upheaval, Poe's contemporaries belonged to the first generation to grow up with a number of the basic fields of modern science in their modern form. The new understanding of chemistry, for instance, dates only from about the time of the French Revolution: the execution of Lavoisier in 1794 provides a convenient date, for during the 1790's, the bugs dropped out of Lavoisier's hypothesis. The gas which Priestley had isolated was, despite its discoverer, oxygen, and, though Priestley tried to cling to his faith that it was "dephlogisticated air" even after his exile to America, the scientific community now quickly moved to oxygen and the new chemistry. Modern geology similarly can be given a reasonably clear birthday in the decades just preceding Poe's birth; zoology and botany were producing what looked like their definitive systems of classification (and interesting anticipations of Darwin); modern physics as a field was older, but revolutionary basic research, such as that of Joseph Henry in electricity, went on during Poe's lifetime. One could go on; suffice it to say that it would be difficult to select a period in which more new and exciting prospects for human knowledge opened up than the early nineteenth century. More is happening in our day, but science has become so complex that the layman responds only to an occasional spectacular "applied" manifestation: an atomic bomb or footprints on the moon. Poe's age was near enough to the era of the universal philosopher to give individuals some hope still of understanding numerous areas of investigation. Several of Poe's biographers repeat the undocumentable story of his passing Jefferson on the steps of the library at the University of Virginia; I find the connection symbolically meaningful. Jefferson was one of the last of the old-style scientists; he had pursued investigations of his own, had been in touch with scientists in Europe and America, and had supported scientific ventures as different as Peale's exhuming the mastodon and Lewis and Clark's exploration of the West. More importantly, he had attempted to generalize from a wide variety of fields, to produce a pragmatically unified world-view.[9]

Poe knew Jefferson's writings on science and was educated in his university.[10] Like Jefferson also, he followed investigation in a number of different fields--one could not read the magazines and avoid it--and like Jefferson, he attempted a synthesis. A measure of the difference in the intellectual environments is the contrast in the world views of the *Notes on Virginia* and *Eureka*. But though *Eureka* is a mystic's work, and *Notes* a rationalist's, each is an attempt to see an orderly universe, purposefully created and meaningfully constituted.

As a landmark of the reaction of artist and intellectual to science, *Eureka* stands halfway between *Notes on Virginia* and *The Education of Henry Adams*. The trouble for Adams is that although he, like Poe, looks for a mystic key, by his day, science had shaken the confidence that there was one to be found. Looking for a means of symbolizing both the ineffability and the complexity of forces in the modern word, he turned to electricity, and called the field of his dynamo "occult." That electrical field, the atomic particles which compose the universe of *Eureka* and the telepathic force which keeps us in touch with Valdemar after his death are in our literature for some of the same reasons.

In a sense, then, "The Facts in the Case of M. Valdemar" is a philosophical story, for it postulates the existence of a "force" which unifies this world and the next. But if one read it in isolation, one might not know that, especially if one knew only the side of Poe's critical thought which concentrates on commercial appeal and effect. The narrator, a practitioner of mesmerism, persuades a dying acquaintance, Valdemar, to be the subject of an experiment. He is put under hypnosis on his deathbed, and hypnotic contact is maintained after his death. The narrator and the other observers, seeing that "to awaken M. Valdemar would be merely to insure his instant, or at least his speedy, dissolution," leave him in this preserved state for seven months, and the story closes with a description of what happened when the decision was finally made to awaken him. The description is horrible, and it is not unfair to say, in those mechanical terms we promised to use, that the most obvious purpose of the rest of the story is to provide a setting in which that description can have its maximum effect.

Poe needs credibility and contrast to achieve his effect. He produces both by adopting a cool and deliberately scientific tone. As the title of this story suggests, the narrator speaks as a relater of facts, trying to clear away exaggerated rumors of a much-gossiped-about affair. The story opens,

> Of course I shall not pretend to consider it any matter for wonder, that the extraordinary case of M. Valdemar has excited discussion. It would have been a miracle had it not--especially under the circumstances. Through the desire of all parties concerned, to keep the affair from the public, at least for the present, or until we had farther [sic] opportunities for investigation--through our endeavors to effect this--a garbled or exaggerated account made its way into society, and became the source of many unpleasant misrepresentations, and, very naturally, of a great deal of disbelief.
>
> It is now necessary that I give the facts--as far as I comprehend them myself. (VI, 154)

Poe is not, in short, presenting another high-strung and unstable narrator; rather the tale is to be told in a straightforward and factual manner. Indeed, quite early in the story, the narrator explains that he is writing from notes taken at M. Valdemar's bedside by a medical student; "...it is from his memoranda," the narrator explains, "that what I now have to relate is, for the most part, either condensed or copied *verbatim.*" (VI, 158)

Contrast the tone of this opening to that of the gruesome conclusion:

> "For God's sake! --quick! --quick! --put me to sleep--or, quick! --waken me! -- quick--*I say to you that I am dead!*"
>
> I was thoroughly unnerved, and for an instant remained undecided what to do. At first I made an effort to re-compose the patient; but, failing in this...I...earnestly struggled to awaken him. In this attempt I soon saw that I should be successful--or at least I soon fancied that my success would be complete--and I am sure that all in the room were prepared to see the patient awaken.
>
> For what really occurred, however, it is quite impossible

that any human being could have been prepared.

As I rapidly made the mesmeric passes, amid ejaculations of "dead! dead! " absolutely *bursting* from the tongue and not the lips of the sufferer, his whole frame at once--within the space of a single minute, or less, shrunk--crumbled--absolutely *rotted* away beneath my hands. Upon the bed, before that whole company, there lay a nearly liquid mass of loathsome--of detestable putridity. (VI, 165-166)

We are dealing with a matter of context-within-context. The effect of the horrible culmination is intensified by the reader's trust of the narrator, who seems to be a scientific amateur of a sort familiar to those who have followed the development of the various sciences in the period. As we have just noted, Poe's era marks the real beginning of professionalized science; the professional scientist was created, so to speak, in response to the increased specialization of the sciences. The older tradition to some extent hung on, however, and the transition from the amateur "philosopher" to the professional researcher is nicely marked both by the appearance of increasingly specialized scientific journals and by the increasing professionalism of the style in which articles in them were written. The eighteenth century treatise or paper often tended to be a personal narrative of the experimenter's adventures in quest of truth--"First, I tried this, then, that failing, I reconsidered my premises, and tried that." By the latter part of the next century, modern scientific jargon was alas, well established, though journals such as Silliman's and *Scientific American* showed continued receptivity to pieces written in the older, more personal, manner. [11] Poe's narrator is speaking a language which could have been familiar to one of Jefferson's correspondents. In that relaxed context, both personal (the narrator tells us a few things about himself and M. Valdemar) and scientific (what he tells us is really relevant to the experimental situation), the impact of the horror is greatly intensified. The narrator has been speaking as though he expects to be believed. Though each event is a bit more unusual than the last, he professes to have been as surprised as we are; he did not know what would happen next.

Besides the context of the story, however, there is the larger context of the magazine. The reader is accustomed to reading in these journals both fiction and non-fiction, and the non-fiction often deals with matters scientific. Moreover, the science involved is very often one of those new areas most sensational in their implications. Mesmerism, we must recall, was taken very seriously in the first half of the century. So for that matter was phrenology. When both fell into the hands of quacks, phrenology died a natural death, but mesmerism, purged of quackery and with its name changed, was to emerge in our own day as a respectable area of investigation. At the time, however, science and pseudo-science were less easy to differentiate. The story "The Facts in the Case of M. Valdemar" works hard to establish credibility, in short, but it has "going for it" the larger context of the magazine environment, in which articles (not stories) similar to it in tone frequently appeared.

Works of fiction based upon fascinating scientific material also appeared frequently. I would say that the difference between Poe's use of such material and that of other writers (often not identified) of his day is that Poe was more patient and a better craftsman. He bothered with credibility and carefully constructed his effects--at least sometimes, for I fear that some of the stories which lean on science are among his weakest. But he was in no sense alone; authors as good as Hawthorne (especially in works such as "Rappacini's Daughter" and *The Blithedale Romance*) and as bad as Griswold used similar materials. Thus the literary environment gave him both the scientific and the horrific elements in this tale. Perilous venture to psychoanalyze an author behaving this "coolly" and professionally.

We opened our discussion of "The Facts in the Case of M. Valdemar" by referring, for perspective, to one of our fixed points, Nathaniel Hawthorne. Let's conclude by referring to our other, Herman Melville, who could turn a reader's stomach at least as well as Poe. *White-Jacket* contains perhaps the most terrifying and grisly operating-room scene in the language. A woman and her child starve to death, in great detail, in *Redburn*, a book which also contains a scene in which, after a dead sailor is shipped as drunk by a crimp, a flame is held near the corpse's face to make sure it is dead:

> ...the yellow flame wavered for a moment at the seaman's motionless mouth...to the silent horror of all, two threads of greenish fire, like a forked tongue, darted out between the lips;

and in a moment, the cadaverous face was crawled over by a swarm of worm-like flames.[12]

Judgment of this sort is of necessity subjective, but it seems to this reader that the horror in some passages in Melville's work comes from deeper sources, and punishes the reader more than anything in Poe. Poe's mind may have been haunted, but Melville had seen the horror with his own eyes: people did doubtless starve in Liverpool. Though Poe's terror may have been, as he said, not of Germany but of the soul, most of the figures in his chamber of horrors came demonstrably from books and magazines. His nightmare visions are compelling, to be sure; that is a tribute for his literary skill. And the horror, I would guess, is not simply pasted in. Poe devoted too much space in his work to subjects which the mind throws up on the fringes of consciousness for this all to be simply a commercial reaction; to some extent the horror must have been experienced. But if it is of the soul, it is also of the genre. More often in Poe than in Melville it seems present for effect.

Moreover, Poe is incomparably more genteel than is Melville, and the gentility applies not merely to sex. There is nothing in Poe, not even in "Valdemar," *Pym* or "The Black Cat," to match the operation scene in *White-Jacket*, and no madman in Poe ever perpetrated as macabre a jest as that which the perfectly sane, and even sympathetic, Lieutenant in the same work plays upon the doctor. Characters rot, murder, and shriek in Poe, but they do not pretend to relish the taste of cancer tissue.

"Valdemar" contains physical horror, but its tone is basically cool. It is, after all, an account of a scientific experiment. The characters involved have done nothing wrong (oh, perhaps they have tampered with nature, but Poe does nothing to indicate that he is concerned with that). Horror in Melville is more often simultaneously moral and physical. Take, for example, the following:

> As strange misgrown masses gather in the knotholes of the noblest oaks when prostrate, so from the points which the whale's eyes had once occupied, now protruded blind bulbs, horribly pitiable to see. But pity there was none. For all his old age, and his one arm, and his blind eyes, he must die the death and be murdered, in order to light the gay bridals and other merry-makings of men, and also to illuminate the solemn churches that preach unconditional inoffensiveness by all to all.

Still rolling in his blood, at last he partially disclosed a strangely
discolored bunch or protuberance, the size of a bushel, low down
on the flank.

"A nice spot," cried Flask; "just let me prick him there
once."

"Avast! " cried Starbuck, "there's no need of that! "

But humane Starbuck was too late. At the instant of the
dart an ulcerous jet shot from the cruel wound, and goaded by it
into more than sufferable anguish, the whale now spouting thick
blood, with swift fury darted at the craft, bespattering them and
their glorying crew all over with showers of gore....13

In *Moby Dick*, such passages always serve some specific
structural or symbolic purpose; the one above, for example,
besides containing that splendid aside about religious hypocrisy,
which is, of course, relevant to the book's theological situation,
offers insight into the personalities of Flask and Starbuck. In
Poe, such is not always the case; the corpse which sits up
accusingly in "Thou Art the Man" does so to accuse a murderer,
but the rotting M. Valdemar rots largely for the effect of
rotting. Within the context of Poe's intention, this is perfectly
justifiable; he is writing short stories, not novels, and has every
artistic right to have impact and unity of effect uppermost in
his mind. That the effect was often morbid may be explained
by reference to his personality, or to the fact that Gothic horror
and beauty, to his imagination, were strangely similar. It must
also be accounted for in commercial terms, for Poe knew that
sensationalism would sell stories. But in any case, it should be
remembered that Poe was not unique in his morbidity. His
contemporaries, fourth-rate and first-rate alike, had pricked the
sore place, and the magazinists and novelists of the day, like
Melville's whalers, worked bespattered with showers of gore.

Chapter VII

The Intellectual Environment

...It appears that the sweltering inhabitants of Charleston and New Orleans, of Madras and Bombay and Calcutta, drink at my well.

"The Pond in Winter," *Walden*

Having discussed Poe's conception of beauty and the influence of that conception upon his fiction, it is time now for us to inquire into the philosophical context of his art. American critics find his taste so little to their liking that they are apt to miss the really rather impressive philosophical unity of his work. And the sensationalism of his best-known productions has tended to hide the fact that even moon-shots or scenes of horror have a place in his cosmological scheme. His prose, too, has tended to throw us off; foreign readers, dealing with translations, generally see the unity more readily than we do. But once the cosmology is explained, there remains the question of the sincerity of Poe's commitment to it, and that is not an easy problem.

151

-1-

Concord and Fordham

When modern readers encounter, in the writings of Emerson, Thoreau and others of their intellectual family, passages quoted from oriental sacred writings, they generally have no trouble accounting for them. The assumptions of the eastern religions seem nicely in tune with the Transcendentalists' way of looking at the world. First, there is the belief that nature is spiritually meaningful; second, there is the closely related idea that some men are in immediate contact with the great truths which nature represents. Within the eastern religions, of course, this is understood literally: the holy man becomes a part of "the eternal one-ness." We generally assume, however, that when Emerson, for example, talks this way, he speaks figuratively. His American scholar, his ideal minister, his free and inspired artist, are mankind's translators of the heavenly signals, perhaps, but only because they have suppressed the worldly static, because they are being true to themselves.

Now, Edgar Poe said that he also subscribed to these ideas about inspiration, and it is tempting to set up an easy equation: in terms of world-view, Emerson=Poe. If the equation is true, it in a sense tends to make Poe seem a trifle less abnormal, a little more a man of his time. Emerson was the chief spokesman in America for these views; the views constitute the single most important component of the intellectual and artistic outlook of the early nineteenth century; they were shared by Shelley, Wordsworth, Blake and other romantics--indeed, they are at the very center of the romantic movement--and therefore Poe, since he also subscribed to them, had a great deal in common with his contemporaries both abroad and at home and should be considered much less of an isolated figure.

Well, that is all true, but if we want to be thoroughly accurate, we will have to admit that in setting up our equation we are ignoring variables. Indeed, there may be so many variables that we will finally be unable to obtain results. The first variable I have already hinted at: we generally do not take Emerson seriously when he speaks of the heavenly signals. We assume, because we are western rationalists, that he is using these ideas of direct inspiration metaphorically. They are his way of saying that the real source of truth and art is within us, if we will only be true to ourselves. Or perhaps we are willing to say that aesthetically he means business and believes in "inspiration," but that intellectually he cannot really think that there is something "out there." If we are to take literally his urging so to supress the worldly static that we become one with the Oversoul, then we will have to call him occultist. Some romantics (Blake, for example) are, but however impressive the reports of Emerson's prophetic manner in his lectures, we balk somehow at imagining him in a mystic trance. Certainly our intellectual historians have played down the irrational implications of this aspect of his work, and probably with good reason. Bostonians, even intellectually rebellious young Bostonians who resign from Unitarian pulpits, are not supposed to have mystical visions. It is only fair to note, however, that if we take literally what Emerson says, he is a mystic and an occultist. You and I may not want to take him literally, but occultists always have.[1]

On the other side of our new and more tentative equation goes Edgar Poe, in whose works we see what looks like a literal working-out of the process of inspiration for which Emerson called. We would suspect this were the only evidence available those stories in which a character, for some reason in a state of heightened receptivity, experiences a sort of vision. But, since in many of these stories the "vision" does not really seem to be the main point, the temptation is strong to conclude that what appears to be philosophical consistency is in fact merely the repeated appearance of a writer's favorite formula. Unfortunately, there is disturbingly strong evidence that the visions of the better-known tales are part of a consistent world view. The evidence consists of a number of stories in which the issue of what is "out there" is specifically under discussion. And even this does not finally settle the matter. Poe says clearly enough in these stories that he is an occultist. Does he really mean it, or is it just another example of his using ideas for effect?

Thus on one side of our equation stands Emerson, who says that he is an occultist (while we doubt him and think that he is talking figuratively) and on the other stands Poe who says that he is an occultist (while we think how seldom he is ever committed to anything). To make things more complicated, both men may be said to embody their theory in their work. The secret of the structure of the Emerson essay is that while

Emerson talks about the intuitive leaps which our minds must make to arrive at truth, his prose itself embodies these leaps. Readers hostile to Emerson thus always complain that he says the same thing in every paragraph; despite this they also say that there are no logical connections between the paragraphs. His admirers know that this is just the point: the connections must be intuited, and that act of intuition is always his subject. Poe, as we have seen throughout this study, included intuitive perception in almost every tale.

Finally there is the famous hostility between Poe and Emerson, hostility which most scholars have considered largely one-sided and mostly Poe's fault.

-2-

Poe as a Mystic

In discussing Baudelaire's first rush of enthusiasm for Poe, Patrick F. Quinn writes,

> It is true enough that in one important respect Baudelaire did err in his comments on "Revelation Magnetique." Poe either knew or pretended to know a great many rather obscure and esoteric authors, but Swedenborg does not appear to have been one of them. In this story and in those other dialogues which resemble it, "Monos and Una" and "Eiros and Charmion," Poe was probably relying mostly on his own individual imagination and not on a thorough acquaintance with that tradition of esoteric knowledge in which the name of Swedenborg occupies a capital place. But the error Baudelaire made in assigning Poe to this tradition was all but inevitable: some American Swedenborgians were convinced that what was revealed in "Mesmeric Revelation" was not only congenial with their master's doctrines but was objectively quite true.[2]

What we would like to know, of course, is whether or not Poe believed that they were "objectively quite true." "Mesmeric Revelation" is one of two similar tales (the other is "The Facts in the Case of M. Valdemar") in which Poe plays with the idea of using mesmerism to establish contact with the "spirit world." In each a man about to die is put under hypnosis and asked questions about the nature of the universe and of God. The answers are philosophically consistent with those in other tales by Poe on the same large philosophical issues: "Shadow--A

Parable" (1835), "Silence--A Fable" (1837), "The Conversation of Eiros and Charmion" (1839), "The Colloquy of Monos and Una" (1841), "The Power of Words" (1845). "Shadow" and "Silence" seem less concerned with philosophical issues than with effect, but the others are quite didactic. All of them have in common a kind of elevation of expression akin to that found in religious prose. In "Silence," for example, "the Demon" tells an unnamed listener of the manner in which he drove from a region of unearthly uneasiness one who longed for solitude:

> And the man sat upon the rock, and leaned his head upon his hand, and looked out upon the desolation. He looked down into the low unquiet shrubbery, and up into the tall primeval trees, and up higher at the rustling heaven, and into the crimson moon. And I lay close within shelter of the lilies, and observed the actions of the man. And the man trembled in the solitude;-- but the night waned, and he sat upon the rock. (II, 222)

Succeeding paragraphs move the narrative ahead by only a sentence or two; for the most part they are given over to repeating phrases from the paragraph above. The effect is almost like that of an incantation.

What these stories have to say is approximately as follows: all things physical and spiritual are inextricably related, and the relationship can be understood physically. All human thought and action literally affects the make-up of the universe. If the spoken word disturbs the air around the speaker, the vibrations thus set up will go on in a theoretically measurable way to affect all the atmosphere and by extension the ether and the cosmos. Oinos, in "The Power of Words," "a spirit new-fledged with immortality," listens as Agathos explains all this. At the close of the story he notices that Agathos is weeping as they hover above a beautiful star which, besides being beautiful, contains fierce volcanoes. Agathos explains, "...it is now three centuries since with clasped hands, and with streaming eyes, at the feet of my beloved--I spoke it--with a few passionate sentences--into birth. Its brilliant flowers *are* the dearest of all unfulfilled dreams, and its raging volcanoes *are* the passions of the most turbulent and unhallowed of hearts." (VI, 144) Agathos' italicized *are*'s come in response to the manner in which Oinos phrased his question. He had asked why the flowers looked *like* a fairy dream and why the volcanoes were *like* the "passions of a turbulent heart." Agathos insists they are not *like* what they represent; they *are* it. John Senior in *The Way Down and Out* explains that an occult artist does not understand "symbol" in the modern critical sense. When an occultist makes one thing represent another, he means literally that it is a part of the other and not merely that they are in some way similar. Poe is very explicit and very consistent on this matter: idea, intuition and creative art reflect and affect the real material world. I have heard this characteristic attitude in Poe called "materialism." We can accept that word if we bear in mind that we are defining it to mean, "A belief in the literal interdependence of matter and spirit."

The dramatic situation which provides an "excuse" for these celestial conversations is, in "Eiros and Charmion," "The Power of Words," and "The Colloquy of Monos and Una," the induction of a new spirit into "Aidenn," and these stories taken as a whole represent Poe's spelling-out of the implications of his world view. What we cannot tell is whether he takes what he says seriously or whether he is merely using it to create fantasies. Certainly he is consistent. "Eiros and Charmion," for example, contains a description of the end of the world. The apocalypse is explained, as one would expect, in physical terms: the earth passes through the tail of a comet; the nitrogen in the atmosphere is removed, and in the pure oxygen of the atmosphere which remains, "a combustion irrestible, all devouring, omni-prevalent, immediate" consumes the earth. Eiros, who was there and saw this all happen, explains in detail the reactions of mankind to the comet's approach. The irony which Poe intended has frequently been missed. Scientists, says Eiros, had explained that the comet was harmless. For once in human history, mankind because of fear turned to science for reassurance and understanding: "Reason had at once hurled superstition from her throne." That is to say, scientific knowledge of the extremely rarefied nature of the gases in the tail of the comet had reassured mankind that there was nothing to be feared. But the plot of the story goes on to tell us that science is wrong: the comet is to be feared. Superstition is right. The story may thus be read as a defense of the power of myth--the old superstitions are grounded in fact. If they say that the world is to end in fire, it is to end in fire.

Because these apocalyptic tales seem different in emphasis and tone from the bulk of Poe's fiction, it should not be assumed that their only link with his usual work is the concern with perception. Other things as well remain the same: the appearance of beauty, for example. Ellison would have been at home in a world in which "...blue rivers ran undammed, between hills unhewn, into far forest solitudes, primeval, odorous, and unexplored."[3] Monos speaks of his sensations after death in terms which the narrators of numerous tales would have understood: "The taste and the smell were inextricably confounded, and became one sentiment, abnormal and intense." (IV, 206) Eiros says that his senses "are bewildered...with the keenness of their perception of *the new.*" (IV, 2) The seven who sit over their red wine in "Shadow" sit in a room described as follows:

> And to our chamber there was no entrance save by a lofty door of brass: and the door was fashioned by the artisan Corinnos, and, being of rare workmanship, was fastened from within. Black draperies, likewise, in the gloomy room, shut out from our view the moon, the lurid stars, and the peopleless streets.... There were things around us and about of which I can render no distinct account--things material and spiritual--heaviness in the atmosphere--a sense of suffocation....(II, 148)

The room is lighted by "seven iron lamps" which are probably the same stage properties used in "The Masque of the Red Death." It might be another parlor in the house which contains the chamber described in "The Philosophy of Furniture," or it might be located in a wing of the House of Usher. And the mental condition of the seven is that of Usher, or Bedloe in "A Tale of the Ragged Mountains." It is "...that terrible state of existence which the nervous experience when the senses are keenly living and awake, and meanwhile the powers of thought lie dormant." (II, 148)

Yet another characteristic of these tales present in the bulk of Poe's work is the emphasis on effect. What is being asserted is, to say the least, radical. Yet the tone is thoroughly confident, almost cocksure. Attributing to man all the power which the romantics felt he possessed is, after all, heretical. Melville knew this; the issue is so strong in his work that one is dealing not with heresy but with outright blasphemy. Poe was no fool; he too knew what all this meant. Let us examine the following passage from "The Power of Words."

> *Oinos.--*...Do you mean to say that the Creator is not God?

Agathos.--I mean to say that the Deity does not create.
Oinos.--Explain!
Agathos.--In the beginning only, he created. The seeming crea-
tures which are now, throughout the universe, so perpetually
springing into being, can only be considered as the mediate or
indirect, not as the direct or immediate results of the Divine
creative power.
Oinos.--Among men, my Agathos, this idea would be considered
heretical in the extreme.
Agathos.--Among angels, my Oinos, it is seen to be simply true.
(VI, 140)

It is not our purpose to note the sense in which Poe here
anticipated what would, a few decades later, become a raging
argument among theologians faced with the Darwinian assertion
of continuing creation; Poe's reasoning quite accurately presages
one line of that debate. What Poe calls heresy would be
seriously advanced in an attempt to reconcile new fact and old
doctrine. What we have to consider is the pat, matter-of-fact
tone of voice of that passage. The most obvious way to account
for it is to say that Poe means what Agathos says: "it is...simply
true." But we must at least consider the possibility that Poe is
less concerned with the "truths" he is propounding than with
the readers' reactions. If we are to assume that Poe is merely
using all of this hermetic mumbo jumbo the way that he uses
horror, then we must conclude that he is simply trying to shock
us with the blandness of his assumptions. If so he certainly went
to great length to achieve a little shock.

Eureka opens with a section in which disembodied voices
discuss the ignorant past. That is precisely what the characters
in the colloquies do; indeed, the passage in *Eureka* should
properly be read as another of the colloquies. The book then
goes on to propose its purely occult thesis, which is nothing less
than an assertion of the interconnectedness of all things.

Emerson once wrote, complainingly, "...the intellectual
men do not believe in any essential dependence of the material
world on thought and volition."[4] He and Poe clearly did.

It is a pity that Poe's immaturity stood in the way of any
close contact with the Concord group, for in a limited sense he
and Emerson might have seen eye-to-eye (or eyeball to eyeball).
Perhaps two passages will suffice to suggest how close Poe could
come to the Emerson line, and how far he was from any fruitful
relationship with Emerson. Monos says,

Occasionally the poetic intellect--that intellect which we now feel to have been the most exalted of all--since these truths which to us were of the most enduring importance could only be reached by that *analogy* which speaks in proof-tones to the imagination alone, and to the unaided reason bears no weight--occasionally did this poetic intellect proceed a step farther in the evolving of the vague idea of the philosophic, and find in the mystic parable that tells of the tree of knowledge, and of its forbidden fruit, death-producing, a distinct intimation that knowledge was not meet for man in the infant condition of his soul. And these men, the poets, living and perishing amid the scorn of the "utilitarians"--of rough pedants, who arrogated to themselves a title which could have been properly applied only to the scorned-- these men, the poets, pondered piningly, yet not unwisely, upon the ancient days when our wants were not more simple than our enjoyments were keen--days when *mirth* was a word unknown, so solemnly deep-toned was happiness.... (VI, 202)

The word "analogy" which Poe italicized is the key to the whole attitude, for to the occultist reasoning by analogy is not a logical error; it is the basis of all paths to the truth and the key to the make-up of the universe.

When Poe spoke of Emerson, he spoke bitterly, but the aspect of Emerson's work which he chose to praise is precisely that aspect which he thought matched the assumptions of the passage above. Poe devoted an entry in his "Autography" to Emerson, and I find it revealing:

Mr. Ralph Waldo Emerson belongs to a class of gentlemen with whom we have no patience whatever--the mystics for mysticism's sake. Quintilian mentions a pedant who taught obscurity, and who once said to a pupil, "this is excellent, for I do not understand it myself." How the good man would have chuckled over Mr. E.! His present *role* seems to be out-Carlyling Carlyle.

His love of the obscure does not prevent him, nevertheless, from the composition of occasional poems in which beauty is apparent by *flashes*....

His MS. is bad, sprawling, illegible and irregular--although sufficiently bold. This latter trait may be, and no doubt is, only a portion of his general affectation. (XV, 260)

Poe's nastiness toward Emerson is wretched, of course, but the nastiness does not entirely obscure the fact that he recognizes a kind of kinship in artistry. The business about beauty and flashes, in the second paragraph, for example, suggests that Poe has in mind his own feelings about the nature of beauty and artistry. The first paragraph is initially more difficult to evaluate. One wonders whether the complaint about mysticism for its own sake is a real complaint based upon analysis of Emerson's work, or simply the result of petulance. Petulance seems the more reasonable alternative, but it is worth pointing out that this response on our part is another example of the working of our rationalistic prejudices. We assume that mysticism is phoney, so when Poe calls Emerson a mystic for mysticism's sake, we assume that he's simply calling Emerson a phoney. There is another possibility. For what cause *should* one be a mystic? A mystic would have plenty of answers: the cause of truth, for one, or beauty, or wisdom, salvation, piety, regeneration, transcendent rebirth. It may be, in short, that Poe is genuinely critical of Emerson for being the wrong kind of mystic, being a mystic *poseur*, as it were, too much concerned with fuzzy exoticism, too little concerned with material fact and with the specific cosmological conclusions which Poe felt were "simply true." The passage, then, may represent not the skeptic scolding the mystic, but rather the "orthodox" mystic scolding an heretic.

This interpretation of the passage assumes a number of things: first, that Poe felt at least some commitment to the mystical world view; second, that Poe felt that mystic faith, though founded on intuitive feeling, yields, to use his word, "material" fact; third, that Poe was actively aware of intellectual and religious currents around him. I am not sure that the interpretation is accurate (Poe may just be grousing), but I am sure that each of the three things I have named is true.

The commitment and the "materialism" I believe I have already demonstrated. The awareness is simple enough to illustrate. Consider, for example, another passage from Poe's "Autography." This time, his subject is Orestes Brownson. The passage is remarkably insightful, especially since it comes so early in Brownson's career. Poe said, of Brownson's *Charles Elwood*,

> In logical accuracy, in comprehensiveness of thought, and in the evident frankness and desire for truth in which it is composed, we know of few theological treatises which can be compared with it. Its conclusion, however, bears about it a species of hesitation and inconsequence, which betray the fact that the writer has not altogether succeeded in convincing himself of those important truths which he is so anxious to impress upon his readers. We

must bear in mind, however, that this is the fault of Mr.
Brownson's subject, and not of Mr. Brownson. However well a
man may reason on the great topics of God and immortality, he
will be forced to admit tacitly in the end, that God and
immortality are things to be felt, rather than demonstrated. (XV,
194)

This is a surprising passage in several respects. Contemporary
scholarship agrees with Poe's estimate of Brownson; this is quite
close to the thesis of the well-known book on Brownson by
Arthur Schlesinger, Jr.[5] The last sentences imply an understanding of the Melvillian dilemma, which arises when one
questions the Transcendental assumptions. Moreover, it is
evident that Poe possessed a certain sympathy for his unhappy
subject. (As we will see in Chapter VII, Poe apparently made an
attempt in an unfinished work to create an Ishmael-like
character who would have had something in common with the
Ishmael-like Brownson.) The difficulty for Brownson, as Poe
understood him, was that if "God and immortality are things to
be felt," the individual might not have the feeling. A warm glow
of faith is not sufficient for all persons.

But we should focus our attention on that last sentence for
its proximity to the Emerson who wrote

> ...when we discern truth, we do nothing of ourselves, but allow a
> passage to its beams. If we ask whence this comes, if we seek to
> pry into the soul that causes, all philosophy is at fault. Its
> presence or its absence is all we can affirm.[6]

It is, in Poe's words, something "...to be felt, rather than
demonstrated." And as for Poe's comment that in the best of
Emerson's poems "...beauty is apparent *by flashes*," Emerson
himself would have admitted that inspiration was a sometime
thing. The basis of his "mysticism" was the attitude of
receptivity; one had to wait for a passage of the beams.

Mr. Senior's *The Way Down and Out* contains a check-list
of occult beliefs. I have checked Poe's professed beliefs against
Mr. Senior's list and regret to report that, if we are to believe
Poe, he is in fact an occult author. The question is, once again,
are we finally to believe him?

To review: the evidence is mixed. On one side we have 1)
The philosophical consistency of his work, in which again and
again characters have "visions," or in which spirits tell us about
the occult unity of all things. 2) The response of authors--

Baudelaire, Rimbaud, Valery--who clearly *were* occultists, and who *did* take Poe seriously as one of their number. 3) Poe's behavior late in his life, and his apparent faith in *Eureka* as his masterpiece. Let me mention also, parenthetically and for fun, 4) Aldous Huxley's observation that occult experiences and mystic visions, whether induced by yoga, drugs, mushrooms or saintly behavior, look disturbingly alike. They "look" in fact, disturbingly like what Poe called "beauty." Since Poe's characters see them when in a visionary state, the connection seems clear. With or without item 4), we have enough evidence to claim that Poe's fiction is a dramatization of his philosophical outlook.

All of these items support the argument that Poe was, so to speak, a devout occultist. On the other side, there is some evidence which might make us skeptical of his orthodoxy. Poe's statement that effect is the main goal of literature seems inconsistent with an occult view of art (though Poe also said that the goal is "Beauty" and, as we have seen, understood beauty in terms consistent with occult belief). So does Poe's occasional Christian fundamentalism. His mocking of the Transcendentalists similarly might make us doubt the sincerity of his convictions. The Transcendentalists, who had strong philosophical ties with occult philosophy, who were forever quoting Eastern occult religious writers, and who share a common belief in the reality of "inspiration" should have been, one would think, his natural allies. Then, too, there is his habit of using ideas without committing himself to them. Our suggestion that his criticism of the Transcendentalists, however bitter and silly, is at least partially constructive, an attempt to show them the error of their ways, would tend to weaken this argument.

My own guess is that Poe for most of his career played with these ideas, but that by the end of his life had probably come to believe in them.

-3-

Dupin as Transcendental Hero

While the matter of Poe's real beliefs is perhaps still debatable, the importance for his fiction of the world-view which we have been discussing is fairly easy to define: Poe was a transcendentalist in that he wrote tales about the act of artistic perception, and his understanding of the nature of that act is substantially that to which the Transcendentalists subscribed. The number of different types of stories which are "about" perception is surprising, especially if one has read the more mechanical passages of Poe's criticism. One might, for example, expect the detective tales to be far removed from the pattern of complex-vision and perception because they seem like logic-games. I think we feel this way partially because of certain preconceptions we have regarding detective tales. We know what the modern whodunnit is like; we see similar features in the Dupin stories, and we conclude that the significant thing about Dupin is that he is a precursor of Sherlock Holmes and Perry Mason. Well, that is true enough, but it is not the whole truth.

When Émile Gaboriau became acquainted with Dupin through Baudelaire's translation, he was inspired to write the first novel-length detective story, and the extent to which the mystery-writing craft is indebted to Poe is indicated by Conan Doyle's words, "If every man who receives a cheque for a story which owes its springs to Poe were to pay tithe to a monument for the Master, he would have a pyramid as big as that of Cheops."[7] Moreover, there are devices in Poe's tales which have proved remarkably durable. The outbursts of amazement from Watson and other "righthand men" are lineal descendents of those of Poe's narrator; they constitute "one of the hardiest devices that Poe gave to the form."[8] There are still other elements which can be traced to Poe: the idea of the detective as a "thinking machine" (one famous fictional detective was so called; several deserve the appellation); the frequent use, in the hero's "logic," of the paradox. The Dupin tales have all these elements which by now are traditional, but they have something else, which becomes apparent when one examines the language with which Poe describes Dupin's method.

Poe's detective succeeds not because of a superior mechanical ability to piece together facts, but because he is an artist, and one who has more than a little in common with the artist described by Emerson in "The Poet." Speaking of the Prefect--prototype of all the literal-minded and unimaginative police chiefs and sergeants of our current detective stories--Dupin observes, "...our friend...is somewhat too cunning to be profound. In his wisdom is no *stamen.* It is all head and no body...." (IV, 192) Dupin's complaint is essentially the message of *Eureka,* or of the "Sonnet--to Science." Science, Poe laments, has become too concerned with minute facts; it loses sight of the beauty of the greater scheme of which the facts are only small details. "SCIENCE! true daughter of the Old Time thou art!/Who alterest all things with thy peering eyes./Why preyest thou thus upon the poet's heart,/ Vulture, whose wings are dull realities?" (VII, 22) Emerson preached the same message in almost every paragraph of his work; Poe, similarly, embodied his conception of inspiration in numerous different pieces. Dupin has a great deal in common with Ellison, the creator of the Landscape Garden, and even something in common with the unnamed narrators of the tales of terror. The common element is to be found in the ways in which these very different people perceive the complex patterns which Poe admired. The Prefect of Police or a scientist following the unimaginative *credo* unfavorably described in Poe's sonnet are analogous to the uninspired scholar against whom Emerson warned in *The American Scholar.*

Poe, as we noted in the last chapter, was not intrinsically hostile to science, but he was hostile to mechanical fact-hunting. He was again surprisingly close to the ideas of the Transcendentalism he professed to scorn. "All head and no body" was the usual Transcendental plea for the instincts. Emerson said "books are for the scholar's idle times"; Poe thumbed his nose at facts-for-facts'-sake. As was very plain in "The Poetic Principle," Poe believed in something very like the Oversoul, which, if not specifically divine, was clearly the source of an artist's inspiration. As one moves chronologically through Poe's work, this "something" becomes more clearly divine and Poe comes to look more and more like an occultist. Hence his attempt, in *Eureka,* to write a prose poem which would, through "inspiration," present a large scientific thesis in an artistic way: if the end of knowledge is merger with "the universal oneness," then art and science are the same.

Dupin is different from Perry Mason because he understands this. He does not merely piece together clues; he creates a beautiful pattern. He uses more than logic. In "The Purloined Letter," Poe has him say of the Minister from whom he recovers the letter, "I know him...as both mathematician and poet, and my measures were adapted to his capacity." (VI, 45) He can imaginatively project himself into the complex personality of another, become one with him.

At the opening of "The Murders in the Rue Morgue," Poe's narrator explains the nature of Dupin's genius as an analyst: "...the analyst throws himself into the spirit of his opponent, identifies himself therewith...." (IV, 147) Analysis, then, involves the imagination, and is an artistic process.

> Between ingenuity and the analytic ability there exists a difference far greater, indeed, than that between the fancy and the imagination, but of a character very strictly analogous. It will be found, in fact, that the ingenious are always fanciful, and the *truly* imaginative never otherwise than analytic. (IV, 149-150)

I have elsewhere mentioned the article in which Robert Daniel points out that Dupin can, with justice, be called "Poe's Detective God." We have also seen that several critics have noticed the similarity between Poe's conception of the role of the artist and that of certain of his contemporaries. One can say, without distorting the literary history of the early nineteenth century, that there is a certain common area shared by the critical theories of men as different as Shelley, Emerson, Coleridge and Edgar Poe, or, indeed, any writer who believed that it was the artist's duty to act as humanity's listening post to the music of the spheres. The artist's gift is defined as an ability to attune his mind to the correct frequencies. Shelley's Prometheus and Emerson's Poet have, in this sense, a common mission; they are heroic examples of man perceiving.

There are curious and paradoxical matters involved here. We have been discussing the philosophical consistency of Poe's fiction. Indeed, we have been demonstrating that the fiction is a dramatization of an esoteric philosophy, one in which the artist is understood to be a "seer," in direct communion with some source of supernal inspiration. And yet, in reviewing the various ways in which these stories illustrate perception and inspiration, we have come to something of a formula, a rather mechanical formula, at that: the easier the perception, the less tension. We may want to state it even more strongly: the easier the perception, the less plot. If the perceiving character in the story is naturally gifted with the artistic ability it takes to see the "vision," the story will be almost without plot. "The Domain of

Arnheim" is hardly more than an extended sketch because the garden is the creation of Ellison; the apocalyptic tales are plotless celestial conversations because the voices belonged to enlightened spirits; the detective stories contain practically no action because Dupin, like Ellison, is one of Poe's ideal artists. Plenty happens, of course, in the detective stories, but it is almost always in the past. Dupin and the narrator discuss it as history, and Dupin intuits its key. There is very little action in the present: Dupin places an advertisement and sits at home to await results, or tells us (again, in the past) how he found the Purloined Letter. We might even borrow a page from Poe, who invited readers to send in cryptograms for him to solve, by claiming to be able to "solve" the plot-structure of one of his stories which we have not read if the reader will send in only a description of the manner in which the perceiving character perceives. The trouble is that in the present case the author has read all of Poe's stories already, and the chances are that most of his readers have, too.

It should really not seem too strange to us that stories which embody an esoteric philosophy should lend themselves this readily to mechanical analysis. The apparent paradox is one for which Poe adequately prepared us in his criticism. As we noted in Chapter One, Poe's criticism acknowledges the importance of both inspiration and craftsmanship. A good craftsman has his favorite procedures, and the fact that we as readers have caught on to them in no sense makes him a formula writer. We may want to claim that we have found a "key" to Poe, but there is no point in claiming that we have unmasked him.

Our main point at present is that the detective stories should not be considered as an isolated handful of experiments in a totally different genre. Rather, they fit in perfectly well with the pattern which we have seen operating in so many of Poe's stories. If we were to arrange Poe's fiction along sort of a scale, running from those in which the narrator has a relatively difficult time in perceiving to those in which he has no trouble at all, the Dupin stories would come near the end of our list. At the other end of the scale would go tales such as "Ligeia," "Berenice," "The Fall of the House of Usher," "The Pit and the Pendulum" and "A Descent into the Maelstrom." What they have in common is that to "get through" to whatever "vision" he is to experience, the perceiver in each of them has to go through a process far more arduous than do Ellison or Dupin. The patterns of crime which Dupin perceives will "take" the usual adjectives. They are ornate, complex, bizarre, but Dupin himself does not have to undergo a harrowing experience in order to see them. (He does, on the other hand, need more help than does Ellison. Dupin takes drugs.)

I do not think that it is overstating the case to claim that Dupin can be understood not merely as the prototype for a large number of whodunnit heroes, but also as an example of the transcendental hero, the character whom the author uses to show the transcendental way, or to demonstrate its hazards. The sense in which Henry Thoreau's work represents a testing of the Emersonian advice is sufficiently obvious; indeed, *Walden* may properly be understood as the "utopian novel" of the movement, and its persona, the modest transcendentalist hero. Similarly, Whitman's bardic pose clearly grows from Emersonian instructions. The mighty "I" of his poems is another example of the type, a God-like super-poet tuned to the broad frequencies of humanity *en mass*, the gain turned up to maximum. Much less optimistic are the versions of the character which appear in the fiction of Hawthorne and Melville. From *Mardi* on, for example, Melville's major fiction deals to a great extent with the attempts of "seekers" to obey the commands within, to step to the personal drumming which, according to the Concord gospel, echoed the eternal rhythms. The result is always disaster. Ahab's *Pequod* sinks into the serene Pacific; Pierre blows out his brains in a jail, and Taji seems doomed to an endless quest; Serenia will not satisfy him once "eternity is in his eye."[9] It seems odd, perhaps, ever to group Poe with "bright" authors, but clearly his Dupin has more in common with Whitman's "I" and with the persona of *Walden* than he does with Ahab, Taji, or Pierre. Poe probably would resent our saying that his character was demonstrating the validity of Emersonian assumptions. He could point out, truthfully, that Emerson did not invent them. But that hardly matters, for the Transcendentalists share them with other writers of their age, and their truth seems sufficiently obvious to Poe for him to assert, in Agathos' words, that they are "simply true." Dupin makes use of them, and they work.

Poe's philosophical position would be clear had he left the

world nothing but *Eureka*, the colloquies, and "The Rationale of Verse," but it would be equally clear, if less obvious, had he written nothing but the major tales. I have been using Dupin as an example of his use of the transcendental hero because Dupin appears in several stories, and is well known, but what I have said about the detective stories really applies to most of Poe's best fiction. Taken collectively, his stories form a great drama in which the hero, as in *Walden*, "The Poet," or "Song of Myself," is the artist in the act of perceiving.

Part Four
SOME FAILURES, SOME SUCCESSES

Chapter VIII

Morality as Theme or Technique

I have a crucifix myself,--
I have a crucifix! Methinks 'twere fitting
The deed--the vow--the symbol of the deed--
and the deed's register should tally, father!
          (Draws a cross-handled dagger and
          raises it on high.)
Behold the cross wherewith a vow like mine
Is written in Heaven!

                                        "Politian"

-1-

Poe as American

Attempts to lay old debates to rest generally fail, but I feel obliged to make the effort. Be it known that I consider puerile the related questions, "Is Poe really American?" "Is there a special characteristic which distinguishes American literature from European?" and, "Has the United States produced a respectable amount of great literature?"

Modern western cultures subscribe to the idea that one

scores points in heaven by supporting the fine arts. As early as the eighteenth century one finds Americans telling one another and Europeans that we'll get around to the arts as soon as we're through clearing trees and chasing Indians. Non-western cultures generally do not isolate the fine arts from the rest of experience; the idea that one measures the "quality" of cultures by the quantity of "great" art and philosophy they produce is itself a culture-bound idea. Poe himself was impatient with it; he argued in *Eureka* and elsewhere that the "artist" should properly be understood as at once scientist, poet, priest, and prophet, a situation which prevails in most non-western cultures, and which makes it impossible to "measure" cultures by counting the examples of fine arts which they produce.

Even if one insists on using the culture-bound hypothesis that a "worthy" culture should "support" the fine arts, one still has no way of determining how much support is enough. Is one great author per century enough? How many composers, philosophers and architects do we need? Should we establish ratios of so many artists per ten millions of population? And who decides what "great" means? My own students are most interested in what they call "the validation process." Study what we do to decide that a work is fine art, they say, and you'll learn about the value-system of the culture. That approach makes sense to me; it yields answers I find useful in understanding our culture. The other, the old debate about whether we're holding our own against Greece, Rome or post-Rennaissance Europe, does not.

One of the first American professors[1] to go to Europe after the Second World War decided, very sensibly, not to concern himself over-much with the second of the questions I listed above. Rather than trying to show distinguishing American characteristics of our literature, he contented himself with a demonstration of its range and diversity. Offering a "Ten Books" course, he had his Austrian students read Emerson's *Essays, Leaves of Grass, Walden, Moby Dick, Huckleberry Finn, The Education of Henry Adams, Sister Carrie, The Short Stories of Ernest Hemingway*, E. E. Cummings' *Collected Poems*, and Edmund Wilson's *To the Finland Station*. It will be noted that the list does not purport to represent the "ten greatest books"; rather, it includes ten representative works which he liked personally. Similarly, although on a much larger scale, the

Carnegie Corporation's volume of recommended reading in American works,[2] intended as a guide for readers who would like to familiarize themselves with our letters, places most of its emphasis upon wide range rather than upon any peculiarly "American" qualities.

This suggests a healthy development away from provinciality; it is even the sort of thinking one would like to see used by those concerned with the task of presenting this country's best face to the world. This is not of course meant to imply that there are not meaningful continuities in our literature, but rather that the painful self-consciousness of the Federal period--which is, ultimately, what is behind most attempts to find "one grand American theme"--is no longer appropriate. When one tells a new acquaintance that one's field is American Civilization, the newcomer usually assumes that the field operates from a defensive attitude. One has to explain that the field deals with the culture as it exists, and not with the problem of whether Americans are yet Civilized.

The ferocity with which young section men snap at the hapless undergraduate who inserts the words "position in the development of American Literature" into his final examination suggests that many of the younger generation of teachers have grown impatient with the old questions. They are not interested in debating either side of, "Do we have an American Tradition?" While only too happy to point out similarities of one sort or another in different authors, they refuse--I think correctly--to assume a defensive position, or to treat any "test" proposed to determine a writer's Americanism.

I remember, for example, hearing an older colleague ask, "Can Poe really be said to belong in a course in the history of American Literature?" His answer, for the most part, was, "No." Similarly, F. O. Mathiessen apparently did not consider Poe part of the "American Renaissance."[3] The question itself seems objectionable. Unfortunately, both the question and a negative answer to it have received considerable reinforcement from that quarter which has given us much of the sensitive criticism of Poe we possess. One of the conspicuous aspects of the French reaction to Poe has been the vilification of the American environment from which he sprang. Poe should have been a Frenchman, these writers say in effect, and we have been on the whole all too willing to agree. Quite recently, for example, one of our most thoughtful critics wrote, "Americans...are likely to be amazed and amused by the high admiration in which the French have held him."[4] I might add that I found this to be true of Latin Americans as well; few of my Argentine or Costa Rican students had even heard of Melville, but all respected Poe.

Patrick Quinn's study makes it clear that there is more to the French reaction to Poe than a general exclamation of pity and approval.[5] The French have been more willing than we have to treat Poe in his own philosophical terms (many of their artists share his occultism), and to read him closely; his work stands up best when read from such an angle. But while the French, as Mr. Quinn demonstrates, have been the first to find a convincing manner of treating Poe, they have been guilty of what seem to me enormous misjudgments and also of strengthening the Poe-isn't-really-American argument. The misjudgments may be typified by their insistence that *The Narrative of A. Gordon Pym* is a great book. While it certainly should be included in any systematic analysis of Poe's work, it is no such thing. The critic who sees patterns in an author's work can be misled into a belief that any appearance of the "pattern" is good, and that a work in which it makes numerous appearances is great; I think it not unfair to suggest that the French critics have been the great pattern-seers in the case of Poe. One feels reluctant to consider the other French argument, at least in the terms first stated by Baudelaire. We do not yet fully understand the relationship between an artist and his environment; it is a subtle social and psychological problem. Poe was badly treated in America, but it is terribly difficult to spell out the precise meaning of this for his work.

On the other hand, it may be useful to make at least a brief attempt to measure Poe against certain other American authors simply to see what he has in common with them. Poe is an American author by virtue of the fact that he was an American who was an author. He should be judged by the value of his work, and not by the degree to which he conforms to any pattern, but of course it is important to know where a writer stands. There are certain lines of development in some of our literature; certain concerns have preoccupied many of our writers.

Poe should also be measured against more general movements and tendencies. Like any author, he was influenced by current intellectual trends, and in his case, these are not especially American. If one wishes to set up "tests," therefore, he should in fairness include both those features which have appeared often in American work and those which appeared here and elsewhere for similar reasons.

Let us, then, line up some tests--superficial as well as significant--which have been used to place our authors. Perhaps doing so will suggest the peculiar position of Edgar Poe. But in doing so, let us again make clear that the issue of Americanism is never in doubt. I see no need for a literary H.U.A.C. Poe lived here and wrote here; this is all we have a right to expect.

Consider first the use of American material. This seems to me a rather shallow test, but it was, after all, taken quite seriously during the Federal period and for some time after, and seemed important enough to the late Professor A. H. Quinn to involve him in a serious investigation of Poe's use of American scenes. This is a nebulous business at best. Rip Van Winkle fell asleep in Upstate New York; Irving was obviously using an American scene. But what he wanted from his *locale* might have been as well provided by the Hartz Mountains as by the Catskills. I think approximately the same thing is true for the America of Charles Brockden Brown. In these cases, the genre called for a certain kind of backdrop, and the author looked around him to find something equivalent. Numerous authors of the early nineteenth century complained of the absence of romantic ruins and buried secrets in the United States. Poe seldom had occasion to use matter-of-fact settings; he ranged through time and space to find settings of the right color. For that reason, I am not sure just how one can relate this "test" to him. Sullivan's Island, where the fantastic first battle of Charleston had been fought during the Revolution, is pressed into service in "The Gold-Bug," and Virginia provided the Ragged Mountains. In those cases, one can say that he knew how to find American settings which gave him what he needed. For the most part, however, if his terror is of the soul, his landscape is of the mind. Even the real places, American or European, which appear in his prose are used coloristically. He used popular notions and preconceptions of places and periods to help create mood; London was the mighty city; Germany the home of the wicked university; the South Pole or the Great

Plains places to seek adventure. Foreign-ness was useful to him
for coloristic reasons, but I see nothing systematic implied by
his settings.

On the other hand, one can speak in a general sense of a
certain personal attachment to places in the United States and
even to the concept of the American dream. The early poetic
works offer the clearest evidence, first, of considerable nostalgia
for childhood scenes, and second, of what can only be called
patriotism. In "Politian--A Tragedy," the orphan Lalage has
been seduced and abandoned by Castiglione. Politian, an
English nobleman visiting the castle of her guardian and
Castiglione's father, the Duke Di Broglio, hears her voice and
falls in love with her. But how, Lalage asks, can you bring a
disgraced woman back to England as your bride?

> How in thy father's halls among the maidens
> Pure and reproachless of thy princely line
> Could the dishonoured Lalage abide?
> Thy wife, and with a tainted memory--
> My seared & blighted name, how would it tally
> With the ancestral honours of thy house
> And with thy glory? 6

Lalage's solution is flight to America. Her suggestion is
written in a manner which implies, I think, not merely an
attempt to move an audience, but the author's own conviction:

> ....Knowest thou the land
> Of which all tongues are speaking--a land new found
> Miraculously found by one of Genoa
> A thousand leagues within the golden west
> A fairy land of flowers and fruit and sunshine
> And crystal lakes and over-arching forests
> And mountains around whose towering summits the winds
> Of Heaven untrammelled flow--which air to breathe
> Is Happiness now, and will be Freedom hereafter
> In days that are to come.

The passage suggests that Poe did not share the opinion of
his French critics about the sterility of the American environment. In Lalage's eyes, at least, it seems a promising place.
Politian's response is stronger still.

> O wilt thou, wilt thou
> Fly to that Paradise--my Lalage wilt thou
> Fly thither with me? There Care shall be forgotten
> And Sorrow shall be no more, and Eros be all. 7

America as the land of freedom, happiness, and Eros no less! It would be well to bear these lines in mind when dealing with oversimplified accounts of Poe's relationship with his environment.

Very useful discussions have been built around what is generally called "the search for a form in which to produce a national literature." This is most often applied to American writers of the first half of the nineteenth century, so perhaps as a second "test," we might try to determine what sort of place Poe might occupy in such a quest. It will be seen that this to some extent overlaps the first heading, especially in the sense that it applies best to writers and critics consciously concerned with nationalism, but I think that the reader will agree that it is more meaningful. Certainly to the teacher of a survey course in American literature, for example, the "search for a form" is a welcome basis around which to organize material. We can not here do justice to this topic, but should at least note that what is usually said is that until extremely strong artists came upon the scene, those writers fared best who found an existing and appropriate manner in which to operate. Once again there is a danger that one is dealing with intangibles, and of course there are the usual dangers inherent in any oversimplification, yet in a general sense it is clear enough what is meant. One would certainly be willing to admit that Cooper should be understood partly in terms of the Scott novel, for example, or Brown in terms of the Gothic novel. There seem clear enough examples, and one should see a kind of development by mid-century. Melville and Hawthorne certainly owe less to contemporary styles than do Brown and Cooper, although, of course, this in itself is no measure of greatness.

Granting the validity of such criteria, Poe's place seems clear enough. Excepting Melville first and Hawthorne second, no American author of prose fiction at the time so thoroughly transformed the material at hand. The popular notion that Poe "invented" the short story is simply not true, but his importance as a theorizer of his form, and the continuing prominence of the short story in this country are certainly worth mentioning. There is a real sense in which he provided a rationale for the procedures of a type of popular fiction and made it available to artists. There is no denying the importance of his achievement, which in this sense, though it probably ranks below those of Melville and Hawthorne, is certainly more important that those of Cooper, Brown and Irving. These latter all seem more heartily indebted to existing forms and procedures than does Poe. This perhaps determines where Poe should be placed on such a scale, but, again, however important such discussion is for an understanding of the problems these writers faced, I do not see anything particularly American about the resulting list except the self-consciousness implied.

Therefore, let us use our third "test" the existence of this very self-consciousness, the concern for appearing American. Such concern is characteristic of many men of letters from the time of the Hartford wits to the present. In our period, Brown, Irving, Cooper, Melville, and Hawthorne all expressed concern with it; Poe, on the whole, did not. Even in the Peter Snook review, in which he complains about the quality of our magazinists, his complaint is not that they are not American enough, but that they are not good enough. Poe was self-conscious about his art, but primarily in other ways. I think, for example, that he was afraid that an author of horror stories might not cut much of a figure. He very much wanted to be a celebrity; the evidence which Mr. Fagin[8] has assembled would suggest that. Despite the good service rendered American letters by his sharp critical outbursts, there is not very much evidence that he worried overly about the stature of American literature as such; in sad truth, his own stature was sufficient cause for worry.

More immediately relevant for Poe is another "test," this time what we might call contact with current intellectual trends. Poe is relatively easy to place here, because, as we repeatedly noted, a great deal of recent Poe scholarship has addressed itself to the problem. To do the job right, of course, we need European as well as American literary history. We now see very clearly those assumptions which Poe shared with eminent authors of his age, with Coleridge and Shelley as well as Emerson.

Similarly, Poe can be shown to have been in contact with current "popular" interests. We noted in our discussion of Poe and science his awareness of subjects which had caught the popular fancy, and the manner in which he deliberately attempted to capitalize upon them in his fiction. A popular author has to have such contact with his audience. Once again our categories overlap, for this has relevance to the matter of understanding the preconceptions of one's audience, and once again we are dealing with a trait not peculiarly American, except in the sense that Poe's was an American audience.

Yet another category in which Poe might fit is suggested by a statement of Paul Elmer More: "The unearthly visions of Poe and Hawthorne are in no wise the result of literary whim or unbridled individualism, but are deep-rooted in American history." More asks why Poe and Hawthorne are so far better than English and German Gothicists, and answers with the suggestion that their Gothicism is more firmly embedded in their heritage, the Puritan imagination which saw evil in the woods and devils in the streets. This would constitute a genuinely American tendency, but I find myself suspicious of it. Before one takes More's hint that Poe's work belongs on the same shelf as Wigglesworth's *Day of Doom*, one feels the need to qualify. I have seen no evidence proposed by any of his biographers that Poe was interested in the Puritan imagination or in contact with its heritage. Though he once called himself a Bostonian, he generally called himself a southerner, and presented himself as hostile to New England intellectuals of his own day. I see no signs of loyalty to, or even interest in, those of two centuries earlier. More is right in this sense: we have had, and still do have, a hauntingly long catalogue of writers who deal in darkness. The darkness is not always the heritage of a Puritan past, but force of numbers and quality of the literary product alone are sufficient to make the catalogue seem a tradition, "this age-long contemplation of things unearthly."[9]

A more important legacy of the colonial period, perhaps, was the intellectual side of Puritanism, that set of hard insights which have been handed down through Christian theology, but which were stressed with unusual strength by the New Englanders. Numerous of the most important American authors have been vitally concerned with the moral problems posed by these insights. There is a kind of tradition in our letters of testing what might be called Calvinist realism--or, if you wish, pessimism--against what might be called romantic optimism.[10] As suggested at the opening of this study, Poe's work, unlike that of so many of the authors we consider "central," does not have this continuing moral underpinning. The moral concern is not a "test" of Americanism, of course, since certain other major writers share it even less than Poe. What troubled Hawthorne and Melville still troubled William Faulkner and Robert Penn Warren, but I do not think, despite "Democratic Vistas," that Walt Whitman lost very much sleep over it. Poe's case is complicated by the fact that he seems to have been aware, but not usually very concerned. His discussion of Brownson, mentioned in the last chapter, shows the awareness, and one of the tales to be treated in this chapter is explicitly a moral tale, although it is other things as well. It is fair to say that in most of his stories which raise moral issues, Poe's central concern is focused elsewhere. One thinks again of his statement about the terror of the soul. In view of the religious implications of that word, and his tendency, generally, to pass by such implications, we might do well, for "soul," to read "psyche."

An author belongs to anyone who reads him, and the French can lay some claim to Poe because, in his century, they read him and used him. They repaid the debt nicely; the Symbolists whom Poe inspired in turn influenced our imagists and T. S. Eliot. But the world of art is international. It is now; it was in Poe's day, and influences ultimately can yield only limited information about national identity. We can use them to show that Poe was a "world author," but we can also demonstrate, through innumerable examples of his involvement in American intellectual life, that he is our baby, too. Poe read heavily in everything that was being published in the United States in his day. As a magazinist and reviewer, he had to. He showed his involvement by fighting to improve standards, by fighting the abuses of the publishing game, by fighting out of personal grievances, real or imagined, and by fighting for the notoriety which fighting brought him on the American literary scene. Moreover, he demonstrated his interest in other areas of American life: he was perfectly obnoxious in his defense of slavery and in his pose as cultured southerner; he followed and commented upon popular topics of conversation, new scientific discoveries, and politics; he expressed opinions on the graphic arts and edited a magazine which devoted almost half of its space to the musical life of New York (see Chapter V). That's enough; it is more than enough. One would like to turn off the debate, to restore his epaulets, as it were; to re-insert him in the

"American Renaissance." He's ours; we should relax and learn
to live with him.

-2-

A Purist's Morality

It should be refreshing to turn from the vague, old and
unsatisfactory debate about Poe's Americanness to the yeastier
subject of Poe's technical relationship to other American
authors.

I have already suggested that, despite the contrast in
emphasis, Poe's tales and Hawthorne's repeatedly must solve the
same problems of technique. All four of the tales we are to
discuss in this chapter have in them technical procedures which
Poe shared with Hawthorne, but of only one of them could one,
say, with any justice, "Now Hawthorne could have written
that." This is not because only one of them raises moral issues;
rather, it is because in only one of them does Poe choose to
stress the moral problems. He used moral issues just as he and
Hawthorne used settings; to emphasize a mood, to evoke a
response from the reader, to increase plausibility: in short, as
color.

Poe shares his most frequent technical problem with all
writers whose subject matter is in danger of appearing incredible. Moral themes come and pass as one reads through
Poe's stories, but this issue of credibility is almost always at
hand. Earlier in this study I discussed "A Tale of the Ragged
Mountains," and the methods I used for analysis are almost
identical to those I use to treat "William Wilson." One of the
stories might be called a "moral" study; the other is devoid of
moral interest. But technically, they are very similar. Were "The
Ragged Mountains" more carefully written, they would be even
closer, but the point is that the existence of the two is evidence
of Poe's independence from moral concern.

In the present chapter I have placed discussions of four
quite different stories. In one, "William Wilson," moral concern
looms unusually large for Poe, and yet the use of setting to
reenforce tone and credibility reminds one of Hawthorne more
than does the moral issue. In one, "The Imp of the Perverse,"
we find a situation of which Hawthorne would have made a

different tale. Poe focused upon a single effect, subordinating what to Hawthorne would have seemed most important.

"Mystification" is a satire, and as such shows moral concern; satire implies disapproval. It is interesting also because it shares a number of specific devices with tales of a more serious nature. Those procedures by which Hawthorne and Poe could make their readers accept the incredible are present, but in a sort of shorthand form. Poe makes no attempt to create the sort of never-neverland in which William Wilson and his shadow move so convincingly, but offers instead a few hasty passes designed, apparently, less to bring it into existence than to suggest what it is the author has in mind. "Mystification" is compounded of less subtle stuff than is "William Wilson," and as a result, Poe's devices stand out in much sharper relief.

The discussion of "The Masque of the Red Death" is not an analysis of the tale's structure, but rather an attempt to illustrate the manner in which Poe utilized preconceptions. "William Wilson" is a far better story, but in terms of moral concern, "Red Death" is more characteristic Poe. Moral issues become part of the backdrop. If one wants to compare them to something in Hawthorne, one should go not to his "moral underpinnings," but rather to his stage-design, for when a moral issue creeps into a tale of Poe's, it is usually there as color, not as subject.

I do not think that this is sinful. A seventeenth century New Englander might have thought so, for it might not seem to him that a literature for effect is a literature for the greater glory of God. One might give him an argument on the point: "Look you here, Goodman--: is not a literature which treats the tortured involutions of the frail human soul, which springs from insights into the manifold complexities of what you call God's most wondrous creation, is not such a literature for His greater glory? Whence spring these effects but from a gifted vision of the workings of the minds of men? To know more of these workings is to know more of the mysteries and wonders of those portions of God's great plan which He permits us to comprehend." (But one would not like to have to answer our New Englander's response, for he might ask why Poe was not properly self-effacing.) The Puritan writers have meaning for even the unreligious today because their insight into the ambiguities of human motivation was so keen that the most

devout among them could doubt the purity of their own most
unselfish acts; their resulting humility is appealing in the light of
any matured understanding of the horrors of which humanity is
capable. Poe's appeal is for different reasons. He was not a
moralist, but a meaningful literature can be created without
explicit moral concern, providing it find some way to evoke
those patterned responses which lie within; Poe found a way.

Indeed, the fact that we feel that an artist need not be a
moralist is to a considerable degree Poe's doing. His insistence
that art should serve beauty and nothing else has been regarded
by many artists and many critics as a sort of manifesto, and has
had effect not merely on literature but upon other arts, notably
painting, as well. Yet in truth even this purist's credo--"Art for
art's sake" is its latter-day wording--had for Poe a residual
morality. After all, *why* should the artist devote himself to
beauty? Why is that good? We must remember that for Poe
beauty was not an abstraction. With his professed belief in
supernal inspiration went the corollary belief that the artist, in
producing the beautiful work, is revealing to his audience a side
of eternal truth. Devotion to beauty is thus an act of piety.
Harry M. Campbell (in a letter to the author) put this very well:
"For Poe, aesthetics was a kind of religion."

In general, however, one wants to concede that Poe is not
interested in a fiction of morality in, say, Hawthorne's sense,
but to add the reservation that this does not make him either
less American or less good. There are strong resemblances
between Poe and other Americans on different matters and in
varying degrees. Happily, we have no final means to determine
whether or not a writer is characteristically American. Alexis de
Tocqueville's fear that our arts would have about them a
"sameness" and a prevailing level of mediocrity has been to a
large extent justified in our media of mass entertainment, but
our major artists have tended to produce extremely personal
art.[11] It may be that their individuality is partly the result of a
reaction against a facelessness which they think they see in the
society around them, but however one accounts for it, our art
has been individual. In my students' terms, perhaps what this
means is that we will only consider art "good" if it *is* individual;
we validate it only if it meets the tests which our values imply.

-3-

Salem and Fordham

Haydn and Mozart were contemporaries who created their music out of a common tradition, and with common devices. Their music tends to fall into the same forms and to be written for the same sorts of groups. One can usually tell the music of one from that of the other. There are times, however, when even the sophisticated listener can be badly fooled. One might say that their paths crossed on occasion. The slow movement of Haydn's "Lark" quartet, played to a listener who knows both composers, but not the piece, would almost always be identified as Mozart, and one has no difficulty finding movements by Mozart which have all the calculated unpredictability so characteristic of Haydn. Of course, there was a period during which they were personally quite close, and could influence one another directly, but their lines of development would have intersected, I think, had they never known one another. Poe's path crossed those of several of his contemporaries, and in "William Wilson" he came as close as he ever would to the road to Salem.

Because "William Wilson" takes place in England, and particularly because its early pages are set in an English boarding school, critics tend to identify the young Poe with the young Wilson. Poe unquestionably did draw upon his memories of his schoolboy days in the Reverend Bransby's school in Stoke Newington, and there is a resemblance between the real school and the school of the story. The school is, however, just one of many elements in "William Wilson," elements which Poe designed to serve specific artistic purposes. He was faced with a difficult technical problem. The story, like many of the best Hawthorne tales, contains, side by side, down-to-earth details and rather miraculous occurrences. It is neither fantasy nor factual narration, but rather something somewhere between the two. Veer too near the former, and one's characters become flat and stereotyped; insist on the latter, and the miraculous happenings seem incredible and out of place.

Poe solved this problem admirably. Early in the story he had his narrator describe himself:

I am the descendent of a race whose imaginative and easily

excitable temperament has at all times rendered them remarkable; and, in my earliest infancy, I gave evidence of having fully inherited the family character. As I advanced in years it was more strongly developed; becoming, for many reasons, a serious cause of disquietude to my friends, and of positive injury to myself. I grew self-willed, addicted to the wildest caprices, and a prey to the most ungovernable passions. (III, 300)

The passage is intended to make credible the narrator's further exploits, and, on the other hand, to set the stage for some rather incredible incidents. The character is to be unusual, so that unusual behavior on his part may seem credible. Poe, as we have seen, used such introductions frequently; many of his narrators are intense, introverted, and neurotic. It is interesting that he here used the device to perform a function different from its usual one. Its usual job is to explain the narrator's morbid sensitivity, the sensitivity which enables him to perceive the wild beauties of the tale of terror. Here it is used to lend credibility to the events of a moral play. As in the tale of terror, however, what is seen is a reflection of the narrator's state of mind; "William Wilson" is a psychological, as well as a moral, story.

A second technique which Poe used to solve the problem of maintaining his tone of credible fantasy in "William Wilson" was a very careful manipulation of setting. As the tale progresses, its locale becomes increasingly vague. Specific place names are given, but they are used more and more impressionistically. Poe tells his readers what Dr. Bransby's school looked like in several very effective passages near the start of the story. The illusion of a child's memories is very nicely conveyed. Here, for example, is an excerpt from his description of the little English town in which the school is located:

My earliest recollections of school-life, are connected with a large, rambling, Elizabethan house, in a misty-looking village of England, where were a vast number of gigantic and gnarled trees, and where all the houses were excessively ancient. In truth, it was a dream-like and spirit-soothing place, that venerable old town. At this moment, in fancy, I feel the refreshing chilliness of its deeply-shadowed avenues, inhale the fragrance of its thousand shrubberies, and thrill anew with undefinable delight, at the deep hollow note of the church-bell, breaking, each hour, with sullen and sudden roar, upon the stillness of the dusky atmosphere in which the fretted Gothic steeple lay imbedded and asleep. (III, 301-302)

The almost fairy-tale air of the passage, coupled with the fact that it is a memory softened by the intervening years since the narrator's childhood, prepares the reader for what is to come; in such a dreamlike town, one will not miss a detail or two, and Poe can be as vague as he wishes.

Wilson's description also provides a vehicle for further sketching-in of his character:

> It gives me, perhaps, as much pleasure as I can now in any manner experience, to dwell upon minute recollections of the school and its concerns. Steeped in misery as I am--misery, alas! only too real--I shall be pardoned for seeking relief, however slight and temporary, in the weakness of a few rambling details....
> (III, 301)

Poe is throwing out hints of what Wilson has become, and also accustoming his reader to the fact that the narration is coming filtered through a rather disordered mind. The description of the school (which follows the passage above) is skillfully done, and a good example of Poe's balancing of the vague with the specific. Poe allows suggestive ambiguities to remain:

> ...the [building's] lateral branches were innumerable--inconceivable--and so returning in upon themselves, that our most exact ideas in regard to the whole mansion were not very far different from those with which we pondered upon infinity. During the five years of my residence here, I was never able to ascertain with precision, in what remote locality lay the little sleeping apartment assigned to myself and some eighteen or twenty other scholars. (III, 303)

William, within the microcosmic school--society of Dr. Bransby's, was, in other words, unable to tell his place in the world. Poe makes full use of the tortuous passages of Dr. Bransby's school. In relating the last episode at the school, for example, he has Wilson begin,

> The huge old house, with its countless subdivisions, had several large chambers communicating with each other, where slept the greater number of the students. There were, however, (as must necessarily happen in a building so awkwardly planned,) many little nooks or recesses, the odds and ends of the structure; and these the economic ingenuity of Dr. Bransby had also fitted up as dormitories; although, being the merest closets, they were capable of accommodating but a single individual. One of these small compartments was occupied by Wilson. (III, 311)

The passage functions splendidly; one knows just enough of William Wilson's surroundings to catch the mood of the locale, and William moving on tip-toes through the passageways of the complex old building becomes William searching out hidden compartments in his memory.

After leaving Dr. Bransby's, William enters first Eton, and then, after another encounter with his double, Oxford. In each case, Poe uses a specific school, but in neither does he offer description. He is, in fact, using them for coloring, playing upon the popular conception of British school life to suggest a rake's progress. Except that William is living in considerable luxury--he has a servant for his "own chambers" (III, 313-314)--and that he is leading a life of dissipation, one knows little of his stay at Eton other than what happened during his climactic meeting with his double. The way in which Poe is merely dropping the names of these institutions to add color is even more evident in his use of Oxford. At Oxford, William is able "to vie in profuseness of expenditure with the haughtiest heirs of the wealthiest earldoms in Great Britain," and Oxford is "the most dissolute university of Europe." (III, 316) Other than that the place is generously supplied with haughty heirs and that it is heroically dissolute, Poe says nothing about Oxford. The injustice of his sketch does not diminish its effectiveness; Poe is merely evoking a popular tradition of student life, in which he himself may or may not have believed, for an effect.

These descriptions fit into the accelerating rhythm of the story. After the relatively detailed handling afforded the scenes at the boarding school come the briefer sections set at Eton and Oxford, and then mere passing references to a number of places. Digressions are possible at the story's opening--the narrator, as quoted above, can dwell upon fondly remembered details--but by the last pages, the leisurely pace has been discarded so that the prose itself matches the accelerated scene-shifting. Exclamation points become more frequent, and cities fly by. Place names are again being used for color.

> Scarcely had I set foot in Paris ere I had fresh evidence of the detestable interest taken by this Wilson in my concerns. Years flew, while I experienced no relief. Villain! --at Rome, with how untimely, yet how spectral an officiousness, stepped he in between me and my ambition! At Vienna, too--at Berlin--and at Moscow! Where, in truth, had I not bitter cause to curse him within my heart? (III, 321)

> [Wilson was] my admonisher at Eton--...the destroyer of my

honor at Oxford,--...him who thwarted my ambition at Rome, my
revenge at Paris, my passionate love at Naples, or what he falsely
termed my avarice in Egypt....(III, 322)

It may be that Poe was indulging in wishful thinking when
he wrote those lines. Fagin's portrayal of Poe as an actor
playing a chosen role throughout his life as well as in his works
has considerable validity. Very possibly, in this case, Poe, who
never had enough cash on hand to be much of a rake, was
imagining himself as the dandyish, aristocratic, thoroughly
corrupted Wilson when he dreamed up Wilson's progress
through the schools and through the glamorous capitals of
Europe. We have already discussed the critical habit of taking
Poe's characters as "masks" for the author. If one is going to do
it, why not take Wilson? He fits the role which Fagin describes
rather well, and though Wilson is a rake and a fop, Wilson as a
daydream is curiously innocent, is he not? Is this a dream of evil
glamor? If it is, it is a naive dream.

Artistically, of course, the dream is irrelevant. It does not
matter whether or not Poe to some extent wished himself into
Wilson's shoes. Biographically, it may be significant in two
senses: first, psychologically, in the very personal terms of
wish-fulfillment; second, "publicly," in terms of the role which
Fagin feels Poe played. Considering the particular channel in
which Poe let his imagination run in this case, a psychologist
might be justified in pointing out a repression based upon Poe's
youthful difficulties with finances, his stepfather and education,
and might term Poe's fancy in "William Wilson," "substitute
activity." In the more public sense, one might argue that Poe
often wanted his readers to identify the author with characters
in his fiction to help sustain a public image he had conceived for
himself. Role-playing on the part of authors is not, after all, so
strange a thing. Many of the writers of the "American
Renaissance" pictured themselves playing specific roles: [12]
Whitman, the bard of his people; Emerson, the prophet; and
Henry Thoreau, the radical-saint. Poe may very well belong on
the list. If it comes to building statues in the park, perhaps we
could use the figure of "the black-cloaked wizard" which Fagin
recommends to us, standing it near Emerson in robes, Thoreau
surrounded by birds, and, while we are at it, Crevecoeur at the
plow, Franklin in his coonskin cap, Hemingway looking clean
and pure and true as Papa, and Henry Adams on the cross.

Poe's dropping of place-names is much easier to explain in technical and aesthetic, rather than biographical, terms. The device serves to move the backdrop before which he has set his narrator. The motion of Poe's background, like the motion of those great rolls of scenery in the early motion pictures, can be varied at will, and the result, in the case of "William Wilson," is an illusion of continuous acceleration. Dr. Bransby's, Eton, and Oxford roll by slowly; the cities whizz past. One knows roughly where the action is taking place, yet one's idea of the specific locale is suitably vague. Poe has, in short, succeeded in subordinating his setting to the total effect of his story, and this device is another of those elements which enable him to solve his very special technical problem. One remains suspended between reality and fantasy.

Yet another device made use of in "William Wilson" is one with which readers of Hawthorne are familiar. A good example of it is contained in the passage below. William has just related his last encounter with his double at Dr. Bransby's:

> After a lapse of some months, spent at home in mere idleness, I found myself a student at Eton. The brief interlude had been sufficient to enfeeble my remembrance of the events at Dr. Bransby's, or at least to effect a material change in the nature of the feeling with which I remembered them. The truth--the tragedy--of the drama was no more. I could now find room to doubt the evidence of my senses; and seldom called up the subject at all but with wonder at the extent of human credulity, and a smile at the vivid force of imagination which I hereditarily possessed. (III, 313)

Hawthorne's ambiguous "may have" has tantalized critics; Poe, it will be seen, at his best, was no less a master of the may-have-been. For the second William Wilson to be effective as a symbol of the long ignored conscience of the first, he must be an unreal combination of man and idea. Without Poe's ever saying whether he is real or not, the reader must slightly doubt his existence. What Poe does implicitly suggest is that he symbolizes conscience to the disordered mind of William Wilson. Wilson, as noted above, is one of those imaginative and excitable Poe narrators. During each of the crucial meetings between the two Wilsons, he has reason to be excited and upset. The first such meeting, at Dr. Bransby's, involves a practical joke which "William I" planned to play upon his double; doing so meant slipping out of bed late at night and sneaking through the twisting corridors of the dormitory wing of the school. The boy is thus tense and keyed-up when he enters the apartment. The reader does not quite trust his discovery that the second William bears features identical with those of the first. The ambiguity of the passage above causes it to function in a similar manner; the reader, like Wilson, can "find room to doubt the evidence" of the young man's senses.

The second major encounter, that at Eton, occurs when the narrator is "madly flushed with cards and intoxication." "Wildly excited with wine," late at night, he topples to the door of his chamber to meet the other Wilson, who hurries to him, whispers "William Wilson" in his ear, and leaves before the stunned narrator can fully recover his senses. (III, 314)

At Oxford, similarly, the whispering William II shows up during a card game, late at night and after the wine has flowed. Wilson I is fleecing a young nobleman. Wilson I himself admits that his conscience was bothering him at the time.

> The pitiable condition of my dupe had thrown an air of embarrassed gloom over all; and, for some moments, profound silence was maintained, during which I could not help feeling my cheeks tingle with the many burning glances of scorn or reproach cast upon me by the less abandoned of the party. I will even own that an intolerable weight of anxiety was for a brief instant lifted from my bosom by the sudden and extraordinary interruption which ensued. (III, 318)

He had again been prepared to meet his other self.

By introducing such ambiguity, Poe keeps his fantasy from being quite a fantasy. That the second Wilson should be an exact double of the first, even to details of clothing, seems impossible on a factual level, yet the reader is continually aware that he is dealing with an erratic narrator who may be inventing the details of his ordeal. Were Poe writing allegory of the clearest sort, with each element standing for something, there would be no need for ambiguity. The story will not stand up either as "real" narrative or as fantasy; it is a bit too specific and a bit too vague. In short, the cards are stacked against it on all counts. Yet it is neither dry, as it might have been had Poe been more systematically allegorical, nor unbelievable, nor silly. Poe holds a trump card. By skillfully twisting and manipulating his setting, his character treatment, and his situations, he is able to make his readers accept as valid an entirely unreal world of his own romantic creation, a world of glamorous European cities and dandified students, within which his moral play seems perfectly reasonable. His last paragraphs are brilliant. Consider, for example, the following, which occurs when the narrator, as usual during these encounters, "had indulged more freely than usual in the excesses of the wine table" and when, also as usual, he is in a state of agitation, this time as a result of "the suffocating atmosphere of the crowded rooms" and "The difficulty, too, of forcing [his] way through the mazes of the company" in order to reach "(let me not say for what unworthy motive) the young, the gay, the beautiful wife of the aged and doting Di Broglio." (III, 323) At this moment, the whispering William appears; the narrator challenges him to a duel, leading him to an adjacent apartment. They fight; the narrator savagely wounds him.

> At that instant some person tried the latch of the door. I hastened to prevent an intrusion, and then immediately returned to my dying antagonist. But what human language can adequately portray *that* astonishment, *that* horror which possessed me at the spectacle then presented to view? The brief moment in which I averted my eyes had been sufficient to produce, apparently, a material change in the arrangements at the upper or farther end of the room. A large mirror,--so at first it seemed to me in my confusion--now stood where none had been perceptible before; and, as I stepped up to it in an extremity of terror, mine own image, but with features all pale and dabbled in blood, advanced to meet me with a feeble and tottering gait. (III, 324-325)

Hawthorne would have thoroughly understood what Poe was about when he wrote those lines. Was there another man in the room? Did Goodman Brown really see the figures in the forest? Wilson thinks his double was there; the reader does not care, for he now fully understands Wilson. It was not a mirror, says Wilson, but "my antagonist--it was Wilson who then stood before me in the agonies of dissolution."

Precisely so. Poe has reached the point at which he can speak of either of the two Wilsons without distinguishing between them. The check represented by the second Wilson, all that the narrator has heretofore repressed, is now to be wiped completely from the narrator's personality.

"William Wilson" has been called a study in schizophrenia; actually, if one must use psychological terms, Wilson exhibits symptoms more nearly akin to a more specific form of insanity, paranoia. Schizophrenia is a very big and very loose term, which includes a number of very different forms of maniac behavior. One of these, paranoia, can be characterized by the illusion of a figure persecuting the sufferer. Schizophrenia does not, therefore, necessarily imply "split personality." Poe's second Wilson does appear to frustrate the narrator at moments when he is about to make conquests in love, revenge, or money; Wilson I is sick enough to think he is being persecuted. As long as the second Wilson wins out, the narrator maintains some contact with his world and its necessary rules of conduct.

It is interesting to note that Wilson hates Wilson for one reason other than his repeated frustrating of well-laid schemes. Early in the tale, Poe has him say,

> I had always felt aversion to my uncourtly patronymic, and its very common, if not plebian preanomen. The words were venom in my ears; and when, upon the day of my arrival [at Dr. Bransby's school] a second William Wilson came also to the academy, I felt angry with him for bearing the name, and doubly disgusted with the name because a stranger bore it....(III, 308)

Not only does Wilson II represent the codes of society which William I persists in flaunting, he also represents Wilson I's human ties to that society. When Wilson I kills him, he cuts the cords which bind him to humanity. It is also clear that Poe is once again making use of his audience's preconceptions. Wilson I wishes that his name were courtly; the reader is expected to react. Wilson's guilt, like that of Prospero, becomes associated with aristocratic pride.

Thus it is possible to set up an interpretation of the tale which does not depend upon the special terminology of psychology. The psychological reading is both relevant and useful, but for once there is also present a moral problem which Hawthorne might have limned out. Wilson has committed Hawthorne's unpardonable sin, or at least that portion of it which involves pride and isolation. Like Ethan Brand, he has tried to set himself off from humanity. That Poe reproduced traits of what is recognizable as a form of mental illness is important for any explanation of the very considerable accomplishment which the story represents, but for the present discussion it is significant that he reflected a sort of moral thinking central to Hawthorne, and that, moreover, when faced with the technical problems produced by his subject, he responded with solutions in many ways analogous with those which Hawthorne used.

And this seems pretty important, for it suggests the strength of the influence of the literary environment in which both men worked. Literary history, as we all know, is too often too far removed from the practical matters with which authors deal. Literary criticism carries an opposite hazard: too much immersion in the printed page of text, too little sense of the artist's world. It seems to me that we have here an unusually resilient piece of evidence, of use to both disciplines at once because it is, at once, technique and history.

-4-

The Walter Mittyish Mr. Poe

Let us turn now from what we must consider one of Poe's major accomplishments to a minor story very different from it in tone and intention. "Mystification" is a satire, and not very well known; it is seldom anthologized. By devoting space to its discussion, I do not mean to imply anything about its relative importance. What I intend to suggest is that, since a number of the same devices which appear in "William Wilson" also appear here, we have further evidence for our general contention that, regardless of his literary pose as a mad genius, Poe was something of a literary craftsman with an identifiable kit of tools. There are elements present in "Mystification" which suggest stories as dissimilar as "William Wilson," "Thou Art the Man" and "Diddling."

The stock idea of a totally corrupt university life, for example, is reminiscent of the same idea in "William Wilson." We are informed that during the period of the story nothing academic was accomplished at "G----n" but "...eating and drinking, and making merry. The apartments of the students were converted into so many pot-houses, and there was no pot-house of them all more famous or more frequented than that of the Baron." (IV, 105)

The story, briefly, deals with a superbly aloof prankster, the Baron Von Jung, and the manner in which he makes a total fool of an obnoxious student. The narrator explains that it was the Baron's arrival which brought work at the university to a

halt, that the Baron superficially appeared to be a serious
person, but that he subtly managed to alter the nature of life at
G----n. He picks a fight with the objectionable Johan Hermann
and is challenged to a duel. The narrator is to serve as
Hermann's second; this office enables him to relate the manner
in which the Baron, preying upon Hermann's stupidity, brings
off his mystification by referring him to a passage in a book on
duelling. The passage is utter nonsense; Hermann is too dull to
realize this, and, unwilling to admit that he does not understand
the book, he accepts it as a full and honorable explanation of
Von Jung's action.

The story is not, I suppose, very funny today, perhaps
because it seems rather long-winded for an anecdote (which is
all that it is), or perhaps because its air of aristocratic
superiority strikes us as offensive. At the opening, the narrator
tells us that he was fortunate enough to have known the Baron
before the Baron's student days at "G----n." Poe needs this bit
of exposition in order that we understand that, although the
Baron's appearance and manner suggest a grave and solemn
personality, he is in fact a droll practical joker. The tone of the
opening, though, is a bit stuffy. The narrator speaks rather too
approvingly of the Baron's noble family and of the string of
adventures too racy to relate which led him to the Baron's
"magnificent" chateau. The reader is perfectly happy to see
Johan Hermann and the *code duello* squelched, but would
probably find the story more digestable were the squelcher or
even the narrator made a bit more sympathetic.

The manner in which Baron Von Jung is portrayed is
especially interesting. Poe, as we noticed, had to make him
appear solemn and even dull in order that the deception could
succeed, but there is something a little uncomfortable in his
treatment of the character who should so clearly be the hero of
the piece: "His forehead was lofty and very fair; his nose a
snub; his eyes large, heavy, glassy and meaningless." (IV, 103) I
think that Poe is protesting rather loudly in this case, and even
wonder whether, by making his hero relatively repulsive, he is
not attempting to hide from the reader what the reader might
otherwise assume--that the author of the story is to be
identified with its clever protagonist. We have already noted
that the psychoanalytical critics play the game of "Poe-mask"
only with the abnormal characters in the most famous of Poe's

horror stories. We have also noted that if William Wilson is one of the nidden masks of the author, all that is being hidden is wishful thinking. Perhaps it would be useful to try the same procedure here. In "Mystification" we are not dealing with deep involvement in morbid subject matter, but rather with the possibility of a painful social situation. This is by no means the only way--or the best way--to read the tale, but the reader is by now doubtless aware that, if one must speak of biography, I find a piece of this nature fully as revealing as, say, "Berenice."

But what sort of biographical material could such a reading of this piece produce? I would suggest that it can produce evidence as relevant as that which can be worked up from the horror stories. We know plenty about Poe's personal inadequacy and his blunders in public situations; the poor fellow was obviously capable of hurting himself socially. Take, for example, the celebrated Boston lecture, an extreme case, perhaps, but characteristic. I am not trying to prove any direct connection between that incident and this story. This story was published long before Poe's adventure in the frog pond.[13] Poe was invited to deliver a talk in Boston, and apparently was unable to face the situation maturely. There are stories that he went to one of his third-rate female poet friends to ask her to write a poem for him to deliver. What he finally did read was a juvenile poem of his own. After his return to New York he published some of the most painfully tasteless prose of his career on the subject. He claimed, for example, that he had gone to Boston to make fools of his hosts by reading them nonsense, that they took it to be fine poetry, and received it politely. The entire affair gives evidence of such excruciating embarrassment as to cause us, for all the century and more that has passed since then, to squirm in our seats. It is sufficient to make one consider the opening passages of "The Imp of the Perverse" the most extraordinarily personal document in Poe's fiction. Anyone who has behaved foolishly or ruined a splendid opportunity through perversity can empathize with Poe, but that one capable of understanding and analyzing such a situation could still have rushed into print to make matters worse by rationalizing his way out of it is a stunning document of Poe's social inadequacy. Poe is worthy both of admiration and of pity, but no honest biographer should attempt to conceal the painful fact that he was something of an ass.

Thus there is probably more justification for considering a character such as Von Jung a Poe-mask than for equating Poe with his mad narrators; in the horror stories Poe demonstrated artistic control and detachment, but here he seems to have created a character by an artistic process much nearer to the sort of compulsion which the older psychoanalytical readings of his work would lead us to believe produced his tales of terror. And there is something pathetic in the resulting equation: mysterious Edgar Poe, reading nonsense to Boston; mysterious Baron Ritzner Von Jung referring the stupid Hermann to a book of nonsense. Perhaps "inscrutable" would be a better word than "mysterious," in which case we should follow Poe on an errand for overshoes, to see whether any vehicles on the streets of his time went "pocketa pocketa."

Let me repeat, so that I am not misunderstood, that I do not intend that the idea of the Baron as a mask be applied directly to the incident of the Boston lecture. A tale about a man who makes a fool of people is, however, the sort of thing which might result from the Mittyish daydreams of a man with a socially ineffective personality. And "Mystification" contains a certain amount of internal evidence that what Poe was doing did bear some close relation to his own social feelings. The description of the Baron is made far more unflattering than it need be; there is in addition the fact that, as Edward Davidson points out, in the original version of the tale there was a long description of Hermann. He was made to appear extremely intelligent. Indeed, Davidson says that he resembled Poe.[14] This might indicate the use of a simple ironic interchange--one builds up a dull Hermann and makes fun of the intelligent Baron. Or it might, as Davidson thinks, show Poe laughing at himself. But I think it more probable that what we have here is another version of the sort of reversal noted in "Thou Art the Man," in which the unpromising and rakish young man, who also sounds very much like Poe, turns out sympathetic.

If both the descriptions of the essential characters and Poe's revisions of them suggest that the author was trying to hide something which made him a little uneasy, there are several other elements present in this little story which could be similarly construed. I think that I can come up with an artistic reason for every one of them, but having set down my list, I find it somehow unconvincing. Poe in every case seems to have gone further than he had to go. Why set the story at a European university? Well, that plays upon the preconceptions of his audience, helps build atmosphere and sustain credibility. But we also know Poe's sensitivity to the matter of his own education. Why Germany? Well, the same reasons, but that also serves to dissociate author and story. Why these lines on the Baron's age: "He was then of no particular age,--by which I mean that it was impossible to form a guess respecting his age by any data personally afforded. He might have been fifteen or fifty, and was twenty-one years and seven months"? (IV, 103) Well, when one has read sufficient Poe or Hawthorne, one can sense, in reading that passage, what Poe wanted to do. The vagueness is part of the usual smokescreen, designed to aid credibility. But that statement is too incredible. Saying that it was difficult to tell the Baron's age would have been sufficient; the reader might have been moved to think of people of his own acquaintance whose ages are not readily ascertained, and all this might help make the Baron more mysterious. Instead the reader becomes suspicious. If an author wants a reader enveloped in fog, he must subtly lead him into the mists, continually assuring him that the landmarks he is passing are of the familiar sort. Poe neither leads his reader into a misty valley nor into a Hawthornian dark forest; he pushes him from a cliff.

These matters are not serious enough to destroy the effect of the story. The satire still works. But there are enough, I think, to support the idea of authorial embarrassment. If we play the game of "Poe-mask," we find that Poe will "work" as well as Hermann as he will as the Baron. To borrow Patrick Quinn's idea,[15] this tale could be read as a dialogue between two manifestations of the same personality, another of Poe's *doppelganger* stories.

-5-

The Short Story as a Musical Form

In a very useful (though grievously mistitled) article, [16] Walter Blair makes clear that Poe thought out for himself many of the practical problems of the construction of effective prose fiction. The practicality and immediacy of these matters make them no less difficult of solution, and signs of Poe's craftsmanlike attitude toward his art, whenever they appear, are encouraging. This article can be regarded as a type of antidote to those readings of Poe, such as that of Joseph Wood Krutch, which see his art essentially as the result of compulsion.

Blair points out, for example, Poe's awareness of the advantages to be gained by giving the reader a character in the tale with whom he can identify. "Psychologically speaking," says Blair, "...he saw a work as the stimulus to a response on the part of the reader." (228) But Blair's contribution is best stated, in more general terms; he has gathered from Poe's criticism passages which discuss each of the important technical problems an author faces in the creation of an effective piece. The surprising thing is that one can find so many, and that Poe's opinion seems, generally, so solidly thought out.

Qualifications are necessary; in order to make Poe's position seem consistent, one has to use the "Philosophy of Composition" rather too heavily. One must also take into account Poe's general tendency to rationalize his own limitations. Nevertheless, the problems are discussed, and there is a complete and really fairly consistent working theory to be gleaned from the sources Blair utilizes.

These Blair applies to "The Masque of the Red Death," to emphasize the extent to which Poe followed his own advice. He deals with what might be called the operatic elements in the tale, pointing out the manner in which Poe parallels the change in the "...feelings of the characters" with changes in the physical backdrop, which he feels is so "...arranged as to account for...mounting fears." (237) Matching these is a controlled shift in tone, used either to provide reenforcement or contrast for the action. The tale's language moves through stages designed to heighten effect, and is in succession formal, quaint, and sensational, as the tale moves from its grotesque opening to the serious conclusion.

Such a reading operates entirely in terms of function, and perhaps suggests that other elements might also be accounted for as they contribute to the story's effect. It has been noted that moral problems occasionally work into Poe's stories, but that when they do, they are usually subordinate to other matters. Tales as different as "The Man of the Crowd" and "A Descent into the Maelstrom" have moral possibilities which, had Hawthorne written them, would have taken over the stories.

But Poe usually used moral problems not for their own sake but as another coloristic device.

This involves distorting the tale, but for the moment we may ignore the orientation of "Red Death," lay out the bare facts, and see what are the underlying moral assumptions. The prince and his noble friends, to avoid a plague, wall themselves up in an isolated castle. "...It was folly to grieve," (IV, 251) so they made the best of their isolation and had a party. Assuming that death is punishment for sin, where have they sinned?

Were the tale clearly about fleeing responsibility, the Hawthorne answer would be, "They have sinned in running from the disease," and there would be present elements which would make the reader feel that the fleeing involved cutting oneself off from the frailties of humanity. Such voluntary isolation is usually sinful in Hawthorne. But such elements are not present. Indeed, in common sense terms, one would be a fool not to run from a plague if one had the means, and there were nothing helpful one could do by remaining to help alleviate suffering. After all, making a martyr of oneself can involve the sin of pride; Hawthorne deals more than once with conspicuous martyrdom.

On the other hand, although it is made clear that the nobles can do nothing to combat the plague, one feels that Poe wants his readers to make some moral judgment. This is implied in Poe's sarcastic, "The external world could take care of itself." (IV, 251) The nobles must be committing some sin. The Seven Deadly Sins are lust, wrath, gluttony, covetousness, envy, sloth and pride. Wrath, covetousness, envy and sloth we can rule out as not especially relevant except as they overlap the others. There remain lust, gluttony and pride. Are these relevant?

Consider the masque itself. It is certainly a big party, but so far as lust is concerned, there seems to be nothing very terrible going on. We are informed that it is the largest affair the nobles have had in the months they have been in the castle; there are an orchestra, dancing, wild costumes, but we may wonder, with Marie Bonaparte,[17] where are the naked women? Sexually, this seems a fairly innocent affair.

More seriously, it is clear that lust is not involved, and that we must look elsewhere to account for our dislike of the celebrants. It may be that the "sin" of the noblemen is the result of their being noblemen at all--or at least being what the man on the street thinks noblemen are. What resentment we feel springs from our prejudices against what we suppose to be a proud and selfish aristocracy. The affair is opulent in the extreme; this might be said to represent the sin of gluttony; moreover, the celebrants are proud. One could, then, with a little squeezing, claim that the tale is about at least two of the Deadly Sins, pride and gluttony. But in truth, one never feels that Poe is making any profound observations about them. One feels rather that he is using them in the most general way. Poe wants us to dislike these people, and he succeeds because he understands our attitudes. The nobles are fiddling while Rome burns; worse, they are fiddling in great style.[18]

One actually feels that to speak of the story in terms of these traditional sins is inappropriate. The tale is not really very much concerned with its own moral problems. It uses common notions of morality as it uses the other elements which Mr. Blair enumerates only as a means to a limited artistic end. Stated unsympathetically, it uses them to justify sensationalism. Mechanical as such a statement is, one can best convey the nature of "Red Death" by saying that it is really not about a moral issue at all, but is really "about" the thrill of horror it hopes to produce in the reader.

Thus the body of conventional moral judgment which Poe used is best regarded as a useful shorthand, to be utilized for the creation of effect. It will be seen that there is more than a little in common between the assumption of the attitudes of the audience in "Red Death" (noblemen: big parties: sin) and the similar, equally shallow assumption in "William Wilson" (university life: dissoluteness: sin). Conventional moral prejudices may, as we earlier noted, be present in "The Pit and the Pendulum" (Catholicism); they are certainly being used in all the tales which have an unsympathetic noble as narrator or protagonist (again, nobility).

More important than any single element such as moral concern in "The Mask of the Red Death" is concern with over-all effect. The tale is an unusually pure example of the more operatic side of Poe's talent. Poe, indeed, seems to have large-scale and spectacular musical productions on his mind. He builds in "Buffoons,...improvisatori,...ballet-dancers," and an orchestra, and alludes to Victor Hugo's "Hernani." The careful stage setting, especially the descriptions of the masqueraders and the famous seven rooms in which the mask is being held, illustrate the theatrical side of this concern. Even more striking is the manner in which Poe's prose is organized. The story is heavily repetitious, and the repetition seems organized not merely for poetic, but also for visual effect. Poe moves his point of view about almost choreographically, sweeping us, for example, through all seven of the rooms several times, and repeating their colors lest we miss the effect. The modern reader, I suppose, might visualize what Poe is about most easily in terms of a cinematic effect; one could say that Poe organizes his piece around a series of sustained shots, dollying his camera along the line of the corridor which he describes as running alongside all seven of the chambers. That corridor, indeed, is something of a theatrical give-away, for Poe introduces it solely in order to light his set: in it stand the tripods bearing the braziers of fire. The light passes through stained glass windows into the rooms of the suite.

Now in such a story, thematic elements are going to be as vague as they would be in a ballet. It's the coloring, the movement, the grouping, the rhythm, the grace, the virtuosity, the costuming, in short, to use Poe's phrase, the total effect, which is really important. This is not to say that this is in any sense a major story; like much of Poe, it is difficult to read seriously today. I'm not even claiming that it is typical of Poe. I'm not sure that there is any such thing as "typical" Poe, and certainly a good deal of his fiction carries more thematic weight than does "The Mask of the Red Death." But it is an extremely good example of those qualities in Poe which have made it possible for his art to have seemed at the same time deeply moving to English speaking adolescents and artistically prophetic to *avant-garde* foreign poets. The youngsters get their goose pimples; the poets, their art for art's sake.

Is the recurrent pattern which we have seen in so many of Poe's stories present here? Indeed it is. Of Prince Prospero, the narrator tells us, "There are some who would have thought him mad." The bizarre *fête* is his creation, and its characteristics illustrate clearly enough what we have called the "look" of Poe's beauty. In fact, the tale can be read as a study in the morality of art. Ellison created the garden in the service of beauty. Dupin creates because he can intuit the patterns beneath human history. But Prince Prospero apparently created

the setting of his ball for pleasure alone. One of my students
suggests, very tentatively, that this may be a part of his "sin":
"Perhaps, if his aims are perverted and his outlook impure, this
is the reason why he becomes trapped in his own creation." The
black room, after all, is his own creation; it is where death
appears. In a sense, then, Poe may be trying to tell us that we
create our own death. In "Ligeia," we recall, he says that we die
only through failure of our own will. Hence this reading seems
consistent with his general philosophy: human power is
limitless, but humanity is generally too weak to know to use it,
or too flawed to use it well. The limitation of this reading is, of
course, the emphasis of the tale upon theatricality.

We have already noted, in our discussion of Poe as a
magazinist, the extent to which this particular story leans upon
the conventions of magazine prose. When all is said and done, I
am not sure that this is not the best way to understand it, for
having noted how little there is in the way of thematic emphasis
(the story tells us little more than that we are all mortal, even
Prince Prospero), and that it is concerned with visual effect,
about all that there is left to discuss is the language itself. It's
pretty awful language, perhaps, but one could make something
of a case for the artistic consistency of this tale if one thought
of the language as just one more prop to be artistically arranged.
Despite the visual interest, this is a surprisingly abstract story,
and I think that whatever force it has (even if this force is only
felt by adolescents) is conveyed by abstract means. I mean
"abstract" here in the sense in which one uses the term in
music. When a composer makes use for the second time of a
theme which the listener has already heard, no meaning is being
conveyed. There is no content which one could summarize. And
yet it is clear that something artistically meaningful is happening. We as listeners respond to it, and an aesthetician would
say that we were responding to pure form. (I am assuming, of
course, that the piece of music has no programmatic content.)
This understanding of abstract form in music is quite close to
Poe's understanding of similar matters in poetry (he once called
verse, in "The Rationale of Verse," "...an inferior or less
capable Music....") and it seems clear enough that "The Mask
of the Red Death" is intended as highly poetic prose. An
over-eager writer of program notes approached Walter Piston
some years ago to ask him whether he had any programmatic

comments to make about a new symphony of his which was to be given its world premiere. The writer had in mind comments which he hoped to make about the rocky coast of Maine, the rugged hills of New Hampshire, and so on. But Piston, who is in this sense another of those twentieth century artists who are heirs to the abstract notions about artistic beauty of which Poe is the most famous early nineteenth century spokesman, responded, "My music is not intended to express other than purely musical ideas."

Comparable ideas are the most important things expressed in "The Mask of the Red Death." For certainly this language does not mean very much:

> But when the echoes had fully ceased, a light laughter at once pervaded the assembly; the musicians looked at each other and smiled as if at their own nervousness and folly, and made whispering vows, each to the other, that the next chiming of the clock should produce in them no similar emotions; and then, after the lapse of 60 minutes (which embrace three thousand and six hundred seconds of the Time that flies), there came yet another chiming of the clock, and there was the same disconcert and tremulousness and meditation as before.
>
> . . . .
>
> But these other apartments were densely crowded, and in them beat feverously the heart of life. And the revel went whirlingly on, until at length there commenced a sounding of midnight upon the clock. And then the music ceased, as I have told; and the evolutions of the waltzers were quieted; and there was an uneasy cessation of all things as before. But now there were twelve strokes to be sounded by the bell of a clock; and thus it happened, perhaps that more of thought crept, with more of time, into the meditations of the thoughtful among those who revelled.

Melodramatic, thematically vague, sensational, and "magazine-ish" in the worst sense, "The Mask of the Red Death" succeeds only, if it succeeds at all, in "purely musical terms." I would guess that Poe had been moved by something he had seen at the theatre, perhaps a ballet scene from an opera, and tried to evoke its effect in prose.

-6-

The Moral Effect

The form of Poe's "The Imp of the Perverse" is a rather

special thing; the story seems as much essay as tale. I have never encountered a generic name for this type of story, but think the genre worthy of study, for it is still very much alive. The brilliant Argentine writer, Jorge Luis Borges, for example, who owes a good deal to Poe, has demonstrated that the form is still viable in the twentieth century. And so many students of Poe have noted the pecularily analytical and philosophical cast of his mind that one should not be too surprised to find among his works quite a number of tales which in one way or another incorporate philosophical discussion.

The critical danger lies in assuming that the philosophical discussion is always the point of the tale. "The Imp of the Perverse" opens with a lengthy discussion of the nature of perverseness, but perverseness is not really what the story is about, and the essay-like introduction turns out, on analysis, to be just another of Poe's devices to heighten effect. We have been discussing the importance (or unimportance) of moral issues in Poe's work, and it is interesting to notice that in this story the total effect for once is what I guess we could call a "moral effect." I hope that the reader finds the phrase "moral effect" a bit offensive. The idea of *utilizing* morality is perhaps not a pretty one, but then, we are discussing Edgar Poe, and not Edgar Guest. Poe is strong medicine, and understanding him sometimes involves swallowing a bitter pill.

"The Imp of the Perverse" opens with the narrator's rather incisive discussion of perverseness as a human characteristic. Indeed, the effect is even cooler than that, for the reader is not yet aware that there is a narrator. The opening pages are completely abstract, and the title might be the essayist's whimsical name for the human quality that he is discussing. The reader is thus tricked from the beginning into the wrong kind of commitment. He is, to use good football slang, "faked out." In a general sense, of course, every short story with a trick or surprise ending uses a variation of this procedure. The stories of some authors, notably O. Henry, suffer from a too-frequent dependence upon it. Perhaps a better modern example of an author who uses the device of luring his reader into a more-or-less deep involvement in the tale only to slap his face for being gullible is John O'Hara.[19] Poe certainly did not invent this device, but it does seem to me that he used it more systematically and more consistently than his contemporaries.

We speak rather loosely of Poe's being the "father of the modern short story," but we could get a little more substance into that claim if we kept in mind how many of the devices of the craft, specific devices such as this one, appear in fully-developed form first in his fiction. This accomplishment is impressive when we look at the list of later writers who used one or another of his procedures; we have already taken note of this in our discussion of the detective story as a form. But an equally impressive argument could be built around comparison of him with his contemporaries, the other contributors to the magazines of his day.

This author participated, in the spring of 1965, in a symposium in memory of the distinguished historian of American magazines, Frank Luther Mott. The university library in which he worked in preparing a contribution to the symposium had recently acquired a set of the University Microfilm series on nineteenth century American magazines, and when the research was completed and the paper written, I found myself fascinated by the texture of these old journals. So I spent an additional month and a half in the microfilm room reading unsystematically in this literature. Because the reading was unsystematic, what follows is a subjective judgment, but it seemed to me that although it was easy enough to find in the works of lesser writers examples of many of the elements which go into Poe's fiction, one never found them combined together for artistic effect except in the works of Poe. One found, for example, numerous brief philosophical essays, often, like the one in "The Imp of the Perverse," motivated by a recent scientific development (we must remember that phrenology, around which the introductory essay in "The Imp of the Perverse" is built, was, during its early years, taken seriously as a science), many accounts of real or fictional horrors, such as the one with which "The Imp of the Perverse" concludes, and even examples of attempts, in one way or another, to fool the reader. But in the works of others, these things seem more like raw materials than like finished products. And it seems clear enough from our discussion of so many of Poe's stories that Poe's use of them in combination is perfectly deliberate and conscious. In this matter of luring the reader into an involvement in the story, for example, we might turn for comparison to "The Man of the Crowd," which we shall shortly discuss. One of the things that makes that strange story so compelling is that the narrator's reasonable tone and plausible account of how he came to be where he is and to feel as he does commit the reader to him, thus intensifying the reader's shock, at the close of the tale, when he discovers that the narrator is also somehow implicated in the unnamed crime.

What fools us into trusting the narrator in "The Imp of the Perverse" is that he seems to have a very good point. He argues that systems which seek to account for human motivation seem to read back into the individual those qualities which *should* exist in an ordered universe, rather than working outward, empirically, from those qualities and faculties which the individual undeniably possesses. Thus the phrenologists, as they systematize their "science," assign to the bumps on their subject's heads qualities which it seems reasonable to believe God intended man to have. The scientist works from peripheral logic and morality back into central experience, "...deducing and establishing every thing from the preconceived destiny of man, and upon the ground of the objects of his Creator," (VI, 146) instead of beginning with experience. In her summary of the tale, Marie Bonaparte says,

> ...the protagonist, by means of a poisoned candle, succeeds in killing....For some time he remains undetected, enjoying the fruits of his crime and his feeling of immunity, while convinced that the deed was done, not at the urge of the Imp of the Perverse but coldly, "rationally."[20]

We have already noted the tendency on the part of psycho-analytical critics to base their interpretations upon the plot-line, and not upon the texture, of the stories. Plot-line, however, is not enough. A plot summary of "The Imp of the Perverse" can deal only with the last page or two of the story. This is not intended as a criticism of the Bonaparte book, whose author did not claim to be making critical evaluation, nor is it intended to suggest that psychoanalytical interpretation is irrelevant in this tale. We shall, indeed, return shortly to psychoanalytical matters. Our point is that analyses of the sort which the Bonaparte book typifies ignore basic facts, such as the fact that the reader, for most of this story, is under the impression that he is being spoken to by an educated man discussing a philosophical problem, only to discover, nine paragraphs from the end, that his narrator is going to speak about himself.

> I have said thus much, that in some measure I may answer
> your question--that I may explain to you why I am here--that I
> may assign to you something that shall have at least the faint
> aspect of a cause for my wearing these fetters, and for my
> tenanting this cell of the condemned. Had I not been thus prolix,
> you might either have misunderstood me altogether, or, with the
> rabble, have fancied me mad. As it is, you will easily perceive that
> I am one of the many uncounted victims of the Imp of the
> Perverse. (VI, 150)

Having learned that he is reading not an essay, but a story, the
reader next discovers, in the following paragraph, that the
narrator is a murderer.

If the reader bothers to reread the opening section of "The
Imp of the Perverse," he discovers that much of it is heavily
ironic, but Poe's intention is for him to miss this during the first
reading of the story. It is important, if the tale is to achieve its
effect, that the reader be quite disoriented, even, one might
hope, troubled by the fact that he flattered himself "in
conversation" with an interesting and intelligent mind, and was
perhaps even pleased by his ability to follow the narrator's line
of reasoning or to criticize its weaknesses. Poe organizes his
opening very carefully. The first three paragraphs constitute an
abstract and highly convincing discussion. Our narrator seems
not merely erudite, but rather witty, and so ironies sail past us
undetected.

> With certain minds, under certain conditions, it [Poe's reference
> is vague; he means the tendency to act without reason] becomes
> absolutely irresistible. I am not more certain that I breathe, than
> that the assurance of the wrong or error of any action is often the
> one unconquerable *force* which impels us, and alone impels us to
> its prosecution." (VI, 147)

The irony here is that the reader assumes that "wrong or error"
means what it usually means. If the narrator is as trustworthy as
he seems, The Imp is to be understood as a force which moves
us, against the dictates of conscience, into immoral action. The
narrator, of course, means nothing of the sort. The Imp of
which *he* speaks had nothing to do with the murder; he is
talking about the force which impelled him to the moral act of
confession.

A further irony which escapes us on first reading is the
phrase "an appeal to one's own heart." (VI, 148) The phrase
and the sentences which follow seem designed to make the

argument more convincing by suggesting the sincerity of the narrator. The real purpose is to heighten the reader's shock when he discovers that the narrator has no "heart." Nowhere in his entire confession is there discussion in moral terms of the murder which he has committed, or evidence of any conscious awareness on his part that the deed itself is reprehensible.

After the first three relatively abstract paragraphs, our narrator, in the fourth, begins to particularize, ånd his examples seem almost embarrassingly apt.

Five deals with the "...desire to tantalize a listener by circumlocution" (VI, 148), and paragraph six with procrastination. The touch is still light; we still seem to be reading the work of a witty and philosophical essayist. It is in these passages that the reader's identification with the narrator is most complete. The rather bookish style of the opening has changed somewhat, and the writing has become more anecdotal. Apparently the author plans to apply what he has said about the Imp to the common foibles of men.

But the tone continues to change. The ending of the fifth paragraph seems strangely strong. Poe is discussing procrastination:

> The last hour for action is at hand. We tremble with the violence of the conflict within us,--of the definite with the indefinite--of the substance with the shadow. But, if the contest has proceeded thus far, it is the shadow which prevails,--we struggle in vain. The clock strikes, and is the knell of our welfare. At the same time, it is the chanticleer-note to the ghost that has so long overawed us. It flies--it disappears--we are free. The old energy returns. We will labor *now*. Alas, *it is too late!* (VI, 148-149)

This no longer sounds like speculation; it is too urgent. The following paragraph continues the strain. The experience described is still a common one, but one which springs from much deeper sources: "We stand upon the brink of a precipice. We peer into the abyss--we grow sick and dizzy. Our first impulse is to shrink from danger. Unaccountably we remain." (VI, 149) Poe is still describing something everyone has felt, but in this case he has selected that single experience which seems the best (because most familiar) common example of the workings of a death-wish. The paragraph is a good reminder that, whatever we may feel are the limitations of Freudian readings, the Freudians are not merely "reading things into" the works which they discuss. Marie Bonaparte said that this story is about a "...perverseness which is never other than eroticized aggression...it is always sadism or masochism." Freud himself repeatedly made the comment that he was not the first to have noticed the connections between such things as creativity, sexuality, and the death-wish. He said that these insights had long been available to certain creative artists. His contribution was to codify them, to attempt to make of them a useful science. A passage such as this one should suffice to explain to us what it is that first-rate authors feel they see in Poe, for generally speaking, before Freud, insights of this dark sort were available only to authors of the first magnitude. They are present in Whitman; in "Out of the Cradle Endlessly Rocking," the young boy, by the seashore, discovers, in the death of the she-bird, the "sweet hell within," and his own realization that he is to be a poet, precisely the same connections. They are present again in Dostoevski and in Herman Melville. Anthropologists and students of myth tell us that they are at the center of that which is most basic in religions. If we recall that the French symbolists were most fascinated with these darker aspects of occult religions, we may see clearly yet another reason for their admiration for Edgar Poe.

The passage also contains another clue to Poe's impatience with the Transcendentalists. That he quite agreed with their mystic premises we have already seen, but it may be that one source of his impatience was that he himself had gone so much farther. All of romanticism, of course, was playing with fire, and the game led inevitably to the explicit diabolism of the symbolists. Herman Melville, on whom nothing was ever lost, understood this tendency precisely. We have discussed the manner in which Ahab could be understood as a transcendental hero; he has also, we remember, joined the Parsee, who keeps his tail hidden out of sight, in fire-worship. In *Moby Dick*, Ishmael delivers a warning aimed explicitly at young transcendentalists standing watch high on the mast ("...move your foot or hand an inch; slip your hold at all; and your identity comes back in horror"[21]). Melville, in fact, included a passage in *White-Jacket* in which the narrator did indeed slip, and in which his identity did come back in horror.[22] It seems to me striking that Melville and Poe both chose to embody this particular insight in the almost universal human fear of and fascination with a fatal fall.

The paragraph on falling in "The Imp of the Perverse" is a complete horror story in itself, and brings what began as an abstract essay to an intense conclusion. One paragraph of summary follows, then the narrator steps forth to make his presence known. One has gone two-thirds of the way through the tale before discovering it is a tale. The surrounding city does not materialize until the last page: "I still quickened my pace. I bounded like a madman through the crowded thoroughfares. At length, the populace took the alarm, and pursued me." (VI, 152) Where? What populace? This is no city, any more than there really is such a thing as the perversity the narrator describes. The narrator is mad; this is the landscape of his mind.

A hard critical problem is involved in determining to what extent the diabolism of this tale is part of a conscious philsophical scheme. In occult religious systems, there are generally two paths to truth, salvation, and merger with the world-spirit. One way is liable to involve such things as fasting, prayer, and conquest of the physical body. The other is "the way down," and it involves quite the opposite--often immersion in horror, and complete surrender to human impulses (for a complete guide to these matters, see footnote 1, Chapter Seven). The narrator of this story is morally monstrous, and Poe has given him in addition all of the usual characteristics of his seer-poets. Like many of the others, he says that people have thought him mad, and like the others, he is, in his madness, capable of great brilliance. Indeed, in a curious sense, he is even capable of "God-like" creativity. The implications of his playing God are quite explicitly blasphemous, but whether this is part of an over-all scheme on Poe's part, or merely an element introduced to intensify effect, is difficult to determine. It does seem worth the while to spell it out, though, because also involved is the issue which we have been discussing, the relative importance of moral issues in Poe's fiction.

At the close of his casual account of the murder, the narrator ironically remarks, "...the coroner's verdict was,-- 'Death by the visitation of God.'" (VI, 151) It is clear enough what that means in moral terms, and in terms of the effect Poe hopes to achieve by his story. The reader is supposed to react, "'Visitation of God,' indeed! How can the murderer himself repeat that?" But it may be that there is something more elaborate intended. The narrator thinks that the only irration-

ality, the only perverse act, is his confession. He is incapable of
seeing that the murder itself is an evil thing. About a page after
his statement about the "visitation of God," when he is
describing the moment of confession, he describes in some
frenzy the operation of the "Imp," and concludes, "...I became
blind, and deaf, and giddy; and then some invisible fiend, I
thought, struck me with his broad arm upon the back. The
long-imprisoned secret burst forth from my soul." (VI, 152)
The two passages taken together produce a perfect moral
inversion. The murder, which we see as morally evil, was an act
of God, while the confession, which we see as morally good,
was the work of a fiend.

It seems indisputable that this inversion is intended; it is
too neat to be an accident. It is also clear that this narrator
bears some of the characteristics of the seer-artist and that Poe
deals successfully in his works with psychological connections
which come from deep sources in human history. But whether
these things are consciously connected in the manner which we
have described it is very difficult to say. However it got there,
Poe's accomplishment is impressive. Despite the high-keyed
prose, despite the sensationalism, "The Imp of the Perverse" is a
minor masterpiece.

Even at the risk of anticlimax, it is worth pointing out that
although one seldom finds them all present at once, plenty of
the elements which Poe utilizes in this story are present in
others of his tales. The metaphysical opening of "The Imp of
the Perverse" is comparable in tone and content to Dupin's
lectures (and one remembers Robert Daniel's insight that
Dupin, too, plays God) or to the equally elaborate logic in "The
Gold Bug" and "A Descent into the Maelstrom." We have
already noted that this narrator is comparable to others in Poe;
he seems an horribly inverted version of Ellison. Even the use of
setting for coloristic effects at the close of this story, when Poe
quickly evokes an imaginary city, is similar to the impressionistic sketching in tales such as "William Wilson" or "The Man of
the Crowd." Evidence of this sort, unfortunately, does not
determine for us whether the total scheme is conscious. The
fact that Poe throughout his career used similar devices suggests
very conscious creation, but it might also be used to document
the argument that these things were clichés for him, which he

used more-or-less mechanically. Perhaps, since we cannot finally resolve this intellectual question, we had best conclude with an aesthetic observation, for if one compares "The Imp of the Perverse" to a story such as "'Thou Art the Man,'" in which Poe also utilizes a number of different elements from his other stories, but in which he fails to achieve the unity and intensity of this tale, one has a measure of the size of his accomplishment.

-7-

Poe, Melville and Hawthorne: The Moral Context

We noted at the very opening of the present study that one of the peculiarities of Poe which makes him difficult to handle is the absence of the sort of continuing moral interest which so characterizes the work of his compatriots Melville and Hawthorne. In the present chapter, we have examined those stories in which Poe dealt with material which seems most clearly to offer opportunities for the moralist. It would probably be an oversimplification to insist that Poe seems to have thought of such issues only as another of the devices one might use to create a strong effect, but if we put his work in moral context by comparing it with that of the two writers we have been using all along as reference-points, we have to admit that there is some truth in it. "Hawthorne and Melville," says Lionel Trilling, "...lived at a time when religion was in decline and they were not drawn to support it. But from religion they inherited a body of pieties, a body of issues, if you will, which engaged their hearts and their minds to the very bottom."[23] There is no comparable engagement for Poe. Occasional passages and a few stories suggest that he was at least aware of some of the issues to which Mr. Trilling refers, but generally he was not interested in developing from them material for his tales.

Even in those few of his pieces which do address themselves to moral matters there is a difference between his usage and that of the others. The moral side of "William Wilson," for example, is almost trite in summary: a young man refuses to abide by society's rules, and, in "killing" his "conscience," dooms himself. To explain the tale's impressiveness, one has to deal with other matters: the psychological insight, the extreme skill with which Poe maintains tone. In isolation, the moral issue seems very conventional; it has little in common with the great questions with which Herman Melville would deal. In "The Imp of the Perverse," if we rule out for the moment the possibility that morality is a concern because diabolism may be present as part of an inverted occult philosophical system, and deal instead with more conventional definitions of morality, we have to conclude that the tale's moral statement is similarly elementary. "The Imp of the Perverse" makes exactly the same statement as "The Cask of Amontillado": What a monster! It is as simple as that.

This conventionality is probably the key to most of the moral concern (if one can use so strong a word as "concern") in Poe. In general, he did not question or "test" commonly accepted moral positions; he used them as devices to move his stories along. If one wishes to relate Poe to the central theological and intellectual struggle to which Trilling alludes, it is necessary to take so long a detour that the trip scarcely seems worth the while. If the reader will excuse our dealing in terribly vast generalities, however, perhaps we can quickly point out at least the direction in which one would have to travel.

Trilling says that religion was in decline. In what sense? Surely not in terms of the number of people who believed in God. I have seen no evidence of a widespread increase in atheism, and since there were far more people in America in 1840 than, say, in 1740, Trilling must refer to a qualitative change. It is true that great changes were taking place in the nature of belief; clearly Americans were on the way to the creation of that "common religion" which Will Herberg calls "The American Way of Life."[24] Major protestant bodies were clearly more anthropocentric; Unitarianism had grown rapidly and quickly become respectable. Emerson's immense success as a lecturer and the rise and impact of Oberlin perfectionism are further signs of the change. A doctoral candidate currently writing a thesis under my direction argues convincingly that the wave of revivals accompanying the perfectionist outburst at midcentury carried surprisingly strong mystical components; he feels he can document a tie to Transcendentalism. Certainly the new religions which would appear later in the century show that tie, both in their general optimism and in their assumption that man could achieve direct contact with the deity or a "World-Spirit." Both Spiritualism and Christian Science, for instance, echo Emerson. In Poe's day, neither had been founded, but the intellectual spade-work upon which their foundations would rest was in busy process. Hawthorne used a stronger image: the celestial railroad was rattling down the tracks.

The conflict as it affected Hawthorne and Melville involved an unusually pessimistic version of Christianity, on the one hand, and an unusually optimistic Christianity, tinged with political conceptions, on the other. On one level, Melville may be said to have tested his own discouraging experience with the world and his Dutch Reform heritage against the new optimism in political thinking and religion. One aspect of the testing process may possibly have some relevance for Poe. Melville was suspicious of the Emersonian confidence that, if man could only cut away all that was extraneous and artificial, his own instincts would provide a sufficient guide. Christianity has generally included certain reservations about the goodness of impulses; the Christianity of the Puritans placed unusually heavy emphasis upon the necessity to control them, and the church training of Melville's youth had a good deal in common with the characteristic Puritan outlook. One can think of Ahab as a soured Emersonian, who insists on his right to strike through on his own to whatever lies beyond. This is Byronic; Ahab wants his freedom. Pierre even more clearly follows his impulses; he tries to be a good Emersonian, but the drumming he hears is not the cadence of the world around him. In Melville the result of such an insistence upon personal right is always tragic, even though no answers are ever offered.

Now Poe deals frequently with impulses, with characters who follow the heart. The sort of religious background which contributed to Melville's manner of looking at the world had, rooted in its traditions, a psychology as well as a theology. Poe was usually quite unconcerned with theology,[25] but the psychological insights he possessed have a good deal in common with those of Melville. The narrators of "The Black Cat," "The Tell-Tale Heart" or "The Imp of the Perverse" are, like Ahab, willing to be guided by their impulses; like Ahab, too, they are monomaniacs, acting out an aspect of the contemporary understanding of mental faculties. Indeed, interest in psychology and its implications is so widespread in the early nineteenth century that no literary figure could have escaped contact with it. Having noticed how frequently it crops up in the magazines,

I recently sent a student to a nearby legal library to find out
how closely legal definitions of insanity match the assumptions
of those of Poe's stories which deal with acts of the "perverse"
will. The project is not yet completed, but it is already clear
that such a contemporary work as Isaac Ray's *A Treatise on the
Medical Jurisprudence of Insanity* (1838)[26] presents an analysis
of mental illness so consistent with Poe's that Ray could well
have used Poe's tales to illustrate his points. Ray, moreover,
claims only to be summarizing and synthesizing standard work
in the field.

Despite Emerson, in other words, science seemed to be
suggesting that "impulses" are not necessarily good. The
"heightening" of a "faculty" of the mind, to use contemporary
terminology, was understood to be a characteristic of mental
disorder. "Heightening" might produce the brilliance of the
artist, but it might also produce monomania or criminality. Evil
in the very "faculties" struck Melville as intolerable; he wanted
to know "Why?" Poe was not interested in placing the blame.
His tales begin on the third day of the Chase, with Ahab as
narrator. The emphasis is not on the reasons for the vengeance,
but on the act itself.

Ahab is a madman, as is Montresor. But Pierre is a "hero"
in the simplest sense of the word; he is a "good guy." He has
not even the detachment of Ishmael, who misses none of the
blasphemous possibilities. Were *Pierre* a successful book, one of
the reasons for its success would be the fact that the reader
would have in Pierre a sympathetic character with whom to
empathize. The book is about the inability of a likable and
intelligent idealistic youth to cope with the world. In terms of
reader response, it is supposed to produce nightmares. Virtue,
ability, and good intentions are not enough. There is nothing in
which one can place confidence.

"The Imp of the Perverse" has most in common with this
aspect of Melville's intention. The reader trusts this narrator as
he would have trusted Pierre (were Pierre only convincingly
presented). He discovers that his trust is not warranted. But
while in *Pierre* the blame for the situation is eventually reflected
back upon the Deity (if, as Pierre comes to wonder, there is
one), in "The Imp" the hint that the murder is an act of God is
intended ironically. There is no real discussion of responsibility;
its absence, indeed is the point, for it tells us that the narrator is

insane. Though, as we noted, an unconventional world-view may be operating in the story, Poe's moral position is conventional. It may not be even sincere. The lurid scandal magazines of our own day play up sensational horror ("Boy, 9, Rapes Four") and profess a moral attitude ("How shocking!"), but we understand that the horror and not the morality is what the editors have in mind. It sells magazines. Marie Bonaparte's conclusions that we are dealing with "eroticized aggression... sadism or masochism," with "...our instinctual urges towards criminal activities..." suggest that Poe, too, is interested in the titillation. So does what we know about the commercial side of Poe, his famous claim that he knew the stuff which would build magazine circulation.

But since we can't prove this, it is probably preferable to say merely that Poe seems less interested in the moral issues and leave it at that. The narrators of "The Imp" and "The Cask" are horrible; that's clear enough. But other Poe characters in the same philosophical situation (creators, that is, of the complex and outré) are clearly good. The morality of the universe does not seem to be on trial.

Let us return to Shelley's Prometheus to explain this. Prometheus' punishment was for usurping godly prerogative; Shelley made of him a hero, and rewarded him. Melville seems to have sympathized, and Ahab insists upon his personal right to find out for himself. But Melville sees the blasphemy inherent in the situation; Ishmael, Starbuck, even Ahab himself understand what the rebelliousness represents. One could illustrate either position with stories of Poe, but Poe seems never to have thought of his stories with such purposes in mind. One could cite Ellison or certain of the characters of the colloquies as examples of God-like creators whose impulses produce beauty; one could cite the narrator of "The Imp" as an example of those whose impulses are evil.

In Hawthorne, any character who presumes to usurp powers he should not have is doomed. Aylmer, in "The Birth Mark," tries, in effect, to do what Ellison does; he wants to create perfect beauty. He removes his wife's single blemish; she dies, for that mark is evidence that she is human, therefore imperfect. In Melville, there is less certainty. To strive for the absolute is to invite disaster, but Melville never says that this is the way things should be, or even that one should not go on striving. Poe is not concerned with the issue. Certain characters can follow their impulses with good results; others are doomed by their nature to do evil. Poe cares only for the state in which the impulses act, the time of creation of the horrible or lovely patterns which he thought of as the results of the exaltation which his characters experience.

To paraphrase Hawthorne, we have climbed high, and our reward is small. I feel rather like the scholar who received a grant to go to Paris for the purpose of preparing a study on the influence of Shakespeare on André Gide, went, worked through the Gide papers, and returned convinced that there was no influence of Shakespeare on André Gide. What I would like all of this to suggest is that Poe should not, in this one matter, be grouped with Hawthorne and Melville. I really think that there is a danger that this will happen; it has happened on other subjects. The general tendency of the Poe revival, as earlier suggested, is to put Poe into closer relationship with contemporary trends; this is a good thing. But were some writer with an ax to grind to come to this subject, he could build up a superficially impressive argument by citing certain stories; Poe might be placed in a central debate in which he had very little interest. This would be an unfortunate distortion, the sort of thing which results from trying too hard to show a unity in our literature when its real strength lies in its diversity.

Chapter IX

Wider Horizons

But for my children, I would have them keep their distance from
the thickening center; corruption
Never has been compulsory, when the cities lie at the monster's
feet there are left the mountains.

Robinson Jeffers, "Shine, Perishing Republic"

In view of the rather limited range in which Poe operated effectively, it is interesting to speculate about what he might have done had he succeeded in developing a broader basis for his art. We have seen that he could get remarkable mileage from that pattern which he used most frequently (the perceiver and something complex and "Gothic" to perceive). The number of variations on the pattern is a tribute to his craftsmanship, and each variation produced a different emphasis. Generally speaking, Poe's formula worked best when the subjective elements were strongest, that is, when the facts of the tale were given to the reader distorted by what Crane would have called the color of the narrator's mind. I suppose one could set up some sort of scale for Poe's stories, running from those in which the narrative is most subjective to those in which the tale is told more clearly

219

from "the outside." At one end, one would have those tales in which the horror has so engulfed the central figure that he is not aware of his own state, tales such as "The Cask of Amontillado," "The Pit and the Pendulum," and "William Wilson." Then would come those in which the hero recognizes his own nervous intensity, and says to the reader, either explicitly or by implication, "I may be mad." These would include the "death of a lady" stories and "The Fall of the House of Usher." Next would come stories in which the heightened sensitivity is clearly accounted for in terms of suffering, loneliness, or an intrinsically perceptive or analytical personality. Here we could list the Dupin stories, "The Gold Bug," the Ellison stories, "A Descent into the Maelstrom," and even "Hop-Frog." Finally, at the other end of the scale, we could place the most coolly-handled stories, such as " 'Thou Art the Man' " and "The Oblong Box."

It will be seen that we have here a rough correlation between the degree of involvement and the degree to which the tales succeed; most of the tales near the start of the list are superior to those which come later. Most of the short stories upon which Poe's reputation, such as it is, rests would be placed near the top of such a scale, and yet I think it is clear that the others are also important for an understanding of his work. Had Poe lived longer, it is from these that he probably would have developed the patterns of a more mature art.

When Poe wrote that the best tales are those which produce the most intense effects, and that such effects cannot be long sustained, he was passing judgment upon his own work. An art which attains its vision through the eyes of hypersensitive personalities is severely limited. One can hardly imagine a novel-length "House of Usher," for the necessary development sections, the biography, so to speak, of Usher, would have to be pitched in a less intense key, and the concentration which gives to the story so much of its force would be lost. We as readers would come to know too much; we would ask too many questions. If Poe chose to be conventionally expository, the surprises which are so important to the impact of the story would have been lost (our discovery, for example, of just how far Roderick Usher's sickness has progressed). If Poe chose instead to attempt to maintain the intensity, we would, I am afraid, simply become fatigued long before page 250. Perhaps what I am saying is merely that the Poe story is stronger than the Gothic novel. I think that this is probably true, partially because Poe is a better writer than the Gothicists, but partially also because he designed a better vehicle for his Gothicism, one which permitted him, for instance, to use the objects of the external world in a manner far more expressionistic than one could get away with in a long work. The materials of the Gothic novel could be transformed into enduring art; *Wuthering Heights* is a good book, as is *The House of the Seven Gables*, but these are a different breed of cow, almost as different from the usual Gothic novel as are Poe's tales.

Two of the works to be treated in the present chapter were attempts by Poe to widen his artistic horizon by producing longer stories. It is probably significant that neither is successful. In one, Poe apparently thought to apply the "Usher" formula to a longer work of fiction; in the other, he experimented--so far as one can tell--with a new and, I think, promising variation on the pattern.

The difference between Ellison and Usher, each of whom is used by Poe as a perceiver, is that Ellison perceives because of an inherent sensitivity to beauty (or at least what Poe called beauty) while Usher perceives because, in his state of extreme nervousness, he is abnormally sensitive. In *The Narrative of A. Gordon Pym*, Poe tried to produce a novel with an Usher-like hero and failed. Now, we remarked that the nature of the perceiving process may be said to determine the structure of the Poe story, and that in the case of Ellison, the ideal artist, because there was no difficulty in perceiving, there was no plot. In "The Journal of Julius Rodman" Poe was probably trying to find a way to create some tension despite the fact that his central character perceived easily without being mad. And so he hit upon the idea of making him lonely, unhappy and isolated.

There are, of course, numerous Poe characters who could be said to be isolated. Dupin is a secluded man, as is Legrand in "The Gold Bug," and one can not imagine the narrators of "Ligeia" or the "Morella" having cronies drop in for a hand of poker. I think, however, that there is nothing very profound implied by such isolation. These people are usually out of sympathy with their surroundings, and their being so is one of the factors which figures in the development of their acute sensitivity, but Poe could do without it. Montresor and

Fortunato seem to lead socially active lives, and Montresor is no less a madman for it. But it seems to me that in "Rodman" Poe wanted to try something new. Julius Rodman is sensitive, but he is not a monomaniac. On the other hand, he does not have as easy a time of it as does Ellison, the ideal poet. Poe sketched him as an *isolato* with certain traits which remind one of the *isolato* in Melville. Such characters in Melville are usually Seekers, and the plot line moves with their quest. Rodman should be regarded as Ellison, made unhappy, on a quest.

To put it in a different way, the usual "mad" characters perceive because of an inner struggle. The ideal poet perceives because he is a poet, and the pieces in which he appears are simply sketches. Rodman was to have been a poet with certain compulsions which would drive him along, providing motivation throughout a longer work of fiction.

The Narrative of A. Gordon Pym represents a failure of the usual pattern applied to a longer work; "Rodman," after a tantalizing opening, collapses completely. The third work to be discussed in detail in this chapter is, in contrast, of the usual short story length and an unqualified success. Like Pym, it uses the supersensitive character, and like "Rodman," it deals with isolation. Although one can be sure that "The Man of the Crowd" is a fine story, and although one can also be sure that it deals with isolation, however, it is difficult to determine just wherein its greatness lies, and just what it has to say about isolation. Clearly it represents an attempt on Poe's part to widen the scope of his art, for unlike almost any of his other works, it seems based largely on observation of the world around him.

-1-

Poe's Lonely Crowd

To contrast Yvor Winters' famous "Edgar Allan Poe: A Crisis in the History of American Obscurantism"[1] with Paul Elmer More's "A Note on Poe's Method"[2] is to gain insight into the remarkable divergence among first-rate critics on the subject of Poe's craftsmanship. A few quotations will suffice to suggest the nature and tone of Winters' *blitzkreig*.

Poe appears never to have grasped the simple and traditional distinction between matter (truth) and manner (beauty); he does not see that beauty is a quality of style, instead of its subject matter. (384)

[Concerning Poe's idea of beauty in poetry:] Poe is...an explicit obscurantist. (389)

Poe had a mind for only the crudest of distinctions.

This is an art to delight the soul of a servant girl....

Poe's theory of Beauty is not understood, and no casual allusion to Plato will ever clarify it. (401)

To accept the latter statements without qualification is to deny the worth of a good deal of very solid work on Poe, but Mr. Winters has a strong point. There is certainly some confusion in Poe's theoretical writing concerning the nature of beauty; that is one reason that the present study operates for the most part not from the theory of beauty, but rather from the "look" of beauty in the tales. This latter, as I hope I have demonstrated, is a fairly consistent thing.

More, in contrast to Winters, says that Poe's artistic personality has a firmness the tragedies of his career never shook; his essay emphasizes Poe's control of his material. Of a portrait of Poe, he says,

But in one thing the face is unlike the type [portraits of defeated men] to which it belongs; there is not the least sign here of that mental relaxation, that loosening of the mind's grasp and determination, which often goes with what must be called...the breakdown of character. On the contrary, the eyes retain the look of intense concentration and logical grip.

...one of the distinguishing marks of Poe's work is just the combination of nervous irritability, running even into the morbid, with rigorous intellectual analysis. (77)

We have previously remarked the danger of generalizing about Poe from any one area of Poe's work--for example, assuming that his only "serious" stories are the ones with mad narrators. To some extent, this sort of assumption is a fault both of Winters' and of More's essays. I do not think I would be distorting these pieces if I said that Winters wrote with Poe's critical statements chiefly in his mind, and that More was thinking chiefly of a certain type of story.

Yet the two evaluations are not thoroughly incompatible. Winters' comment regarding Poe's habit of regarding beauty as subject, rather than style, is significant, but need not, as he seems to feel, imply mediocrity. Poe frequently attempted to create stories which would serve as frames for pictures of his special sort. One can easily see why the idea might offend a classically oriented critic such as Winters, but Poe could transcend his own theory. We can forgive Poe his shallow notions whenever the end product, the story, gives evidence of a convincing unity. When Poe utilized the kind of "logical grip" of which More says he was capable, he could create effective stories through the very process which Winters finds objectionable: viewing beauty as "subject matter."

We do not condemn Nathaniel Hawthorne because the often hearty and solid material limned out in the notebooks seldom appeared in his work, or, when it did appear, turned up somehow rarified. In theory (his own desires) he would have liked to have been another Trollope; in practice he had to invent a manner all his own. We should not condemn Poe because the critical theory which he rationalized out of his own experience does not seem to be the sort of code which can guide the creation of literature. Even if, as Winters insists, it was not really an organic theory of art, it came from an art which was, at its best, organic. If, in examining Poe's criticism, it is possible to show a shallowness on this matter of organic structure, in examining his fiction one can often show a practical understanding of the manner in which tone, plot and texture should all contribute to an artistic whole. Often the story which frames the "beauty" in Poe is itself beautiful.

We suggested that, significantly, Winters' essay grows from an examination of Poe's criticism, while More has his eye on certain works of fiction. Consider More's treatment of "The Man of the Crowd." This story he compares to Hawthorne's "Ethan Brand."

> Poe's is a grim and unforgettable story, as original as Hawthorne's but different. Its power over our imagination depends upon the analysis of the sensations connected with crime, whereas in *Ethan Brand* the interest is centered upon the search for the idea of evil in itself. (79)

He has selected a fine example of tight and careful craftsmanship. Suppose, however, that he had chosen "Hans Pfaall," "'Thou Art the Man,'" "A Descent into the Maelstrom," or one of the obscure satires, stories in which Poe was less successful precisely because of a lack of "rigorous intellectual analysis." From these one could document Winters' essay rather well, for in them the "distinctions" are indeed "crude."

"The Man of the Crowd" is all More says it is. Nowhere in Poe is the detachment of the author and his absolute control over his materials more evident, and nowhere does he seem more modern. But the modernity is a difficult matter to account for. More's comparison of the story to "Ethan Brand" is a good place to start. Hawthorne turned similar materials to different ends. The moral parable is the very type of Hawthorne's artistry: the tableau is presented, and its meaning appears clear. Brand has searched for sin, but the searching itself involves the sin, and he is consumed by fire. The story would not exist were not Hawthorne what he was and his times what they were. He was moved by the moral insights which were the finest legacy of a specific passing age. The insight has meaning for all times, but the story itself has its historical location written large upon it. It is clearly the product of a man who sees the validity of insights which have existed in Christian thinking from the start, which were a cultural force in Puritan times, but which he feared were largely ignored or discredited by his contemporaries.

Poe's story, in contrast, is strangely timeless, and also strangely modern. Change its language in different ways, and it might be a tale by Hemingway, Stephen Crane, Henry James or Faulkner, or a passage from a Melville novel. It might have occurred to any author concerned with the sensations of psychological insight, who was also, at least at the time, reticent to spell out a "message."

The unwillingness of Poe in this tale to build fiction for moral ends ties him to the twentieth century as Hawthorne's need to do so ties him to the nineteenth, with this difference: many modern authors forbear moral spelling-out in explicit terms, yet so strongly imply judgment in their tone and situation that their works cannot be fully understood without an awareness of such moral concern. In its very unwillingness to preach, Crane's *Maggie* is a very sentimental book, which cries "shame!" throughout its length. The "coldness" of Dreiser's *Sister Carrie* fools no sensitive reader. The reader who misses Faulkner's approval of the moral strength of the traditions which bolster Dilsey and her brood misses the point of *The*

Sound and the Fury. And Hemingway, for all his callous pose, can be almost sentimental in his insistence on getting across his "message." This is perhaps most evident in his weaker work. He stops the action of his *To Have and Have Not* as his hero is brought in dying on a boat because he is ashamed to preach, yet wants to make clear the way he feels. He takes his readers on a tour of the yachts in the harbor, where the futility of the lives of the sleepless wealthy is symbolized brutally in the person of a woman masturbating. All this because the heritage of naturalism has left him unable to say openly that Harry Morgan's ragged life, if violent, is more meaningful.

In this sense, then, these authors, because they feel the need to say somehow things it is unfashionable for an author to say, are nearer to Hawthorne and Melville than to Poe. In his disciplined unwillingness to make moral commitments, the Poe of "The Man of the Crowd" seems *avant-garde* even today, when we find ourselves again dealing with young artists whose intentions puzzle us, and whose real commitments are deliberately hidden.

Through its very impersonality and unwillingness to specify, "The Man of the Crowd" achieves a kind of universality. It is one of the most haunting visions of the modern city in our literature, and yet even the city itself may be regarded as a coloristic means to an end. Herman Melville sent his young Pierre to New York, and Pierre's descent from the soft "green sward" of his country home to the harsh cobblestones of a nightmare New York is the American visit of Aeneas to Hell. It is also one of the great passages in Melville. That New York and Poe's London are the same city. Compare the experiences of Pierre's entourage to Poe's catalogue of faces in the crowd. Melville writes:

> [The approach to the city] ...the coach gained the top of the long and very gradual slope running toward the obscure heart of the town, and the twinkling perspective of two long and parallel rows of lamps was revealed--lamps which seemed not so much intended to dispel the general gloom, as to show some path leading through it, into some gloom still deeper beyond--...

> [The cobblestones] The coach seems rolling over cannon-balls of all calibers. [Pierre explains them to Delly] "...the buried hearts of some dead citizens have perhaps come to the surface." [To Isabel he says,] "Milk dropped from the milkman's can in December, freezes not more quickly on these stones, than does

snow-white innocence, if in poverty it chance to fall in these streets."

[The shops' shutters clank shut] "...the town's-people are going to their rest." [says Pierre; Delly responds,] "Please God they may find it."[3]

The coach then turns into a "side gloom," and Pierre finds no lights on in his cousin's house. Of the silence of the city, Pierre explains, "'...brick and mortar have deeper secrets than wood or fell, sweet Isabel.'" (323) They arrive at a police watch-house; the policeman tries to help, then becomes suspicious. Pierre leaves Delly and Isabel and walks to his cousin's home; he is approach by a prostitute: "'My God!' shuddered Pierre, hurrying forward, 'the town's first welcome to youth!'" (331) His cousin Stanley Glendinning refuses to recognize him; Pierre returns to the watch-house. It has become a place of horror:

> In indescribable disorder, frantic, diseased-looking men and women of all colours, and in all imaginable flaunting, immodest, grotesque, and shattered dresses, were leaping, yelling, and cursing around him. (335-336)

A catalogue of horrors follows, and Melville concludes,

> The Thieves'-quarters and all the brothels, Lock-and Sin hospitals for incurables, and infirmaries and infernoes of hell seemed to have made one combined sortie, and poured out upon earth through the vile vomitory of some unmentionable cellar. (336)

This is what Melville found in "the obscure heart of the town," and what Poe symbolized as "the worst heart of the world." (IV, 145) Poe's review of the populace of the city at night is organized on precisely the same principle; we move through successively lower strata.

Poe's city may even be the more horrible because it is seen through the eyes of an abnormally sensitive narrator. "I had been ill in health," he says,

> but was now convalescent, and, with returning strength, found myself in one of those happy moods which are so precisely the converse of ennui--moods of the keenest appetency, when the film from the mental vision departs....--and the intellect, electrified, surpasses as greatly its every-day condition, as does the vivid yet candid reason of Leibnitz, the mad and flimsy rhetoric of Gorgias. Merely to breathe was enjoyment; and I derived positive pleasure even from many of the legitimate sources of pain. (IV, 134-135)

Happy or not, this is an unwholesome sort of health. If this narrator is not mad, he has had at least the usual supernormal abilities of the perceiver in Poe: extraordinary sensitivity, and the capacity to lose himself in the contemplation of objects. In this sense, for example, he has a good deal in common with that prototype of such Poe personalities, the monomaniac narrator of "Berenice." That Poe took the trouble to present him to the reader with such qualities may be taken as a hint that there is some grotesque pattern to be perceived. One knows in advance that the pattern will function both for its inherent dramatic effect, and also as a reflection of the narrator's mental state.

Considering the Winters essay, however, it is important to note that, while the "pattern" which the hypersensitive mind perceives might be called beauty-as-subject-matter, there are patterns of other sorts present. These are related to the presentation of the "beautiful" subject, and as structural devices make of the tale an organic whole. The central pattern grows from the psychological insight around which the story revolves, but one must also consider the structural rhythm of this carefully fashioned tale.

Poe has been very methodical, so much so that it is worthwhile to trace the mechanical elements--matters such as the time scheme, the weather, and the gradual movement from abstraction to action. The story opens "about the closing of an evening in autumn," (IV, 134) but the narrator takes one back a short step to explain how he came to feel as he does, so that the earliest action (if one excepts the "long months" of illness) takes place in mid-afternoon. The narrator sits in the coffee-house amusing himself with trivia: advertisements in the paper, the changing company of the establishment, the people in the street.

In paragraph three, "the darkness came on"; (IV, 135) the narrator turns all his attention to the street. The fourth details a further shift; he begins to pick out individuals. Already we have come a long way. The first paragraph was abstract speculation about "mysteries" so evil they "will not *suffer themselves* to be revealed"; (IV, 134) in three paragraphs Poe has us ready for the long catalogue passage, paragraphs five through ten, which takes up most of the central portion of the tale.

In number eleven, "the night deepened," the street lights came on, and in twelve "The wild effects of the light" enchained the narrator's attention "to an examination of individual faces." Once more the reader is reminded here of the intensity of the narrator's perception when he speaks of his "peculiar mental state." (IV, 139) Then, in paragraph thirteen, the man of the crowd appears. He has grown organically out of the last paragraph of the catalogue, but also out of the darkness, and out of the mind which has so seen the city.

In paragraph fifteen it is "fully night-fall," with "a thick humid fog...over the city." The narrator's reaction to the fog is revealing: "...the lurking of an old fever in my system... [rendered] the moisture somewhat too dangerously pleasant. Tying a handkerchief about my mouth, I kept on." (IV, 141) What we see, Poe tells us, we see through feverish eyes.

And now begins the pursuit. In the language of the radio announcers, here are time and weather checks: in paragraph fifteen, half an hour passed; in sixteen an hour, heavy rain, and cool. "A few minutes" (IV, 142) more, and, in seventeen, the scene in the bazaar: an hour and a half is spent there. Eighteen: it is eleven P.M. Nineteen: no one is on the streets but the most depraved. Of the man of the crowd, Poe says, "the spirits of the old man again flickered up, as a lamp which is near its death-hour." By paragraph twenty "It was nearly daybreak." (IV, 144) A full day passes in a single sentence of this last paragraph, and the pursuit ends "as the shades of the second evening came on." (IV, 145)

The pace itself, then, has to be considered a structural device, and part of our aesthetic response is our reaction to this purely formal element. To say that Poe suceeds is, of course, to make a subjective judgment: I like the story and think that he succeeds. My point, though, is that if this tale is aesthetically successful, its success has to be understood in terms of manner and not just matter. Rhythm is an abstract quality, and has to do with manner. Winters' comment seems almost totally irrelevant. What is beautiful in this story is Poe's manipulation of his materials, not the materials themselves.

This is no accident; it is almost a truism that Poe is very good at handling structure. One thinks of the carefully-timed effects to which he builds in "The Facts in the Case of M. Valdemar," "The Black Cat," "The Fall of the House of Usher," "The Pit and the Pendulum," "Ligeia" and other successful tales, or of the pacing of "William Wilson," which is very much like what we see in "The Man of the Crowd."

Wilson's stays in the various European cities are treated in progressively less detail as the story's action accelerates. Even if one dislikes some of these stories, one has to concede Poe's skill.

"The Man of the Crowd" has some special qualities that differentiate it from much of Poe's work. Though we are given the usual "margin of credibility," what the narrator sees seems to reflect the real world to a greater extent than is usual in Poe. The sick narrator rushes through the city in increasingly foul weather; doubtless his vision is colored, and the reader has the option of considering the entire affair as the distorted vision of a sick mind. Yet there is enough of reality here to keep the tale from being merely abstract. This is an accurate enough picture of the city at night, as anyone whose work-schedule requires him to patronize the all-night joints of any large city can testify. The tattered old men who are, as the sociologists tell us, the only real inhabitants of a city's center, still shuffle along echoing streets. In the few all-night places, where policemen go for coffee, a cigarette, and a little rest, are sick-eyed men, prostitutes, and shabby exhausted workers too tired and too lonely to face bed as yet.

Hemingway understood what Poe saw in the city, and wrote a story which is really concerned with the same thing. Hemingway's old man is not depraved, though he despairs of life.

> "Last week he tried to commit suicide," one waiter said.
> "Why? "
> "He was in despair."
> "What about? "
> "Nothing."[4]

He has a need in the night, and one of the waiters in the "clean, well-lighted place" understands the need. He has it himself.

> He disliked bars and bodegas. A clean, well-lighted cafe was a very different thing. Now, without thinking further, he would go home to his room. He would lie in the bed and finally, with daylight, he would go to sleep. After all, he said to himself, it is probably only insomnia. Many must have it. (481)

But there are significant differences. Hemingway's old man is alone, but has at least the sympathy of one of the waiters. And that waiter suspects that there is a community of lonely men. Although it is not satisfactory, he has a sort of code by which to live his life, a code hinted at in his feeling of duty towards his job as waiter. There are men who need the cafe; keep it clean and well-lighted, and do not rush them out.

Poe's narrator reacts not because of sympathy, but because of a curiosity which turns to revulsion at the close of the tale. There is no positive horror in "A Clean Well-Lighted Place," that is, no hint of terrible crime or violence. The horror is of a negative nature; there is no rule to guide life. Life threatens to be meaningless. Love is no longer possible for the old ones; religion is also gone:

> Our nada who art in nada, nada be thy name thy kingdom nada thy will be nada in nada as it is in nada. Give us this nada our daily nada and nada us our nada as we nada our nadas and nada us not into nada but deliver us from nada; pues nada. (481)

If there is nothing to be given, at least there is nothing to be delivered from. In Hemingway's story, the fact that religion has gone out of the lives of the characters is a sign that everything which can make life meaningful has been lost. The tale may be said to be about patternlessness.

In "The Man of the Crowd" the hint of religion comes in the closing sentence. "The worst heart of the world is a grosser book than the 'Hortulus Animae,' and perhaps it is but one of the great mercies of God that 'er lasst sich nicht lesen.'" (IV, 145) Religion is not really involved in the moral situation in the Poe, and the danger is not meaninglessness, but rather the existence of a meaning too deadly to be known. Hemingway's waiter thinks vaguely that he needs "...a certain cleanliness and order"; (481) Poe's man needs anonymity, and Poe's narrator finds himself peeping into secrets too horrible to name.

Thomas Mann has a comparable involvement in horror to relate in "Mario and the Magician," that surrealistic account of a hunchback entertainer whose hold over his provincial audience becomes more horrible when the reader realizes that even the urbane narrator finds himself "under the sway of a fascination which emanated from this man who took so strange a way to earn his bread."[5] Like "The Man of the Crowd," this story derives a good deal of its horror from the drama of our narrator's discovery of his own absorption. Both narrators finally fear being swept along by the unnamed power.

Mann's credibility is maintained by wordy disclaimers on the part of the narrator. He is continually saying, in effect, "It was really strange, but you'll believe me if I give you all the prosaic details--I had the wife and children along; there were people we knew in the audience; we were embarrassed." Poe knew that technique, and explained it in detail in his review of *Sheppard Lee.* But in "The Man of the Crowd," he accomplishes the same thing more economically by hinting at his narrator's unbalance. Mann's tale does not have the sort of gradual adjustment of the lens--until the reader sees, in sharp focus, how deeply he is involved--which is the secret of Poe's structure. Mann's narrator has difficulty shaking off the spell; Poe's awakens with a shudder.

Consider the catalogue passage, paragraphs five through ten, and compare it to the splendid catalogue in section fifteen of Walt Whitman's "Song of Myself." Whitman's holds together here (sometimes his catalogues do not) because there is a kind of continuity of emotional and associational responses. This is a difficult matter to demonstrate, and any spelling-it-out seems pedestrian, but here is an example:

> 1 As the woolly-pates hoe in the sugar-field, the overseer views them from his saddle,
> 2 The bugle calls in the ball-room, the gentlemen run for their partners, the dancers bow to each other,
> 3 The youth lies awake in the cedar-roof'd garret and harks to the musical rain,
> 4 The Wolverine sets traps on the creek that helps fill the Huron,
> 5 The squaw wrapt in her yellow-hemm'd cloth is offering mocassins and bead-bags for sale,
> 6 The connoisseur peers along the exhibition-gallery with half-shut eyes bent sideways,[6]

To explain how the catalogue holds together, one has to list associations: 1. South, 2. South; music, 3. Music; cedar and rain, 4. Hard out-door life; Indian, 5. Indian; business, 6. Business; art; social attitude. This, of course, should be intuited, not explained; too many "little things" stay with the reader to be analysed. A page later, and the "half-shut eyes" will spring to mind when an opium-eater is described as having "just-open'd lips." (36)

Whitman's catalogue contains sufficient images in common with Poe's so that when he deals with the city, it is recognizable as the same city seen in the same panoramic manner. But the purposes of the two are different. Whitman wants to force the reader to make the kind of intuitive leaps which will allow him to see the Transcendental unity of all men; he is building to the line which closes the section, "And of these one and all I weave the song of myself." (37) Poe's purpose is more immediate; his catalogue must give birth to the man of the crowd. And so he starts it in the late afternoon with satisfied businessmen, and gradually works down through layers of society to the loathsome dregs and lees of urban life. Whitman feels a communal tie to the prostitute who "...draggles her shawl" and whose "bonnet bobs on her tipsy and pimpled neck." (36) Poe's crowd has in it lepers, prostitutes and "reeling, inarticulate" (IV, 138) drunkards, but they are present not as brothers, but as the vast, moiling womb from which will emerge the detestable man of the crowd.

Mann, Hemingway, Whitman, Melville and Poe: An odd grouping, no doubt. One does not want to overstress the similarities. What their visions of the city have in common is considerable enough, however. There is horror in the city, and the issue with which all deal is our involvement in it. Whitman will embrace everything, but what he embraces will kill Pierre. Hemingway's old man will find some order of his own to cling to in the face of the city; Poe's narrator will discover that the horror is not merely external; it is within him, too. Part of the tale's modernity must be the result of the fact that Poe had discovered an important modern subject.

Poe's style and his tale's structure both reflect deepening involvement. His tone, for example, shifts from good-humored if incisive social commentary (paragraph five) to a deadly serious parade of straggling horrors. Even sentence structure changes. The formality of paragraph six ("Setting aside a certain dapperness of carriage, which may be termed *deskism* for want of a better word, the manner of these persons seemed to me....") (IV, 136) is unlike the jumbled and heavily hyphenated paragraph ten.

And what of the final meaning of "The Man of the Crowd"? Patrick F. Quinn, in a very perceptive discussion of the story, says,

> Now the meaning of this story seems to be that the narrator encountered and failed to recognize a prophetic image of his future self. But this meaning is nowhere directly stated. Perhaps no other of Poe's stories proceeds so much by indirection and faint clues as this one. Yet the clues are there, and when they are

read aright the reason for Poe's reliance on implication rather than straightforward exposition becomes sufficiently clear.[7]

This is certainly consistent with the mood of the story, although this reader personally feels that even this is too specific a statement. I think that Mr. Quinn has indicated the *sort* of thing the story is about, but am not convinced that the meaning can, finally, be stated. The narrator's sickness Quinn takes to mean something very different from what this discussion suggests, and I think it is because of his feelings on this point that Quinn is willing to specify a meaning. He says,

> The important thing to notice is that "The Man of the Crowd" is not a realistic story. Its time-span is virtually impossible....It would be possible for such a pursuit to last through one night, but that it should continue through the following morning and afternoon is most improbable. And since the narrator remarks at the outset that he has only recently recovered from an illness, the probability of so extended a chase is nil. Another odd detail is that the pursuer consistently manages to avoid being seen by the man he is following....More surprising still, when he finally does confront the old man, no notice is taken of him: "he noticed me not." If taken realistically, this would be another baffling detail. But the significance of the episode is that the narrator, facing his future double, fails to see and recognize himself. (230)

In one sense, as we noted, the story is more "realistic" than most of Poe: what the narrator sees from the coffeehouse is really visible in any large city. The only other of his tales which seems as soundly based on personal observation of the external world is the satire "The System of Doctor Tarr and Professor Fether," in which the insane asylum is described on the basis of Poe's own familiarity with one which he visited.[8] In the sense in which Quinn uses the word, certainly "The Man of the Crowd" is not realistic, but I think that the sickness is not the factor which makes the chase impossible, but rather precisely what makes it possible. It also determines the very special manner in which the narrator sees the city, and the way he sees the man of the crowd himself. By telling us that he is sick, the narrator leaves open, as often in Poe and Hawthorne, a "realistic possibility." The reader who will not believe the chase has the option of saying to himself, "Well, this fellow is delirious. He says he was sick; obviously he still is. These are the visions of the feverish. Perhaps the entire story is about his sickness."

The unending and ambiguous inconclusive chase: is this not the very stuff of which dreams are made? We pursue or are pursued with a desperate urgency which makes us toss in our sleep, and gallop slow-motion through a nightmare landscape, never knowing what the chase is about. Ideas indeed arise "confusedly and paradoxically" within our minds, but on awakening we can not single them out.

Folklore may help us out here. The popular notion of such dreams is that if they should end conclusively--should the dreamer catch or be caught, or, in another dream, should his fall from dizzy heights ever be completed--he would die. One can even read this tale as a specific account of the crisis in a serious illness, in which the sick narrator, at the final moment of revulsion, comes as near as he is to come to the unnamed mysteries of death, and then flees. The will to live asserts itself, the seductive temptation to give in suddenly seems not seductive but horrible, the crisis passes, and with it the fever.

Even this is probably too specific; it would be better to say that this is the *sort* of response which the story evokes. One might be able to settle conclusively upon one of these readings were the story clearly "realistic" or clearly fantastic, but as we have seen, while there is too much that is terribly accurate in the vision of the city at night, there is also too much that is in the nature of fantasy in the pursuit. Had Poe made the choice, a final reading might be possible, but we would be dealing with a far less imposing piece of fiction.

Quinn says,

> As its author...Poe was presumably conscious of what this story means. It is too expertly managed, its details too finely controlled and mutually managed, to permit of any other conclusion. Furthermore, the evident reflections of Poe's own character that are found in "The Man of the Crowd" make it unlikely that he did not work this story out very carefully as a parable of his own life. (231-232)

But it is just this expert management and fine control which prevent a clear "meaning" from becoming apparent. If this story is primarily a psychological study --and I think it is--and not a moral parable (except in the most general sense), then it is reasonable to assume that Poe did not know specifically what it meant, or knew and refused to say, or was not interested in knowing and was rather interested in the process by which a mind arrives at a vision of a final horror. Winston Smith in George Orwell's *1984* discovers that the final horror varies from person to person. Poe, like Orwell, takes us to the door of the room which contains that which we most fear, but Poe can not or will not tell what is inside; to do so would make the story less universal.

The general sense in which "The Man of the Crowd" can be taken as moral parable is by no means easy to state. The terms one might apply to a Hawthorne tale do not quite fit. This story is not about the discovery that there is terrible evil in the world, nor even that there are terrible horrors. Rather, it is about the mind's discovery that there exists within itself the fear of these things. The accuracy or "realism" of the vision is intended to emphasize the immediacy and strength of this fear, and the sickness is, in this sense, a device to allow the author to present his vision with maximum clarity. In short, the story is like Hawthorne only up to a point; Hawthorne would have used it to present the discovery of evil. Poe has, if one insists on a moral reading, presented the discovery of the fear of evil.[9]

It may be, however, that we are being too careful with "The Man of the Crowd." The story seems to have a more obvious meaning. Or, perhaps, it seems as though it ought to have a more obvious meaning. Perhaps Hawthorne will be of further use to us in this matter. Isolation, in Hawthorne's world, is an extraordinarily dangerous condition, for it can cut off the individual from that sympathy with his fellows which is necessary for his humility and his salvation. However, although it is dangerous, it may be necessary for the artist; there is at least a chance that the "Sights from a Steeple" will be worth the climb. What isolation means in Poe is less clear. We do not, in the final analysis, know why he put the gentleman in the lighthouse.

Perhaps this tale simply means that there is terrible evil in the city. The man of the crowd typifies the city; he "'is the type and the genius of deep crime.'" (IV, 145) The narrator is present merely to give movement to a vision of evil. This simple reading is certainly at least partially valid, and it conforms to the usual pattern we have noted whenever a moral issue arises in Poe, namely, that such matters concern Poe not for their own sake, but as a means to an end. They are used as color, to heighten an effect.

But such a reading leaves several puzzling matters unexplained. An evil man compulsively seeks company; he must hide himself in the crowd. What does that mean? Contemporary discussions of crowd psychology and "groupism" stress the danger of conformity, but is that at issue here? A growing body of recent books and articles emphasize the danger that, in Melville's image, the individual will become a cipher added to a long group of ciphers. But Poe's man of the crowd is not like the crowd; he is worse than anything in the crowd. Is he an evil man so tormented by his guilt that he cannot bear to be alone? Yes, for Poe says, "Now and then, alas, the conscience of man takes up a burthen so heavy in horror that it can be thrown down only into the grave." But this only heightens the mystery, for the next sentence reads, "And thus the essence of all crime is undivulged." (IV, 134) Once again Poe seems unwilling to develop the moral line ("conscience" and guilt); his concern is with the sensations involved. Probably, in Hawthorne's hands, the sinner would have become the narrator, who, instead of reacting with the sympathy which one sinful being should show to any other, runs away in terror. The fact that Poe does not even hint that this possibility exists will serve as a measure of the vast contrast in emphasis in the art of the two authors.

I think that I will stand by my statement that one of the hidden sources of this tale's strangely compelling effect is that, finally, *er lasst sich nicht lesen.*

-2-

Poe's Novel

The Narrative of A. Gordon Pym will not let itself be read, either, but in that case, the phrase takes on an additional ironic meaning. Poe does not say where his novel is going; he may not know himself, and, what is worse, the reader may not be willing to read far enough to find out.

With the vigorous revival of interest in Edgar Poe which the past two decades have seen, it is not surprising that a good deal of critical attention has been focused upon the longest piece of fiction which Poe produced. According to Patrick Quinn, *Pym* has long been considered a masterpiece by the French. Quinn himself calls it a "crucial text" for an understanding of Poe, and he approves of Gaston Bachelard's conclusion that it comes from the very center of Poe.[10]

All this is a trifle surprising. *Pym* is certainly an important document for studies both of the nature of Poe's imagination and of his technique, but what seems to me the most obvious fact about it, and the fact which should qualify critical discussions conducted from any approach, is that it is a very bad book. I do not mean that it is a great work with some technical lapses, such as *Moby Dick*, or that it is a fairly good book with moments of greatness; or even that it is a workmanlike piece of hack writing. It is worse than any of these possibilities. No editor, even of the lower-grade adventure pulps, would consider publishing as loose and disorganized, confused and ineffective a work as *The Narrative of A. Gordon Pym*, because the veriest hack writer can turn out for him a piece more unified. *Pym's* closest structural relative is the cliff-hanger serial novel, which in each issue leaves the hero in some awful danger, and each installment rescues him from the previous issue's predicament, but even the cliff-hanger has a certain unity and purpose. The hero battles the elements, mechanical failure if machines are involved, and the merciless agents of the enemy; after twenty installments he rescues the secret documents and the lady, and the thing ends in a blaze of speeches, medals, and a wedding. Poe's novel--if it deserves the name--has not even that much clarity of purpose. But even more striking is the matter which every reader who opens the novel notices before he reads very far: the book reads badly.

Mr. Quinn detects a central theme in *Pym*; he feels that it is a book about treachery, and points to the continuing examples of betrayal, mutiny, revolt, overthrow of authority, and the underdog taking over. He says that the key to the whole is that nothing can be depended upon to remain stable. I see two alternative explanations for this instability, and neither seems a sign of a work written out of a central theme. First, the nature of Pym's world and Pym's adventures certainly might be considered a reflection of Poe's neurotic and uninformed social attitudes, and, as such, fine ground for psychoanalytic study, but only so long as the writer of such a study keeps in mind the second explanation. This is that *Pym* is an extended piece of space-filling hack work. Poe very obviously had difficulty keeping his book going. It is atrociously episodic, because Poe had to keep thinking of new adventures; the adventures become increasingly weird. The environment of any cliff-hanger is unstable. Some readers doubtless remember the cliff-hanger movie serials, currently being revived by film clubs, in which fair Pauline faced innumerable cliffs, buzz saws, railroad trains and greasy dudish men with knives. Now, there was an unstable environment. It had to be if the episode was, in twenty minutes, to build tension and suspense. One had to fear that danger lurked behind every door, and that the floor might at any moment give way to plunge Pauline into a bubbling cauldron (though of course next week it would turn out that as she plunged she managed to grab the trap-door and hang on).

Edward Davidson also makes *Pym* seem too systematic. He feels that this is a story about a boy turning into a man.[11] He says, "The tale begins...where most of Poe's tales and poems on this subject [growing up] had begun, with the high degree of responsiveness of a young and simpleminded boy." (166) Yet, as Mr. Davidson himself points out, Arthur Pym at the start of the book is a liar and a cheat. Again, Pym is "...an arrogant young American go-getter." (176)

Fortunately, both Quinn and Davidson also have useful insights to offer. Mr. Davidson, noting a general tendency throughout the book, says that "...as Pym matures and gains control over outward circumstances,...the external world seems to dissolve." (174) This is in keeping with Mr. Davidson's feeling that all the horror in Poe represents

> ...the fading of any moral law into an apocalypse of man's last "distempered" things in which anything may happen; [character- istic of this state is] ...the total freedom of the will to function, at the same time that there is nothing to will "for" or will "against." (124)

Thus in *Pym*, as one nears the close of the work, the will becomes the protagonist, and Arthur himself fades away; "...he nearly ceased to have any existence at all." (179) This is an interesting idea, for there is an evident change in the nature of the narrative as it progresses. I think the fading of Pym, however, represents more a failure on Poe's part to devise any manner in which to develop his young hero than any planned scheme of disintegration. Cliff-hangers are not notable, on the whole, for their subtle development of character; usually, as in *The Narrative of A. Gordon Pym*, the adventure overshadows the hero.

Patrick Quinn shows an awareness of the defects of the book. He says that Poe had no plan; indeed, he chooses to make his general observations on poor craftsmanship in Poe in the chapter of his study which deals with "Poe's Imaginary Voyage." Poe's blunders, he notes, are usually violations of precisely those tenets of composition which Poe suggested in his criticism: careful construction and unity of impact. One also gets the general sense that Mr. Quinn understands that whatever accomplishment there is in *Pym* involves the manner in which Poe manages to move from the relatively prosaic opening to the strange ending. This, once again, I feel is less a matter of plan than expediency, but it is only fair to admit that the reader is not quite as unwilling to believe the events of the close, when they occur, as he would have been had they come earlier in the story.

Mr. Quinn has an attractive hunch that Herman Melville knew this book. He compares Ishmael to Pym, each of whom may be said to hunt doom, notes the common use of Nantucket, and points out the common use of the "colorless all-color" white. It would certainly be nice to have this firmly established; one would like to think that the young Melville had this tie to his older colleague. If, however, one wants to go to Melville for an argument with which to defend *Pym*, the volume to take down from the shelves is not the dog-eared copy of *Moby Dick*, but rather the less-used copy of *Mardi*.

Pym's structure is so terribly episodic that I find it difficult to defend it at all, but an argument could be devised along the following lines. Just as Melville, in *Mardi*, desired to remove his hero, Taji, several stages from reality, so Poe with Arthur. If one examines the opening chapters of the Melville work, one finds that it takes the narrator forty chapters to reach the islands in which Melville sets his allegory.[12] Those chapters contain some of the best adventure narrative Melville ever wrote, and will stand quite nicely on their own without any explanation of their extreme importance as a testing ground for devices to be used again in *Moby Dick*, but for the present purpose, it will be sufficient merely to point out that structurally they perform the function of leading the hero and the reader into another world. The adventures are progressively more strange, and the characters who are Taji's companions become increasingly extraordinary. Indeed, Melville tends to kill

Taji's companions as the story goes on, so that Taji's ties to the very real and specific world of the opening of the novel are continually being cut as he moves into less well charted seas. By the time one reaches the mythical isles of Mardi, the stage has been perfectly set for strange adventure, and the tragedy is that Melville was unable to match the extremely high standards set in the opening; the allegory is dishearteningly flat.

At least Melville had something planned for the moment Taji arrived. Pym is also removed several stages from reality. The characters of one section tend to die before the next section, and the adventures, as in Melville, become stranger as one moves to less known climes. But *Pym* comes to a close at about the point that it really becomes interesting. The trouble seems to be that Poe, who worked out a splendid formula for writing a particular type of short tale, never hit upon a corresponding recipe for an adventure story, a long one in particular. *The Narrative of A. Gordon Pym*, far from being an exalted masterwork, seems rather the best example of Poe's difficulties. It fails for the same reason that shorter works outside the central pattern of the Poe tale also fail. *Pym* runs off in too many directions.

I do not detect anything within the rambling frame of *Pym* which deserves to be called great, but there are patches of perfectly good writing. The opening pages, in which Pym's character is sketched and one of his adventures with his friend Augustus related, are effective. Arthur is a familiar Poe type, another narrator with an "enthusiastic temperament, and somewhat gloomy, although glowing imagination." (III, 17) But what differentiates this book from the best of the stories which share this type of hero is that Pym's peculiar characteristics, far from being utilized throughout the work to give it intensity, tend to disappear as one reads along. A similar change occurs in *Mardi*, for after Melville gets his hero to Mardi, Taji gradually fades out of the story; the long conversations in the allegorical section are carried primarily by the narrator's Mardian companions, and Taji's quest for Yillah become almost a token reason for visiting the islands, to be revived only at the novel's close in an ending which seems almost as much an afterthought as the ending of *Pym*.

The story line of *Pym* is so filled with wild adventure and narrow escape that, beyond wondering why Poe bothered to introduce him so elaborately, one soon forgets Pym's personality. The adventure passages are passably well handled, although Poe certainly never rivaled the great authors of sea-adventure stories. He did, however, plunge whole-heartedly into the traditions of the craft. In the pages around Chapter VII, to pick one example, he kills off characters at a great clip in the lustiest *Mutiny on the Bounty* manner. All the familiar elements of a sea story are present; there are a mutiny, several fights, and a starvation scene, complete even to cannibalism, but it is clear in any one of them that Poe is attempting to adapt his short story techniques to a longer piece, and not succeeding very well. At the close of the story, he again changes his manner; the last chapters are science fantasy, and hardly related to what comes before--indeed, Pym and his companion, Peters, are about the only characters who survive from the earlier portions. These chapters involve a different ship, a new crew, and adventure in the Antarctic. Since very little was known about the region, Poe was able to give free rein to his imagination; he invented a strange island, placed upon it a new race of men, killed off another shipload of sailors, and sent his hero floating over milky seas toward a steaming South Pole. The hints Poe drops that the natives are on islands known to the Egyptians, together with his increased use of whiteness as the adventurers proceed southward, make these pages fairly interesting. The island discovered had no white upon it; the natives, in fact, feared and worshipped white, but as Peters and Pym, having escaped from the island, drift southward with the captive Nu-Nu, they drift into a world of white, and the novel closes with a passage we have mentioned before:

> And now we rushed into the embraces of the cataract, where a chasm threw itself open to receive us. But there arose in our pathway a shrouded human figure, very far larger in its proportions than any dweller among men. And the hue of the skin of the figure was of the perfect whiteness of snow. (III, 242)

The last chapters might succeed in raising a goose-pimple or two upon admirers of this type of science fantasy, but they seem out of place in what started out to be a sea novel.

  Sidney Kaplan argues that this close of *Pym* is an allegory indicating that "...the scriptural-genetic defense of slavery" rests upon nothing less than the will of God.[13] His case is, I think, quite impressive. Poe's feelings about Negroes are ugly, and the elements in the intellectual atmosphere which Kaplan says contributed to this section of the novel were without question familiar to and influential upon Poe. I am not so sure that Poe was really "a Biblical fundamentalist of the most orthodox sort" (xxiii). It would be more accurate to say that he was so when he was being stuffy in print. One can't honestly construct anything religiously systematic by quoting Poe, because these proper and orthodox statements, often delivered in the snobbish tone he used in his editorial magazine work (the "Marginalia," the "Pinakidia" "Autography," etc.) conflict so strongly with the mystical beliefs evident in so many tales, sketches, critical pieces and in *Eureka*. When Poe speaks of "The Human Aspiration for Supernal Beauty," as he does in "The Poetic Principle," he speaks as a romantic and a transcendentalist (small "t"), and we know that he understands the theological implications of his aesthetics. As we noted in Chapter VI, Poe seems another of the numerous Western authors since Blake who have flirted with occultism, and in his case the flirtation gives every evidence of having become very serious.

Poe's bigotry may seem curiously inconsistent with the high ideals of his artistic theory, but it is unquestionably a part of the man. Perhaps his pose as a southern gentleman in some manner involved both religious fundamentalism and bigotry: as though any aristocrat would know that Blacks were inferior, and would also regard religious liberalism as foolish and pernicious heresy. In reality, of course, aristocracy has nothing to do with this complex of ideas. Today we know about the connection between such attitudes and the Southern psyche, and Poe's attitudes seem all too familiar to us. To intolerance and fundamentalism we can also add a particular snickering nastiness which is present both in Poe and in a type of more modern Southerner. One of the most useful services which Marie Bonaparte performed was to explain the "dirty" implications of some of Poe's writing. I say "dirty" instead of "sexual" to differentiate this level of discussion from her more general Freudian reading of his works. She tells us, for example, that we are to read "penis" for "nose" in the tale "Lionizing." I am certain that she is right, and that, in such cases, Poe's obscenity is intentional. We do not need her analysis of Poe's supposed sexual inadequacy, though we may choose to believe that, too;

there is enough evidence of an entire syndrome without it. We no longer are surprised to find people who are bigots, who profess fundamentalist beliefs, and whose imaginations run to nastiness, but it is surprising to find all three characteristics of this cast of mind in an artist and an intellectual. Poe's biography gives us clues as to why they are there, but they are unquestionably there.

We have already noted that when one is steeped in the popular culture and issues of Poe's day, one hears their echoes continually in his work. It is thus altogether reasonable to suppose that Poe tucked an allegory on race into *Pym*. Kaplan is very sly about not connecting his good explication of this portion of the novel with his review of critical attitudes towards the book as a whole. He goes over a century of criticism, concluding with the favorable opinions of Davidson, Levin and Patrick Quinn, but does not tie his analysis of the close of the book to their opinions. I would guess that he sees their illogic and wants simply to make his contribution uncontroversially. He says very little about the rest of the novel. Perhaps he would agree with Poe's own statement, which he quotes, that *Pym* is "a very silly book" (viii).

Kaplan's explanation raises one difficult problem. His contention that black is bad and white is good makes it necessary that we understand that as Pym is carried toward the white figure, he is about to be saved. The figure is God. The native Nu-Nu ("to deny") dies at the moment of approach, which makes Kaplan's thesis seem more plausible, yet every reader takes the final event to involve supernatural horror and mystery. Although Pym supposedly survives to tell the tale to Poe, many readers take the ending to mean that he is killed.

Kaplan quotes S. Foster Damon, who thought so, and adds "[!]" to the quotation to clarify the issue: "'The nature of the horrible whiteness which sucked Gordon Pym down to his death [!] at the South Pole.'" (xv) Damon is a distinguished scholar, not prone to errors of simple reading. That he makes one as basic as this suggests that Poe's ending so strongly implies disaster, not salvation, that even good readers are fooled. If Poe intended the close to show Pym saved, in the embrace of God, he failed to get across the idea or the emotion involved.

The closing scene has been cited as the prime example of the novel's greatness, but while it is true that one can build an

impressive argument for it on symbolic grounds, it is also true
that it does not strike one as a great passage when one first
comes upon it. Things have been getting whiter as Pym moves
southward; now here is a white man. The reader innocent of
Kaplan's analysis can only assume that Poe was trying hard, as
he wrote the last chapters, to think of something to do with the
whiteness, and that, unable to devise anything, decided instead
to intensify what he had on hand to a pitch which might be a
little impressive, and let it go at that.

Very little in *The Narrative of A. Gordon Pym* can really
be said to develop. Mr. Davidson, as we noted, suggests that the
story is about a boy's maturing, but he also says that Pym
emerges from the action of the book "the same as he went
into" it. (127) It is difficult to reconcile the two, especially if
one adds to them Mr. Davidson's other generalizations, that the
progress of the story reveals Pym's heightened powers of
perception, and that Pym gradually fades out of the book.

Even Poe's documentation is open to criticism. There is
another and less favorable comparison to Melville which will be
useful here. If one tried to match *Pym* and *Moby Dick* in terms
of the use made of such material, it would quickly become
evident that, even on this mechanical level, Poe's book is a
sloppy job. To the reader who has in mind the masterful
manner in which Melville makes his chapters on sea-lore and
cetology work for him, for example, a documentary passage
such as the one in Chapter Six of the Poe seems terribly weak, a
haphazard collection of odds and ends inserted to add authen-
ticity, to fill space, to impress the reader, but not for any
important structural or dramatic reason. For all the use that Poe
makes of the importance of packing a hold correctly, he might
have made his point in a sentence, instead of covering several
pages. When Melville brings up a point of this sort, as in his
discussion of hemp, one can be sure that he has a reason, and
that somewhere in the book the strand will be picked up. The
documentary material in Poe's Chapter Sixteen is a little more
functional; it serves somewhat as a preparation for the
adventure to come, though not in any profoundly symbolic
sense.

It is true that several of the "preoccupations"--that is,
those repeated horrible elements which are supposed to reflect
Poe's morbid subconscious machinery--crop up in *Pym*. Pym is

twice buried alive, once when he hides in the hold as a stowaway, and once when he is trapped underground on the mysterious island. No connection between the two experiences is suggested; indeed, one half suspects that Poe, when he wrote the second, had forgotten the first. If he were really obsessed with fear of entombment, or even very interested in it, why did he not, in the second case of it in the same work, at least refer back to the first, if only to give his work some weak semblance of unity? Writers of serial novels who publish the first installments before the last are written, frequently come to passages which they wish they had more thoroughly prepared, but they usually make at least some effort to "cash in" on the earlier instance of whatever it is they are treating. Poe was not even this careful.

Once one has read one of the short stories in which Poe handles burial alive, one fears burial alive, just as most of us fear sharks. I have never seen a shark (excluding a sand shark I once brought up on a drop line while fishing), but I am terribly afraid of the things. Herman Melville and the authors of the numerous "I Spent a Month on a Raft in the South Pacific" books which came out during the Second World War are to blame. I am sure that Poe feared premature emtombment; he had read a good deal about it during the period in which he steeped himself in popular magazine literature. In his case, it is literally impossible to determine the extent to which his fear was produced by personal traumatic experience, and the extent to which it derived, like my fear of sharks, from reading. Moreover, because he was a cash-hungry journeyman writer, Poe's choice of subject matter can not be explained entirely in psychoanalytical terms, and, indeed, there is no available evidence which will even support speculation regarding the *extent* to which his choice was unconscious.

Now, in his short stories, Poe could make a topic such as burial alive very effective and very haunting. "The Premature Burial," for instance, is a fine story. It opens by denying that it is a piece of "legitimate fiction," (V, 255) and spends its early pages documenting burial alive with a series of graded examples, each a trifle more horrifying than the preceding. In terms of the psychology of the reader, these are intended to lend credibility to what is to follow, and also to open up for the reader the awful possibilities of such a predicament. Such functional documentation, of course, contrasts sharply to the haphazard documentation in *Pym*. Toward the close of "The Premature Burial," the reader discovers that he is reading not an article on burial alive, but a personal anecdote in which he, because he thought it a factual essay, is more involved than is comfortable; he, too, is now afraid of premature burial. The narrator tells his tale, accounts for his experience in medical terms, and the tale, which had opened conversationally, closes impressively.

I do not see how one can say that *Pym* represents any sort of central document for Poe's preoccupation when a tale such as "The Premature Burial" exists. The tale is so much more effective than the novel that one feels that the burial theme was introduced twice in *Pym* only because Poe needed a good many dangerous situations, was running low, and did not care enough for his novel to bother to make the burials effective. Poe had premature burial remarkably under control for a man who supposedly was haunted by a fear of it. "The Premature Burial" will never rank as one of his great stories, but never was there a piece in which the reader's mental furniture was more carefully arranged by the author. Here is no emotional rush of terror-filled language, but a calculated, completely premeditated construction of a single effect. This is not to deny the possibility that there was something in the topic that struck a responsive chord in Poe, but if one insists that such a factor is really important, clearly one good tale of this sort is worth a dozen *Pyms*. It will serve much better as a "central document."

Although *The Narrative of A. Gordon Pym* is superficially complete, its lack of development gives to it the general feel of a fragment. Had Poe thought it out more carefully in advance, or, lacking that, even bothered to write more carefully within each of the better episodes, this would not be so. Perhaps an example from one of the more interesting passages will be useful as an illustration. In Chapter XXIII, Pym and his companion at this point, Peters, explore the caves in which they have been locked by the landslide which the natives precipitated upon their unfortunate shipmates. Poe offers sketches of the shapes of the caves, and hints that some "singular-looking indentures" (III, 225) in the wall of one section may be writing of some sort. His hero, Pym, does not think so, but in the "note" which closes Poe's book, we are told that the engravings are indeed writing. The fragments are tentatively translated "To

be shady," "To be white," and "The region of the south." The
"characters" are reproduced for the reader's edification, and the
first group ("To be shady") has in it "letters" which, if one
looks back a few pages, exactly match the shape of the caverns
Pym sketched. (III, 244-145) The "Note" speaks of Ethiopian
and Egyptian roots for these words. In the last pages of the
"Narrative" proper, as Peters, Pym, and their native captive
float on the milky Antarctic Ocean, the two adventurers
question Nu-Nu and discover that there are "eight islands in the
group--that they were governed by a common king, named
Tsalemon or *Psalemoun....*" (III, 239)

We are dealing here with a standard device of science
fantasy, the vague hint of mysterious historical presences. All
this is supposed to produce in the reader an awed feeling. The
Egyptian words and King Solomon are intended to set off a
thousand speculations. Are these natives a lost tribe of Israel?
(That seems especially doubtful, but it does occur to one.) Are
the caves in reality Solomon's fabled mines? Is there a passage
from the South Pole to the Middle East? We have mentioned
that the idea of a great opening at the poles was seriously
entertained during Poe's day. Indeed, one of the factors which
influenced an American Congress during the nineteenth century
to finance an expedition to the far south was just this old
tradition that the earth was, in fact, open at the ends. Poe had
picked the right part of the world for a setting.

But there is a difference between this and most science
fantasy. "Pym's" introductory notes and "Poe's" editorial note
at the close form an improvised frame for the tale, and, taken
together, give to the whole narrative the aspects of another
hoax. Fantasy usually stands on its own; if it is any good at all,
it will hold its readers on the merits of its material and
treatment. The hoax element was evidently introduced here
because Poe was aware of the weakness of the tale itself, and
wished to bolster it up at both ends. To make things worse, the
two notes to the reader are inconsistent. The first, which
purports to be by Pym, says that he has placed his manuscript
in Poe's hands. The latter, by Poe-posing-as-editor-of-the-
manuscript, regrets the fact that no trace remains of the last
chapters. We will never know, he says in effect, because poor
Pym is dead. But according to the prefatory note, Pym and Poe
had worked together closely. When the tale first began to

appear in serial form, it was presented as fiction, but, says Pym,
Mr. Poe and I decided to be frank about it, and to admit that it
is a true story. If so, one wants to ask, and if Poe worked over
the manuscript with you, why doesn't he remember how it
ended?

There is a certain playfulness inherent in these notes. Poe
was leaving open the possibility that the entire affair was a
grand joke on his readers. Such behavior on the part of the
author of a serial was not unusual in the last century, and critics
of writers like Dickens have a good deal of fun with the author's
occasional references to his characters as though they were real
people. I think Hawthorne was amused by this procedure,
because in *The Scarlet Letter's* famous preface, "The Custom
House," he not only claimed to have found the documents
which recorded the story, but also to have the very letter. There
is a relationship between that passage, one of Dickens'
statements that he has not the heart to kill such-and-such a
character, and Poe's pose. But one can not chuckle good-
naturedly at the Poe passages as one can at the others.
Hawthorne's serve a clear function; he wants at least a hint of
credibility to come across. The letter still seems to produce a
burning sensation when one holds it to one's chest. Dickens'
reflect an author's hearty confidence in his art. Edgar Poe's
seem merely an unhappy attempt to salvage something from a
job poorly done. Even "Pym's" modest disclaimer--he hints that
the portions transcribed by Poe are better written than his
own--does not seem graceful; one feels that Poe is covering up
his sloppy workmanship.

If the *Narrative of A. Gordon Pym* is a "central document," then, it is one of a very peculiar sort. Though it contains
examples of an impressive number of ingredients found elsewhere in Poe's fiction, they are clearly not evidence either that
Poe is in full control or that he is deeply committed to the work
at hand. Like the bad cook who has already put too many
expensive things into the pot to be willing to throw the whole
out, Poe adds still more in a futile attempt to save a bad job.
And so his stew contains the usual sensitive narrator, burial
alive, adventure on the high seas, anthropological science
fiction, science fantasy, and the hoax. Not one ingredient has
been properly prepared, though each has remained painfully
visible beneath the sleazy surface. Because of the half-hearted

manner in which each is handled, it only adds to the unsavory lumpiness of the final product. *Pym* is the central document of Poe's poor craftsmanship, and the best evidence that his usual recipe for fiction was the only one that consistently worked for him.

Pym, of course, does not represent his only attempt to break away from his tested formula; we have in this study noted several shorter works which will also serve as examples of his difficulty. At the opening of *Pym*, one thinks that the book is going to be an extended example of the tale of horror, a sort of trip round the world with a younger Roderick Usher. This is because Pym shares certain qualities with the perceiving characters of Poe's characteristic good fiction; he is sensitive, morbid, and, as several critics have noted, a hunter of doom. Poe might have used Pym as the usual supersensitive artist-perceiver--indeed, I think that was his original intention--instead of allowing him to fade from the story. Such a plan might have produced an interesting novel. Pym, we may suppose, would have been thrown by his experiences into increasingly sensitive states of mind. As the experiences became stranger, so would the narrator, until, at the tale's conclusion, Poe would have had a narrator whose madness might account for the nature of the wonders he perceived. Pym complains loudly about the agonies he undergoes, but I see no continuing development. Poe instead uses trite formulas (Pym's suffering repeatedly "cannot adequately be imagined") which do not vary throughout the work.

The Pym of the opening pages is snobbish, moody and sensitive, the very type of the narrators of the horror tales who are so frequently in Poe the perceivers of the wild beauty. *Pym* might have grown from this portrait of the artist as a young man to a final vision of the world through the eyes of a man of whom the outer wonders have made a kind of Usher. Then might the incidents of the adventure truly seem a reflection of an inner wonder; then would "Poe's Imaginary Voyage" seem the monumental work it is supposed to be.

In saying that *Pym* is a failure, we are not saying anything very terrible about Poe's stature. There is no reason that, because we are interested in Poe, we should become biased advocates of everything he wrote. Structural analysis, reader response and common sense all tell us that this is not a good book, but we can learn almost as much from a writer's failures as from his successes. In a general sense, it is probably safe to say that Poe's peculiar mentality did not lend itself well to the form of the adventure-novel. In the more specific terms in which the present study has been operating, we can say that the cluster of closely-related ideas and procedures which we have seen in all of his successful work seem to be absent from *Pym*, or insufficiently realized. Poe's taste, which ran to the complex and the outré; his aesthetic, which involved the creation of the beautiful effect; and his artistic philosophy, which was based upon the romantic assumption of transcendent inspiration, determine the content, structure and technique of his best fiction. The beautiful effect is what the sensitive character perceives; the manner in which the perception takes place determines the plot; the philosophical implication, whether or not in a given story Poe chooses to emphasize it, is that the inspired mind can transcend the usual limits of consciousness to glimpse a deeper and more complex, but beautiful and unified reality which is the real source of both ultimate truth and artistic beauty. In *Pym*, these component traits of Poe's successful formula appear only in fragmentary form. What is more striking, they do not interact. The "outer wonders" are there in pretty good supply, and Pym himself is an appropriately hypersensitive observer, but the outer wonders do not become ambiguously equated with his acute sensitivity in the manner which we have seen so frequently. Instead, Poe allows us to forget Pym's personality while he racks his brain for new adventures through which he can run a hero so unimportant by the middle of the novel that he might as well be called "What's-his-name."

Pym is thus in a curious sense reassuring evidence that our sweet science of literary criticism is not the sterile or mechanical field we sometimes, in our insecure moments, fear it is. We have been claiming an organic unity and a high level of craftsmanship for the best of Poe's works, which makes them succeed in spite of the fact that changing tastes have made his prose style and his subject matter seem very foreign to modern sensibilities. We can analyse these good works, demonstrating the relationship between structure, content and meaning, but we have difficulty with the poor ones. There is some satisfaction in knowing that the ones which are fertile to analysis are also the ones that hold their audiences, in spite of changing tastes. I have used my good students to check the accuracy of this estimate. Students are a wonderful resource. Their honest reactions are a way of keeping one's judgment in touch with the everyday world in which literature ultimately operates. I have tried sending them to *Pym* primed to like it, telling them how much certain critics think of it (W. H. Auden's remarks[14] impressed them particularly), and building their curiosity (few of them know that Poe once wrote a novel). No good; they come to class a few days later displeased with the book and even a little angry with me for having misled them. On the other hand, no amount of negative thinking succeeds in convincing them that the better-constructed of the tales are really dated. They can see that the prose is preposterous; I have told them that the subject-matter is unoriginal, and quoted Yvor Winters' famous attack on Poe, yet they conclude (I am quoting a student literally), "If only adolescents like Poe, I guess I'm an adolescent." It is interesting that the more sophisticated quickly come to see that most of the poetry is, as Poe says, merely experimental, not major, but nothing will shake their conviction that the tales are so rich and so beautifully contrived that they still come off in spite of the fact that almost any other example of extreme literary Gothicism seems of interest today only to scholars and antiquarians. I can think of no stronger tribute to Poe than the statement that his best work still has the ability to hold and move bright young readers. The great value of *Pym* is that, since it can not hold an audience, it indicates conclusively the importance of those elements in Poe's work present in his best tales and absent here.

-3-

Judaism, Plagiarism and the Wild West[15]

The gloomy and isolated character who figures in so many of Poe's best tales is, as we have seen, closely related to the ideal artist whom Poe portrayed in "The Landscape Garden." In Poe's one other attempt to write an extended piece of prose fiction he presented a character who in some ways represents a merger of artist and *isolato*. *Pym* is a frustrating book partially because Arthur Pym promises to be so much and disappears; the opening pages of "The Journal of Julius Rodman" are even more promising. I think in the figure of Julius Rodman Poe had a character who could have solved for him the problem of applying his short story technique to a long work of fiction. In reading the speculation above about what *Pym* might have been, the reader has perhaps been struck by the fact that to write such a book would have been, at best, an enormously difficult artistic task. What would be an appropriate tone of voice to maintain, say, while the narrator gradually went mad under the strain of the horrors within and without? And what of the adventures themselves? When the situation came up in a short story, Poe could leave matters ambiguous: the events are either real or the productions of a fear-racked mind. To achieve a transition from clear reality to such a state, and then to sustain it for the length of a novel, would have been a mighty job.

But with Rodman, Poe added certain extra elements which might have made the job possible. Rodman was a sensitive and lonely man, but these qualities were not entirely constitutional. He was more the Ellison and less the Usher, though he shared qualities with each. Poe may have been groping towards something which today would seem more obviously in the tradition of Melville and Hawthorne: he seems to have been tinkering with the reader's involvement not merely in strange states of consciousness and strange views of the external world, but in a fully-realized personality. It is striking even in much of Poe's best fiction how little attention is paid to what might be called conventional interest in character. It is true that what Poe projects in the fantasies which compose his plots is often psychologically valid; he knows a good deal about states of consciousness, about the way a disturbed mind responds, about subconscious associations, and so forth. Moreover, he uses such insights in all of his major work. But while the reader often feels that the world which the character sees is an accurate reflection of the character's inner state, he seldom feels committed to the character in exactly the manner in which he does when reading most fiction. Indeed, a critical reader has good reason to wonder whether the character is not often merely a device to make the expressionistic effect, the "outer wonder," possible and credible.

Now, "character development," to use the old-fashioned term, is clearly less often important in short stories than in novels,[16] but Poe's apparent indifference to the involvement of his readers in his characters is striking even when his tales are compared to other short fiction. He wants his readers involved in his tales, to be sure, but often the character's main function seems merely structural: he is a lens through which Poe can project a special view of "reality." Distortion in the character will produce distortion in "reality."

Is this merely a way of saying that Poe deals with an abnormal world, and that it is hard to identify with abnormal characters in it? To some extent, but even writers who deal with fantasy or near-fantasy generally give us more in their characters. *Moby Dick* walks the thin line between realism and "romance," and Ahab is as mad a visionary as any in Poe, but we remain interested in his personality. Indeed, we become more intensely interested as the book goes on. And whenever we are sure that Ishmael is speaking, we feel his personality in a way we never do, say, in the case of the narrator in Poe's "The Pit and the Pendulum."

Julius Rodman may well be an incipient Ishmael. Like Ishmael, who went to sea whenever it was "a damp, drizzly November" in his soul, or whenever his "hypos got...an upper hand," Rodman went to the wilderness to seek escape.

> The hunting and trapping designs, of which he speaks himself, in the beginning of his Journal, were, as far as we can perceive, but excuses made to his own reason, for the audacity and novelty of his attempt....He was urged solely by a desire to seek, in the bosom of the wilderness, that peace which his peculiar disposition would not suffer him to enjoy among men. He fled to the desert as to a friend. (IV, 10-11)

Whether Poe would have elaborated along the line suggested by that splendid last sentence it is impossible to say, for he never finished the story. But Julius Rodman possesses many of the characteristics of an "isolato." He is, for example, a Jew, and as such the only character in Poe this writer can recall, with the possible exception of the narrator of "The Pit and the Pendulum," whose religion has such direct relation to his psychological make-up. His background reenforces the theme; he is a wanderer, out of contact with society. After members of the Rodman family came to America, Poe says in his introduction to the Journal proper, they

> first settled in New York; but afterwards made their way to

Kentucky, and established themselves, almost in hermit fashion, on the banks of the Mississippi near where Mills' point now makes into the river. Here old Mr. Rodman died, in the fall of 1790; and, in the ensuing winter, both his daughters perished of the small-pox, within a few weeks of each other. Shortly afterwards (in the spring of 1791), Mr. Julius Rodman, the son, set out upon the expedition which forms the subject of the following pages. (IV, 11)

Poe's introduction is interesting. Besides the portrait of Rodman, it contains a long summary of the various expeditions which had been made to the far west, which Poe culled from other books.[17] He presents his story as though it were a factual account of a real trip; in a sense, this is another one of his hoaxes, and the introductory material serves to make the whole seem veracious. But in this case the hoax is directed to ends more questionable than usual. Poe is not merely trying to fool his readers; he is trying to swindle them. And Poe's plagiarism seems especially objectionable in this work, because "Rodman" promises so much. The characters who surround Rodman could have been made into as colorful and as meaningful a cast as walked the decks of the *Pequod*.

In the early pages of the work, Poe's borrowing seems less objectionable. He was picking up traditional elements of this sort of narrative, selecting character types he thought might be useful later. His crime becomes serious later, when the time comes to describe their adventures, and he turns to the glue-pot rather than the inkstand. But at the outset, one feels that these characters could have forced Poe into a type of realistic writing one is not accustomed to finding in his work. A splendid foil to the sensitive Rodman would have been John Greely, who

> had the reputation of being the strongest man, as well as the best shot, in Kentucky....He was full six feet in height, and of most extraordinary breadth across the shoulders, with large strongly-knit limbs. Like most men of great physical strength, he was exceedingly good-tempered, and on this account was greatly beloved by us all. (IV, 25)

Then there are five Canadians,

> good boatmen, and excellent companions, as far as singing French songs went, and drinking, at which they were preeminent....

Toby, a Negro, is presented as a loyal old servant, and comes into prominence later, in a passage lifted from one of Poe's sources,[18] when his appearance astonishes some friendly Indians.

The scene is based upon the humor of racial stereotype; it is true also that Poe would repeat southern arguments about Negroes. One could argue that this racist humor, for such it is, seems less objectionable in Poe than it would today. Indeed, considering that other stereotype--of Poe himself as brooding drug addict--its common coarseness is almost refreshingly offensive.

> At first they doubted the evidence of their own eyes, spitting upon their fingers and rubbing the skin of the negro to be sure that it was not painted. The wool on the head elicited repeated shouts of applause, and the bandy legs were the subject of unqualified admiration. A jig dance on the part of our ugly friend brought matters to a climax. Wonder was now at its height. Approbation could go no further. Had Toby but possessed a single spark of ambition he might then have made his fortune for ever by ascending the throne of the Assiniboins, and reigning as King Toby the First.

Thornton, another member of the expedition, is a fine story teller; he and his dog, Nep, provide another humorous scene. Thornton has been telling some pretty tall tales of adventure with the Indians:

> Whenever any particularly incredible circumstance was related, Thornton would gravely refer to him as a witness. "Nep," he would say, "don't you remember that time? "--or "Nep can swear to the truth of that--can't you, Nep? "--when the animal would roll up his eyes immediately, loll out his monstrous tongue, and wag his great head up and down, as much as to say: "Oh, it's every bit as true as the Bible." Although we all knew that this trick had been taught the dog, yet for our lives we could not forbear shouting with laughter, whenever Thornton would appeal to him. (IV, 40-41)

One would be grossly overstating the case if one called Poe, on the basis of this one passage, a writer of tall tales, but Poe was obviously sufficiently acquainted with native traditions of humor to recognize and appreciate a good liar when he ran across one.

One other character deserves mention.

> His name was Alexander Wormley, a Virginian, and a very strange character. He had originally been a preacher of the gospel, and had afterwards fancied himself a prophet, going about the country with a long beard and hair, and in his bare feet, haranguing every one he met. This hallucination was now diverted into another channel, and he thought of nothing else than of

finding gold mines in some of the fastnesses of the country. Upon
this subject he was as entirely mad as any man could well be; but
upon all others he was remarkably sensible and even acute. He
was a good boatman, and a good hunter, and as brave a fellow as
ever stepped, besides being of great bodily strength and swiftness
of foot. (IV, 26)

A right good crew, all told--a group of colorful Canadian
boatmen, a "faithful old Negro," a teller of tall tales, a veritable
Bulkington of a man, very much like the type of "handsome
sailor" Melville describes at the opening of *Billy Budd*,
physically impressive, good natured, and immensely popular
among his fellows[19]--and, in command of the expedition, a
Wandering Jew.

But, of course, "Rodman," in the state in which Poe left it
to us, cannot be defended. We noted, in comparing Poe to other
American authors, that it is to his credit that he was not heavily
dependent upon his sources in his best work. As one reads
through the very extensive literature which discusses those
works which influenced him, one becomes convinced that what
Poe created was really very different from and artistically far
superior to what had come before. Why, then, in this promising
work, did he resort to unethical practices? If we can not defend
what Poe did in "Rodman," we can at least understand his
motivation: plagiarism must be a strong temptation to a writer
continually pressed for copy.

In the older studies of Poe, when he is attacked, it is
usually on grounds of drunkenness, dope addiction, or behavior
even more unsavory. Since A. H. Quinn's labors in the maze of
biographical material, such attacks seldom seem justified. No
reputable scholar claims that Poe was a strong person, but the
time has probably come when we must shift our emphasis, both
in defense of Poe and in attacks upon him. His faults are
undeniable, but usually they can be explained in terms which, if
no more flattering, seem at least less unhealthy. The case of
"Rodman" strikes me as far more damaging to Poe's reputation
than any example of more blatant vices, but at least it can be
accounted for without speculation into aspects of his character
about which, in truth, we know next to nothing. Let us do Poe
the honor of attempting to account for characteristics of his
work in terms of the practical problems of a journeyman
author. I have attempted to use this method in the discussion of

the magazine environment; the results there were, on the whole, flattering to Poe. I would like to see the same procedure followed in cases in which it is obvious that Poe sinned.

The boldness of Poe's venture in "Rodman" has about it qualities which seem uncomfortably familiar. Poe, knowing there was a market for journals of voyages, set out to make one up. It reads like a journal because it is largely stolen from journals. There is something in the procedure which brings to mind the robber barons, the audacious and unethical manipulators of the years after the Civil War. We know that Poe was aware of unscrupulous methods and swindling; he devotes two very interesting tales, "The Business Man" and "Diddling," to the subject. Perhaps had Poe lived thirty or forty years later than he did, when unethical manipulations were being perpetrated on a scale far larger than in his day, he might have become a literary scoundrel of great magnitude. Certainly the barbaric methods of big business did carry over into unexpected fields; the Cope-Marsh war is a famous episode in the annals of, of all things, American paleontology. Perhaps had Poe been around at the time, they would have appeared in literature as well.

It is pleasanter to speculate about the sort of book "Rodman" might have been had Poe written the Indian fighting, nature description, and day-to-day account of the trip himself. We would not object to his going to sources for inspiration, and the task of unifying the book would have been more easily manageable than was the case in *Pym*.

Rodman, with his loneliness and his sensitivity, could have provided Poe with the greater flexibility which might have enabled an adventure story to succeed. In order to unify *Pym*, Poe would have had to make use of the more extreme traits of Arthur Pym. An extremely high-keyed tone would have had to be maintained; that would not have been necessary in "The Journal of Julius Rodman." It could have been a rambling and more genial book, alternating whatever adventures Poe could create with passages of description in the general manner of "The Landscape Garden," although, of course, here nature could not be so artificially arranged. Poe, however, was capable of superimposing his special vision of beauty upon an unaltered landscape. Patrick Quinn makes a good deal of a slight sketch, "The Island of the Fay," in which Poe does just that.[20] And perhaps the characteristics of the isolated seeker which Rodman possesses might have been used to produce a significant contribution to the tradition of the picaresque novel. But whatever its structure, it would have had our interest in the personality of Rodman to lend a tone not present elsewhere in Poe.

Indeed, the "Journal of Julius Rodman" may be thought of in some senses as an interesting document of a major change in the tenor of romantic fiction. In much of earlier romanticism, it seems reasonable to say that personality is subservient to structure or to effect. The imagination of the artist produces something which he wants to project; he then designs a personality which will enable him to project it. This is true, for example, in almost any Gothic novel. Terribly strong examples of it appear also in the deeply sick world of the Marquis de Sade, where personalities are almost entirely a series of devices on which to hang erotic fantasies. Many writers have noticed the troublingly close relationship between Poe's approach and Sade's. So far as I know, the fact that there exists also this technical similarity has not yet been spelled out. In the bulk of later romantic and modern fiction, in contrast, personality is presented largely for its own sake. Poe is intellectually far more adventurous than most of his romantic contemporaries; indeed, than most of his successors. But in this one matter, he was never able to make the transition to the newer kind of fiction. Contrast Poe to Dickens, to Trollope, to Melville, to Dostoevski, to James, to any of a widely assorted list of very different writers and the contrast becomes immediately clear.

I like to think that in "Rodman" Poe originally intended to attempt the transition, and there is considerable evidence in Rodman's personality to suggest that the idea occurred to Poe. Julius Rodman was to have been the ideal poet on the road. Here is Rodman's description of a scene he admires:

> I...was enchanted with the voluptuous beauty of the country. The prairies exceeded in beauty anything told in the tales of the Arabian Nights. On the edges of the creeks there was a wild mass of flowers which looked more like Art than Nature, so profusely and fantastically were their vivid colors blended together. Their rich odor was almost oppressive. Every now and then we came to a kind of green island of trees, placed amid an ocean of purple, blue, orange, and crimson blossoms, all waving to and fro in the wind. These islands consisted of the most majestic forest oaks,

> and, beneath them, the grass resembled a robe of the softest green velvet, while up their huge stems there clambered, generally, a profusion of grape vines, laden with delicious ripe fruit. The Missouri, in the distance, presented the most majestic appearance; and many of the real islands with which it was studded were entirely covered with plum bushes, or other shrubbery, except where crossed in various directions by narrow, mazy paths, like the alleys in an English flower-garden; and in these alleys we could always see either elks or antelopes, who had no doubt made them. (IV, 41-42)

Rodman sees the West as Ellison sees his landscape garden; the preconceptions which shape nature to the ideal pattern are the same. If we must have Poe-masks, here is the best mask of all. What Rodman might have been--the lonely but exquisitely sensitive poet, seeing the world through his special bias--is what Poe might have been. What "Rodman" is--unsatisfactory, incomplete, a fragment of its own potentialities--is what Poe's career turned out to be. "The Journal of Julius Rodman," like other episodic novels, could have been symbolic of the journey of the perceptive soul through life. Let us for the moment try to forget that what Poe called beauty seems to us peculiar, and that what men of his cast of mind expected of "Nature" is not what we expect, and read Poe's sketch of Rodman as it was intended, a promise of things to come.

> He was possessed with a burning love of Nature; and worshipped her, perhaps, more in her dreary and savage aspects, than in her manifestations of placidity and joy. He stalked through that immense and often terrible wilderness with an evident rapture at his heart which we envy him as we read. He was, indeed, *the man* to journey amid all that solemn desolation which he, plainly, so loved to depict. His was the proper spirit to perceive; his the true ability to feel. (IV, 13-14)

The promise was unfulfilled, but Rodman was to have been Poe's Seeker as clearly as Ahab was Melville's. Ahab sought truth, and Rodman beauty.

Epilogue

He Fled to the Desert as to a Friend

Tel qu'en Lui-meme enfin l'eternite le change
Stéphane Mallarmé, "Le Tombeau d'Edgar Poe"

We opened our study with a fragment; we have closed with
a fragment. The first, "The Light-House," promised to conform
to that pattern which we have used to link the tales. The latter
promised to transcend it, to open new paths. Poe never trod the
new paths. For him the road ended on the second floor of the
Washington College Hospital on October 7, 1849. It ended
abruptly, like a story in which the author has lost interest.

What can we conclude? What do we say about his life,
about his place in literary history, about his worth as an artist?

About his life we know less now than we thought we knew
thirty years ago. Our certainty about his really bad behavior has
disappeared. In its place we have somewhat more information
about the business side of his literary operations and about his
relations with some of his contemporaries. This book has not
been about his life, for the most part, but to the extent that our
examination of the works has biographical implications, it
would seem to suggest that he was somewhat more a craftsman,

261

somewhat less a madman, than the older stereotype would allow. The subjects of his tales still seem strange, still seem psychologically revealing, but this fact is tempered by three things: 1.) The literary environment. We know where his subjects came from. 2.) His craftsmanship. There can be no question, in his good work, of his control over his material. 3.) His aesthetic, which would have given him reason to deal with consciousness-beyond-death, with madness, with drugs and nightmares even had he been a perfectly stable person. We can, in short, provide plausible and normal professional or artistic motivation for almost everything he did in his art. But to tell the truth, reasonable motivations alone will never convince us that we are dealing with a reasonable personality. We sense that, however naive their methodology, there was a large measure of truth in the older Freudian interpretations of Poe. When one lives with Poe for a long period of time, reading trivia as well as major pieces, reading material in the magazines around him as well as his own work, one sometimes feels on the verge of knowing the man. The sensation never lasts; the next letter, the next story or squib, could not have been written by the fellow one was visualizing.

His place in literary history, in contrast, seems perfectly clear. Poe is one of those writers who remind us that Romanticism was not merely rebellion. It was not even merely rebellion against reason, an assault of the heart against the head. Rather, it was for some artists deeply conservative, an attempt to restore art to the place it had held in all but modern Western societies. Poe was among those artists who understood, long before the anthropologists explained it to the rest of us, that in most cultures art and magic and religion and science are indistinguishable. He shared his view with a great many of his artistic contemporaries; indeed, he did more than most to make the implications of his world-view explicit.

About his worth as an artist we need several judgements. If one evaluates him in terms of his influence on later writers there cannot be much doubt that Poe is an artist of the first magnitude. We feel his force directly in Symbolism, we feel it at least indirectly (and often directly) in the modern poetic novel, in the entire genre of the short story, in commercial fiction from science-fiction and the detective story to the world of the slick magazines, in places as unexpected as Spanish-language *modernismo* and the mystical underside of naturalism, in writers as different as Baudelaire, T. S. Eliot, Norris, Bellamy, Borges and Nabokov. To a surprising extent, the contemporary arts are in tune with Poe: our novelists are more than toying with mysticism; our cinema uses methods of psychological association which have clear precedent in Poe; our poets insist on the validity of transcendent inspiration (and, like Poe's heroes, will use artificial means if necessary to attain it); even our painters speak of themselves as lenses through which we may glimpse the great Unity in the great Diversity. We owe even the popular image of the artist (as a hungry fellow, scorning and scorned by society) largely to Edgar Poe, who has come to stand as a symbol of the alienation of the sensitive.

About the absolute worth of his literary output it is harder to reach a clear decision. Sometime ago, this writer was attacked in print for saying, in a review, that the author of a book on Poe was making a foolish judgment when he claimed, without qualifications, that Poe is the greatest American writer. The author of the book in question insisted angrily that literary worth is a matter of opinion, and that he was entitled to believe that Poe is our greatest writer. To tell the truth, if he had merely claimed that Poe is the American who has had the greatest impact upon world literature, I am not sure I would not agree. These things are hard to measure, but Poe's influence has been very great indeed. His work itself is much more difficult to evaluate. Much of it is minor, or dated, or too topical for the modern reader to follow. A sophisticated reader can demolish most of the poetry. We earlier mentioned Poe's own estimate of the poetry; the passage is worth quoting at length:

> In defence of my own taste...it is incumbent on me to say that I think nothing in this volume of much value to the public, or very creditable to myself. Events not to be controlled have prevented me from making, at any time, any serious effort in what, under happier circumstances, would have been the field of my choice. With me poetry has not been a purpose, but a passion; and the passions should be held in reverence; they must not--they cannot at will be excited with an eye to the paltry compensations, or the more paltry commendations, of mankind. (VII, xlvii)

It is tempting to apply what Poe says about his poems to his prose as well. Yet there are some very good poems, and plentiful evidence that Poe had the makings of a major poet.

Moreover, the "paltry compensations" did not so completely interfere with the tales as with the poems. (Had it not been for "paltry compensations," indeed, Poe might never have become a prose author.) There is a certain body of his prose, which, despite its relatively narrow range, despite its high-flown language and rhetoric, still retains the power to move readers. We are surprised, every time we return to some familiar tale which we think we know almost by heart, to see how much there is in it which we did not notice before, how skillfully it is put together, how rich are its philosophical implications. Yet clearly his medium prejudices us against him; it leads us to associate him with hacks rather than genuises. To call him the greatest writer since Shakespeare, as some critics do, does seem foolish to me. Yet Poe is better than most academic writers have been willing to admit. He deserves the large audience which he has continued to hold.

Poe means too much to us as Americans and as students of literature for us to go on using him to support questionable generalizations about our culture and about literary history. If there are things about him which we can never understand, there is much that we can handle quite comfortably. We can see very precisely how close are his ties to artistic and intellectual tendencies in his day; we can spell out his interests in popular culture as well. His sources we see plainly in the literature and sub-literature around him; his aesthetic thinking is clearly articulated, and generally exemplified in his work. Even the contradictions in his theoretical writing are easy to comprehend, and in no sense a barrier to understanding his feeling that the artist is at once seer and creator.

FOOTNOTES

Preface

1. I have discussed both works--Arthur Hobson Quinn's *Edgar Allan Poe: A Critical Biography* (New York, 1941), and Edward Wagenknecht's *E.A.P.: The Man Behind the Legend* (New York, 1963)--at some length in "Scholarly Strategy: The Poe Case," *American Quarterly*, XVII, 1 (Spring, 1965), 133-144.

2. *Ibid.* Since that article appeared, Burton R. Pollin has published the very best book-length study of influences on Poe: *Discoveries in Poe* (Notre Dame, Indiana, 1970). I recommend it.

3. "Edgar Allan Poe: A Crisis in the History of American Obscurantism," *American Literature*, VII (January 1937), 379-401.

4. *From Poe to Valery* (Washington, 1949).

5. The essay is Mr. Auden's "Introduction" to the Rinehart paper-back *Edgar Allan Poe: Selected Prose and Poetry* (New York, 1950), and is warmly recommended as a perceptive introduction to Poe. I find myself in disagreement in only one important matter; Mr. Auden thinks that Poe's *The Narrative of A. Gordon Pym* is a great book (vii). The quotations are from vi and vii.

The View from "The Light-House"

1. *The Selected Poetry and Prose of Edgar Allan Poe* (New York, 1951), 344-345. This is not, of course, contained in the Virginia Edition which we will use as a standard text for the other tales.

2. The most accessible location for this sketch is Norman Foerster, ed., *American Poetry and Prose*, 3rd ed. (Cambridge, Mass., 1947), pp. 598 ff.

3. Foerster quoted this from Hawthorne's notebooks, *ibid.*

4. See footnote 1, Preface.

Part One: The Aesthetic

Chapter One

1. "Our Cousin, Mr. Poe," *The Man of Letters in the Modern World: Selected Essays 1928-1955* (New York, 1955), p. 134.

2. See, for example, Norman Foerster, American Criticism: *A Study in Literary Criticism from Poe to the Present* (Cambridge, Mass., 1928), esp. 1-51; John Paul Pritchard, *Return to the Fountains: Some Classical Sources of American Criticism* (Durham, 1942); George Snell, "First of the New Critics," *Quarterly Review of Literature*, II (Summer, 1945), 333-340; Margaret Alteston, *Origins of Poe's Critical Theory* (Iowa City, 1925); Killis Campbell, "Poe's Reading," *University of Texas Studies in English*, V (October, 1925), 166-196.

3. James A. Harrison, ed., *The Complete Works of Edgar Allan Poe* (New York, 1902), XIV, 194-195. This is the "Virginia Edition," and will be referred to as Poe, *Works.* For the reader unable to obtain access to this edition, the author recommends Eric Carlson's intelligently organized

Introduction to Poe: A Thematic Reader (Scott, Foresman and Company, 1967). The author's own edition of the prose fiction will shortly be published by Bobbs-Merrill.

4. *Ibid.*, 290.

5. *Furioso*, VI (Summer, 1951), 45-54.

Chapter Two

1. Poe, *Works*, II, 229. The actual narrator of the tale is not, of course, the perceiving character. Most of the story comes in the words of the Norwegian, who is our real subject in this discussion.

2. *Romances of Herman Melville* (New York, 1931), pp. 1341-1342, hereinafter referred to as *Romances.*

3. See, for example, Floyd Stovall, "Poe's Debt to Coleridge," *University of Texas Studies in English*, Number 10 (July 8, 1930), 70-127, which contains an excellent summary of previous work on the subject; Coleridge's influence on Poe's critical thinking was especially strong. Indeed, Poe's critical writing often contains almost word-for-word borrowings from Coleridge. The article can also be recommended as a brief summary of Poe's critical position. Darrel Abel, "Coleridge's 'Life-in-Death' and Poe's 'Death-in-Life,'" *Notes and Queries*, CC (May, 1955), 218-220 deals primarily with "Berenice." Articles dealing with the sources of "Maelstrom" are Arlin Turner, "Sources of Poe's 'A Descent into the Maelstrom,'" *The Journal of English and Germanic Philology*, XLVI (July, 1947), 298-301, and Adolph B. Benson, "Scandinavian References in the Works of Poe" *JEGP*, XL (January, 1941), 73-90. Turner found a story in a French magazine similar in some ways to Poe's, and discussed also Poe's use of two articles in the *Encyclopedia Britannica;* the Benson article traces *Britannica's* sources.

4. Carroll D. Laverty, "Science and Pseudo-Science in the Writings of Edgar Allan Poe," Duke University Doctoral Dissertation, 1951, unpublished.

5. To the best of my knowledge, Mr. Griffith has not published a full exposition of this splendid approach. I am borrowing the phrases from my notes of his lectures at Harvard during the academic year 1952-1953.

6. Since we are only going to discuss one of these tales at any length, it is worth noting that while these tales have, as I say, a common position in relation to Poe's method of using the perception-perceiver pattern, they are by no means of a piece in certain other aspects. There is a continual danger inherent in "grouping" Poe's tales; one is liable to imply that they are more stereotyped than they are. I find myself progressively more impressed with the variety he achieved even within as clear a group as these stories.

7. "Poe's 'Ligeia' and the English Romantics," *University of Toronto Quarterly*, XXIV (October, 1954), 8-25. The first page or two of this article imply what seems to me a marvelous feeling for Poe, and a fine over-all reading of his work, but as noted in footnote 5, Mr. Griffith has not expanded his idea in print.

8. *Poe: A Critical Study* (Cambridge, Mass., 1957), p.247, fn. 1.

9. *Selected Essays*, 143.

10. "The Interpretation of 'Ligeia,'" *College English*, V (April, 1944), 363-372.

11. *Selected Essays*, 139-140.

12. "The Universe of Roderick Usher," *Personalist*, XXXVII (Spring, 1956), 147-160.

13. *Ibid.,* 160.

14. "A Key to the House of Usher," *University of Toronto Quarterly,* XVIII (January, 1949), 176-185. For further indication of the range of interpretation, see J. O. Bailey, "What Happens in 'The Fall of the House of Usher,'" *American Literature,* XXXV (1964), 445-466; and Joseph Gold, "Reconstructing the 'House of Usher,'" *Emerson Society Quarterly,* No. 37, 74-76.

15. One of the most patient and scholarly of such studies is Ruth Leigh Hudson's "Poe's Craftsmanship in the Short Story," University of Virginia Doctoral Dissertation, 1935, unpublished. Miss Hudson makes few specific claims for the sources she discusses; her central point is rather that Poe was in the midst of a large-scale popular tradition. She says, "...the essential Poe can best be discovered by an examination of him and his literary backgrounds at the beginning of his career...." (629) The work, especially considering its date, is commendable for several reasons. For a discussion of the methodical manner in which Poe turned to fiction, see Chapter Two of Miss Hudson's thesis, pp. 79-248.

16. For a discussion of the type of current literature which might have provided material for this particular story, see D. L. Clark, "Sources of Poe's 'The Pit and the Pendulum,'" *Modern Language Notes,* XLIV (June 1929), 347 ff. Ruth Hudson discusses its sources in her thesis (cited above), pp. 102 ff. It would now seem obvious, thanks to the numerous "source" studies, that Poe's subject matter was not usually his own invention. This would seem to me at least partially to invalidate a great deal of that Freudian criticism which insists that Poe produced his art, so to speak, compulsively.

17. "The Angelic Imagination," *Selected Essays,* pp. 113-131. See especially p. 126.

Part Two: The Horror

Chapter Three

1. *The Complete Novels and Selected Tales of Nathaniel Hawthorne,* ed. Norman Holmes Pearson (New York, 1937), p. 920, hereinafter referred to as *Complete Novels.*

2. The story runs as follows. The narrator, sailing from Charleston to New York, is puzzled by the behavior of an artist friend, Wyatt. Wyatt is newly married, and supposedly has a beautiful and vivacious young wife. But he is depressed and moody. The woman introduced as his wife is neither beautiful nor vivacious. His travelling companions--his two usually cheerful and witty sisters--keep strangely to themselves. To add to the mystery, Wyatt has engaged three staterooms, when two--one for the sisters and one for himself and his wife--would seem to be sufficient. Most mysterious of all--although the narrator believes it to contain nothing but a painting--is an oblong box which Wyatt keeps in his room. When the narrator discovers that the supposed Mrs. Wyatt leaves Wyatt's room each night and sleeps in the extra room, he guesses that the couple is separating, and keeping the broken marriage secret, but he is still puzzled to hear Wyatt open the box each evening after she leaves. Wyatt, when asked jokingly about the box, had laughed hysterically and fainted.

The ship runs into a storm, the pumps fail, and the passengers and crew abandon it. Wyatt, in the lifeboat, insists on being taken back to get his oblong box; when this is refused, he jumps overboard, swims to the sinking ship, emerges with his box, lashes himself to it, and leaps into the sea. To the narrator's surprise, he sinks. The captain, because of the presence of Wyatt's sisters, refuses to explain the phenomenon to the narrator, but, a month later, when the narrator meets him in New York, he tells the whole story. Wyatt's wife had died, and Wyatt had wanted to return her body to her family. Because he knew that the passengers would object to having a corpse on board, he had her first embalmed, and then packed in salt in the box. Hence his distraction, and the sisters' loss of vivacity. The supposed wife was a serving maid acting the part of the wife, hence the extra stateroom.

3. See, for example, the collection of his short stories, *Someone Like You* (New York, 1953).

Chapter Four

1. *The French Face of Edgar Poe* (Carbondale, Ill., 1957), p. 254.

2. See Malcolm Cowley, "A Natural History of American Naturalism," in John W. Aldridge, ed., *Critiques and Essays on Modern Fiction, 1920-1951* (New York, 1951), pp. 370-387.

3. Marvin Felheim, "The Cask of Amontillado," *Notes and Queries*, CXCIX (October 1954), 447-448.

4. This is by Donald Pierce, in part III of the same article, 448-449.

5. See, for example, the tasteful treatment of water in Poe in the chapter "The Pool and the Portrait," pp. 257 ff. of Patrick Quinn's *The French Face*.

6. Sam Moon, "The Cask of Amontillado," *Notes and Queries*, CXCIX (October, 1954), 448.

7. Rene Wellek and Austin Warren, *Theory of Literature* (New York, 1956), p. 182.

8. Sam Moon; see footnote above.

9. *American Quarterly*, XIV (1962), 198-206.

10. A commonly accepted critical notion concerning Poe's settings is that they always depict an unreal, even sentient, environment. We might note parenthetically that Poe several times makes use of "normal" settings, if only to set off a narrator's intensity.

11. This reader finds the sustained tone broken only once, and then in a minor way. The narrator cracks a joke about how he got his servants out of the house by telling them to stay. Even this is functional in that it demonstrates Montresor's cynicism.

12. In point of fact, Amontillado is not an especially rare wine; it is now, and was in Poe's day, a readily available kind of sherry.

Part Three: The Environment

Chapter Five

1. A good example of it is the editorial chatter about "coming attractions" in XXI, 5 (Nov., 1842), 288.

2. First appearance: October, 1830; second appearance: May, 1831.

3. A fuller list of the magazines with which Poe did business is available in Charles F. Heartman and James R. Canny, *A Bibliography of the First Printing of the Writings of Edgar Allan Poe* (The Book Farm, Hattiesburg, Mississippi, 1940). Robert D. Jacobs' *Poe: Journalist and Critic* (Baton Rouge: Louisiana State University Press, 1969) is a recent detailed study of his editorial career.

4. *A History of American Magazines 1741-1855* (New York, 1930), 354.

5. *Ladies' Magazine* III, I (January 1830), 47. The review, presumably by the magazine's editor, Mrs. Sarah Josepha Hale, is quoted in Heartman and Canny, *A Bibliography*. Quinn (165) attributes it to her.

6. The context of Poe's remarks about the Boston lecture is, of course, not a place in which one would expect reasonable opinions. Poe was excruciatingly embarrassed by the Boston experience, and foolishly rushed into print again and again with rationalizations of what had happened. He claimed, finally, that he deliberately went to Boston to read trifling juvenilia, that these were accepted as high art by the frogpondians. But what he says about the quality of his early poetry, despite the context, seems of a piece with his famous preface to the last volume of poetry which he published, in which he said, I think with perfect candor, that he really thought that he had the ability to be a major poet, but had been so pressed all through his career by the practical problems of producing something saleable so as to make a living that the poems in the volume should best be regarded as ideas and experiments. I think that Poe, in that little preface, was trying to speak to posterity. We shall discuss these matters in a later chapter.

7. Mott, *A History*, pp. 344, 357. See also the good recent discussion of the influence of this copyright situation upon Poe's career in Sydney P. Moss' *Poe's Literary Battles: The Critic in the Context of his Literary Milieu* (Durham, N.C., 1963). See my review of it in *MASJ*, IV, 2.

8. These are from *The Anglo American: A Journal of Literature, News, Politics, The Drama, Fine Arts, etc.*, IX (1847). The system of capitalization is inconsistent.

9. *Ibid.*, 1 (Saturday, April 24, 1847), pp. 14-15.

10. For Melville's relation to the world of the magazinists, see Perry Miller's *The Raven and the Whale* (New York, 1956).

11. Mott, *A History*, p. 359.

12. XXI, 4 (October, 1842), facing page 156. It is, I believe, the cover of the issue, though the manner in which my copy is bound makes it difficult to be sure.

13. Facing page 288 in *Graham's* XXI, 6 (December, 1842).

14. *Atkinson's Casket*, XV, 1 (July, 1839) facing page one, accompanied by a poem by Miss E. H. Stockton. The drawing is by W. Danniell, R. A., the engraving by B. Woodman.

15. *Our American Music: Three Hundred Years of It* (New York, 1929-1958), Third Edition.

16. A good description of the contents of *Graham's* is in James Playsted Wood, *Magazines in the United States* (New York, 1949, 1956) 50-53.

17. John Tasker Howard, *Our American Music*, 164-168.

18. See footnotes 7 and 10 for the Moss and Miller volumes. Allen's (New York: Oxford University Press, 1968) offers excellent new evidence that magazinists had to understand how to appear to be elite artists while retaining journalistic standards of "popularity."

19. *Edgar Allan Poe: The Man Behind the Legend* (New York, 1963).

Chapter Six

1. A. H. Quinn, *E.A.P.*, 215.

2. Meredith Neal Posey, "Notes on Poe's *Hans Pfaall*," *MLN*, XLV (1930), pp. 501-507.

3. Chapter 9 of Pollin's treasure-trove of curious continuities in Poe, *Discoveries in Poe* (see footnote 2, Preface).

4. The major extant study of science in Poe, Carroll D. Laverty's

"Science and Pseudo-Science in the Writings of Edgar Allan Poe" (Duke University Doctoral Dissertation, 1951, unpublished) concerns itself primarily with the sources and nature of Poe's use of science and pseudo-science.

5. Poe, *Works*, V, 238. Mr. Laverty says that Poe lifted entire passages from the writings of balloonists. The references to equipment are authentic. The present passage seems to be Poe's own invention, although other writers had hypothesized the same phenomenon. Amusingly enough, one version says "concave," another "convex." Laverty, p. 146.

6. A writer who specializes in parodies of the genre is Arthur C. Clarke. See his *Tales from the White Hart* (New York, 1957), for example.

7. Yvor Winters, "Edgar Allan Poe: A Crisis in the History of American Obscurantism," *American Literature*, VIII (January, 1937), 401.

8. *Complete Novels*, p. 413.

9. The best-known discussion of Jefferson's world view and the science upon which it is based is Daniel Boorstin, *The Lost World of Thomas Jefferson* (New York, 1948). A paperback reprint is available: (Boston, 1960-1964).

10. See our discussion of "The Journal of Julius Rodman" in the concluding chapter. Poe actually plagiarized from Jefferson!

11. For a detailed description of the early scientific journals in the United States, see Donald de B. Beaver's "Altruism, Patriotism and Science," *American Studies*, XII, 1 (Spring, 1971), pp. 5-19.

12. *Romances*, p. 1618.

13. *Ibid.*, pp. 974-975.

Chapter Seven

1. For a brilliant discussion of the relationship between occultism and romanticism see John Senior's *The Way Down and Out: The Occult in Symbolist Literature* (Ithaca, N. Y., 1959). One of Mr. Senior's most convincing arguments concerns just this matter of when to take an artist seriously when he says that he is an occultist. The book is also the best scholarly reputable introduction to this intellectual tradition. See also my "'In the Mystical Moist Night Air'." *American Quarterly* XIV, 2 (Summer, 1962), 198-206. My thesis in that article is, briefly, that however much we may consider the occult view of the universe a crackpot view, a significant number of our important artists have either taken it seriously or believed in it wholeheartedly.

2. *The French Face of Edgar Poe* (Carbondale, Ill., 1957), p. 93.

3. "The Colloquy of Monos and Una," *Works*, IV, 202.

4. "The Poet," in Reginald L. Cook, ed., *Selected Prose and Poetry* (New York, 1955), pp. 316-317.

5. *A Pilgrim's Progress* (Boston, 1939).

6. "Self-Reliance," *Selected Prose and Poetry*, p. 177. The standard study of oriental mysticism in the works of Emerson is F. I. Carpenter, *Emerson and Asia* (Cambridge, Mass., 1930). I have corresponded with the author on this matter, and believe that he agrees with my interpretation.

7. Quoted in Valentine Williams, "The Detective in Fiction," *The Fortnightly Review*, CXXVIII (September, 1930), 381-392. This is a sprightly and informative article.

8. Robert Daniel, "Poe's Detective God," *Furioso*, VI (Summer, 1951), 49.

9. *Romances*, 742.

Part Four: Some Failures, Some Successes

Chapter Eight

1. Alfred Kazin.

2. Eric Larrabee, ed., *American Panorama* (New York, 1957).

3. *American Renaissance: Art and Expression in the Age of Emerson and Whitman* (New York, 1941). Yet Mr. Matthiessen contributed an extremely sensitive essay on Poe to *Literary History of the United States,* ed. Robert Spiller, Willard Thorp, Thomas Johnson, Henry Seidel Canby (Revised Edition, New York, 1953), pp. 321-342.

4. Lionel Trilling, in *American Panorama,* Entry 248, p. 267.

5. *The French Face of Edgar Poe, passim.*

6. My quotations from "Politian" are from the complete version published in the "Appendix" of Floyd Stovall's new *The Poems of E.A.P.* (Charlottesville, Virginia, 1965), 301-340. 325.

7. *Ibid.* 327. I have made the changes in spelling, though not in punctuation, which Stovall mentions on p. 348.

8. N. Bryllion Fagin, *The Histrionic Mr. Poe* (Baltimore, Md., 1949).

9. "The Origins of Hawthorne and Poe," Shelburne Essays, *First Series* (New York, 1904), pp. 51-70. See also Harry Levin, *The Power of Blackness: Hawthorne, Poe, Melville* (New York, 1958).

10. For an interesting discussion of a variant of this idea, see the essay "The Meaning of a Literary Idea," in Lionel Trilling, *The Liberal Imagination: Essays on Literature and Society* (New York, 1950), pp. 272-293, especially pp. 292-293.

11. I have elsewhere published a fuller discussion of the relationship between artist and audience in America: "Some Observations on the Concert Audience," *American Quarterly,* XV, 2 (Summer, 1963), 152-166.

12. For this idea I am indebted to Afred Kazin's lectures, mentioned above in fn. 1 of the present chapter.

13. A. H. Quinn, *Poe,* pp. 486 ff. Mr. Quinn also feels that this is a biographically significant story.

14. *Poe, A Critical Study,* 144.

15. *The French Face, passim.*

16. "Poe's Conception of Incident and Tone in the Tale," *Modern Philology,* XLI (May, 1944), 228-240.

17. *The Life and Works of Edgar Allan Poe.*

18. How little Poe makes of the most obvious moral problem which this story poses may perhaps be demonstrated by contrast. Consider, for example, the painful situation portrayed in "Roger Malvin's Burial," a Hawthorne tale which deals with the problem of leaving a dying friend (indeed, one's future father-in-law) when there is clearly no "practical" good to be achieved by remaining. Hawthorne's story is built around the subtleties of the moral situation, the implications of which he considered sufficiently troubling to justify a tragic conclusion. Poe's tale operates in the most general and impersonal terms; Hawthorne's in the specific and personal terms of a troubled man's conscience.

19. I am indebted for this idea to Professor Albert Van Nostrand of Brown University.

20. *The Life and Works of Edgar Allan Poe,* p. 463.

21. *Romances,* p. 853.

22. *Ibid.,* pp. 1341 ff.

23. "The Meaning of a Literary Idea," 290.

24. *Protestant--Catholic--Jew: An Essay in American Religious Sociology* (New York, 1955, 1960), especially Chapter V.

25. One commentator, discussing *Pym*, feels that it is concerned with theology, and that its position is fundamentalist. See Sidney Kaplan, "Introduction," *The Narrative of Arthur Gordon Pym* (New York, 1960); see also our discussion of *Pym* in Chapter IX.

26. Edited by W. Overholser (Cambridge, Mass., 1962).

Chapter Nine

1. *American Literature*, VIII (January, 1937), 379-401.

2. *New Shelburne Essays*, I (Princeton, 1928), 77-87.

3. *Pierre, or the Ambiguities* (New York, 1929), pp. 320-321.

4. *The Short Stories of Ernest Hemingway* (New York, 1938), p. 477.

5. Robert B. Heilman, *Modern Short Stories* (New York, 1950), p. 422.

6. *Leaves of Grass and Selected Prose*, ed. Sculley Bradley (New York, 1953), p. 35.

7. *The French Face*, p. 230.

8. I am indebted to Miss Jean Hardy for information about Poe's knowledge of contemporary treatment of the insane.

9. Because of the fact that one must carefully qualify the "meaning" of a tale the action of which is relatively simple, "The Man of the Crowd" rather strongly suggests Henry James' "The Beast in the Jungle." In each piece one discovers on reexamination that he is dealing with matters more subtle than were at first apparent.

10. Mr. Quinn's discussion of *Pym* in Chapter VI of *The French Face*, 169-215. It earlier appeared in *The Hudson Review* ("Poe's Imaginary Voyage," IV [Winter, 1952], 562-585).

11. *Poe*, p. 166.

12. For a full discussion of the sea-adventure chapters of *Mardi*, see my "Melville's 'Voyage Thither'," *Midwest Quarterly*, III, 4 (Summer, 1962), 341-353.

13. Sidney Kaplan, "Introduction," *The Narrative of Arthur Gordon Pym* (New York, 1960) vii-xxv. xxv.

14. From his "Introduction" to *E.A.P.: Selected Prose and Poetry* (Revised Edition, New York, 1955).

15. A good deal of the material in this section appears in my "Poe's *Julius Rodman*: Judaism, Plagiarism and the Wild West," *Midwest Quarterly*, I, 3 (Spring, 1960), 245-259.

16. Fred Lewis Pattee's *The Development of the American Short Story* (New York, 1923) is the standard older treatment of this subject.

17. For discussions of Poe's borrowings in this work, see Hervey Allen, *Israfel: The Life and Times of Edgar Allan Poe* (New York, 1927), II, p. 463, fn.; George E. Woodberry, *Edgar Allan Poe* (Boston, 1885), I, 235-236; H. A. Turner, "A Note on Poe's Julius Rodman," *University of Texas Studies in English* (July, 1930), 147-151; Polly Pearl Crawford, "Lewis and Clark's *Expedition* as a Source for Poe's 'Journal of Julius Rodman,'" *U. Texas Studies*, XII (July, 1932), 158-170. Poe's primary sources were Jefferson's introductory section to *The History of the Expedition under the Command of Captains Lewis and Clark*, Irving's *The Adventures of Captain Bonnerville*, and Irving's *Astoria*. Crawford discusses the extent to which Rodman may be modeled upon Meriwether Lewis (159), but I think it safe to say that Poe made him his own.

18. Crawford, p. 168.

19. One might also mention Jack Chase, the marvelous captain of the foretop in *White-Jacket*. This is a type Melville often used.

20. *The French Face*, pp. 262-265, 268.

INDEX

How to use this Index:

I tried, in writing this book, to keep my main discussion of each tale more or less in one place. I had in mind the reader who wants a quick introduction to a single story. For his sake, such discussions are indicated in **bold type** in the Index.

The Index lists major ideas in the texts, works by Poe, authors and bellelettristic books referred to by Poe or by the author, and all proper names. It does not include the *titles* of modern critical or scholarly works; those may be located by referring to their authors' names or by referring to topics.

Topical headings in general refer to Poe throughout the Index. Thus "Beauty, perception of" means, "Poe's ideas on the perception of beauty." The heading "Poe, Edgar" is thus kept as brief as possible.

275